The Invisible Hand in Virtual Worlds

Video games are not merely casual entertainment: they are the heart of one of the fastest-growing media industries in the world, and a cultural phenomenon in their own right. In the past 50 years, gaming has evolved from a niche pastime relegated to the back rooms of arcades into a global business that rivals film and television. In the process, games have created new art forms and social arenas—as well as their fair share of political controversy—and become the subject of endless public debate. This book shows that games also provide a unique space in which to study economic behavior. Games, more than any other form of media, demonstrate the power and creative potential of human choice—an idea that is also the foundation of economic thinking. Whether it is developing trade relations, or the use of money, or even complex legal institutions, virtual worlds provide a captivating and entertaining arena for studying economic behavior in its most dynamic forms.

The chapters in this book combine theory with gaming practice to create an original story about the economics of virtual worlds and about the game industry. Various economic themes are represented, from long-established ideas about the benefits of the division of labor and trade to new work on the evolution of social institutions and governance. The contributors explore these ideas within the virtual worlds of games to show how economic behavior evolves over time to resolve conflict and promote social cooperation. The overarching theme of the volume is the economic order that governs virtual worlds and the many ways individuals work together, often without knowing it, to govern their social relations in digital space. The chapters also offer a wide range of practical implications for both gaming and economics, implications that span research, teaching, and public policy.

Matthew McCaffrey is associate professor of entrepreneurship in the Alliance Manchester Business School at the University of Manchester.

The Invisible Hand in Virtual Worlds

The Economic Order of Video Games

Edited by

Matthew McCaffrey

Cambridge University Press

CAMBRIDGE
UNIVERSITY PRESS

University Printing House, Cambridge CB2 8BS, United Kingdom

One Liberty Plaza, 20th Floor, New York, NY 10006, USA

477 Williamstown Road, Port Melbourne, vic 3207, Australia

314 to 321, 3rd Floor, Plot No.3, Splendor Forum, Jasola District Centre, New Delhi – 110025, India

103 Penang Road, #05–06/07, Visioncrest Commercial, Singapore 238467

Cambridge University Press is part of the University of Cambridge.

It furthers the University's mission by disseminating knowledge in the pursuit of education, learning and research at the highest international levels of excellence.

www.cambridge.org
Information on this title: www.cambridge.org/9781108839716

First published 2021

Printed in India by Thomson Press India Ltd.

A catalogue record for this publication is available from the British Library

Library of Congress Cataloging-in-Publication Data

Names: McCaffrey, Matthew, editor.
Title: The invisible hand in virtual worlds : the economic order of video games / edited by Matthew McCaffrey.
Description: Cambridge, United Kingdom ; New York, NY : Cambridge University Press, 2021. | Includes bibliographical references and index.
Identifiers: LCCN 2021005368 (print) | LCCN 2021005369 (ebook) | ISBN 9781108839716 (hardback) | ISBN 9781108884891 (ebook)
Subjects: LCSH: Video games—Economic aspects. | Video games—Social aspects. | Economics—Psychological aspects. | Video gamers—Psychology. | Video game industry.
Classification: LCC GV1469.3 .I48 2021 (print) | LCC GV1469.3 (ebook) | DDC 794.8/4—dc23
LC record available at https://lccn.loc.gov/2021005368
LC ebook record available at https://lccn.loc.gov/2021005369

ISBN 978-1-108-83971-6 Hardback

Contents

Introduction

Matthew McCaffrey

At first glance, using economics to study video games seems counterintuitive. After all, is not economics all about work, and are not games about play? How much do they really have in common? It is certainly true that when we talk about economics, we are usually speaking about our commercial lives: buying and selling, our jobs, the interest rates on our mortgages, and lots of other things we rarely think of as fun or entertaining. But our economic decisions are about much more than what we do in the marketplace, and economics actually has a lot to say about how and why we play.

Economics is the study of human action and choice, and it applies nearly everywhere in life, including games and entertainment. Whether we are playing the stock market or *The Legend of Zelda*, we are always making economic decisions and living out economic principles, even if we do not realize it. More important for this book, our actions when we play also help to create large, complex economic systems that rival real-world economies. Virtual worlds develop specialization, division of labor, trade, money, entrepreneurship, and even legal institutions that enforce social norms and protect property rights. Thus, virtual economies are often anything but simple simulations, and their economic development gives the lie to the claim that they are little more than diversions from "real" life. In fact, if we look at them from a wider perspective, a picture begins to emerge of an extraordinary *order* that exists in and around games. This order develops from the actions of individual gamers and developers, who together create a vast system of social cooperation that links millions of people around the world and influences even the highest levels of industry.

The purpose of this book is to explore this (often hidden) order. It asks what economics can teach us about video games and reveals the intricate economic logic that underlies so much of what happens in games and the gaming industry. Whether we approach video games as researchers, industry professionals, gamers, or something else entirely, knowledge of economics is valuable and even vital. Thinking of games in an economic way helps explain their social implications and opens up new possibilities for academic research, but it also allows for greater communication between gamers, professionals, and academics. The economic point of view is also highly practical; to give only one example, it is crucial for understanding the relationship between gaming and public policy—a controversial topic for several decades and one in desperate need of attention from serious scholars. We hope that this book will provide a strong foundation for investigating these kinds of problems.

In this task, we have two audiences in mind: economists who want to know more about video games, and people who play, make, and research video games and are curious about their economic side. Yet, appealing to both groups presents a problem: too much detail about games risks alienating the economists, while too much economic talk discourages the gaming community. We have therefore tried to walk a fine line between these extremes by making each chapter accessible to economists, who lack a detailed knowledge of games, as well as noneconomists and nonacademics, who simply have an interest in video games and want to know more about the social science behind them. As explained later, there is an overarching narrative to the book and the chapters are arranged in a logical progression; however, they are also largely self-contained and can be read in any order.

It is also important to say a few things about what this book does and does not hope to achieve. It does explain how gaming provides a unique space in which to study economic behavior. Games, more than any other form of media, demonstrate the power and creative potential of human choice—an idea also at the foundation of economic thinking. Whether they are developing trade relations or the use of money or even complex legal institutions, the worlds of gaming provide a captivating and entertaining arena for studying economic behavior in its most dynamic forms.

In addition to exploring these specific topics, the book is generally intended to show the value of applying economic analysis to the study of video games and the gaming industry and can serve as a handbook for doing such research. Unfortunately, despite providing some fairly obvious benefits, economic research makes up only a small part of the work being done on video games—even in work purporting to study economic problems. It is understandable, of course, that most game research is undertaken by scholars in communications and media studies, as games are fundamentally linked to these disciplines. It is far less forgivable, however, that so much of gaming research either proceeds with a bold disregard for economic analysis or relies only on economic ideas that have long since been discredited and exiled to disciplines such as critical theory.

Despite the ambitious scope of this collection, however, there are definite limits to the research presented here. Importantly, the purpose of this book is not to explain every important economic idea in gaming. Instead, the chapters are organized around several key areas of overlap between economics and gaming. As the title of the volume indicates, the overarching themes are economic order and disorder in the world of video games. The question of order has been a crucial aspect of economic thinking for centuries and remains one of the most important contributions of economics to human knowledge and well-being. The Scottish philosopher-economist Adam Smith is usually credited with being the first writer to systematically explore the idea of economic order and the role it plays in human moral and social life. His investigations inspired the now-famous metaphor of the "invisible hand"—Smith's way of describing how, in the marketplace, there exists a harmony between individuals' interests. His idea was that by participating in the division of labor, we create a system of mutual dependence, in which, in order to improve our own lot in life, we must first improve the lot of others. As we produce, trade, and consume, we adjust our behavior to the needs of different people, and thereby create an order in economic life—and perhaps in our moral and cultural lives as well.

Importantly, Smith recognized that this social order can be unplanned—it can appear *spontaneously*, as the result of human action but not of human design. Many of the orders studied in this book are of this type. To take one simple example, individual gamers in massively multiplayer online games often play with their own interests in mind, yet still contribute to the well-being of other players as well as the workings of in-game economies or social groups. Of course, not all orders are spontaneous and not all spontaneous orders are "good," either morally or economically. But the idea of an unforeseen, unplanned order is nevertheless valuable for analyzing the kinds of social interactions that occur in and around games.

Shifting from economics to the games themselves, it is also important to note that this book does not study every important game economy or even every genre of game; the sheer number of titles published in the past forty years or so makes it impossible for us to study more than a small fraction of them. As a result, we have had to be extremely selective in our choice of individual games to discuss. To avoid being too narrow though, we have mainly focused on recognized "classics" that combine commercial success with economic depth. *EVE Online* and the games in the *Diablo* franchise, for instance, have stood the test of time and amassed large fan bases that remain active years or even decades after their initial releases. These kinds of games, we argue, are far richer and more fascinating than the much-maligned "AAA" franchises so common today whose annual installments leave behind no economic or cultural footprint.

The remainder of this introduction outlines the narrative of the book and the content of the individual chapters. The material in Part I ("The Political Economy of Gaming") sets out many of the key economic concepts and theories that are then applied throughout the rest of the volume. Chapter 1 explains the broad domain of video game economics and how, at the most fundamental level, games and play can be understood using economic ideas. Essentially, video game economics can be divided into three main branches: exploring the economic meaning of video games and play, the study of in-game economies, and the economics of the gaming industry. These three are intertwined and influence each other to a significant extent, and each is also represented in one or more chapters in the book. The majority of Chapter 1, however, discusses the first branch: the economic interpretation of games.

There is now an enormous literature studying games and their role in individual and social life. Unfortunately, the relationship between games and economics is not studied very often in this research, mainly because economics is thought of in narrow terms that makes it irrelevant to the world of play. If economics is restricted to work and commercial activity, as in the famous construct of *homo economicus*, then it would indeed have little to say about the subject. However, economics, properly understood, is a broad and rich social science based on the concepts of action and choice. In fact, economics is, in a sense, simply the teasing out of these ideas under different conditions. And because play involves action and choice, it too can be analyzed using economic reasoning.

In the world of video games, economic ideas play a vital—though often unseen—part in structuring gameplay. Actually, the defining characteristics of games are often economic conditions in disguise: the most obvious example is that games create challenges by introducing artificial scarcity into the world of gaming, and players respond by economizing in their use of resources. Their choices about how to do this comprise an essential part of games in many genres. Game design similarly evokes problems of choice, trade-offs, opportunity costs, specialization, trade, and entrepreneurship. In fact, some genres depend entirely on these concepts to create compelling play experiences. As a result, simply by playing games and being familiar with their conventions, gamers are already becoming used to the economic way of thinking, even if they do not realize it. Nevertheless, it remains an open question just how similar virtual worlds are to the real world and whether economics translates exactly into digital space. Chapter 1 therefore concludes with a discussion of the similarities and differences between the two, especially with regard to the role of governance and economic policy.

Whereas Chapter 1 studies individual action and its immediate effects, Chapter 2 expands on the themes of social interaction and social order. In particular, it explains the key concept of spontaneous order, also known as "emergent" order. The chapter argues that early video games had mostly spontaneous narratives due to hardware and software limitations, which were then gradually replaced with more structured, on-rails narratives of increasing complexity. Throughout the first two decades of the twenty-first century though, there was a resurgence of interest in the spontaneous generation of narratives, which many argue provide a kind of richness in the game experience not found in linear narratives. Spontaneous games create stories that, as Adam Ferguson said of emergent order in general, are the "result of human action, but not the execution of any human design." In fact, the video game medium is particularly well suited to this kind of interactive and open-ended storytelling, giving it a unique place among artistic media.

Part II of the book, "Economic Order and Chaos in Virtual Worlds," begins a series of discussions of economic order and chaos in specific games. Chapter 3 opens by examining how in-game economies develop legal systems to deal with conflict and create institutional stability. In many real-world cases of self-governance, individuals are able to rely on the threat of simple ostracism to induce cooperation. Yet in the relatively populous and anonymous world of online virtual societies, this mechanism is often ineffective. Indeed, even some exceptional solutions that have emerged to induce cooperation in cases where ostracism has proven impossible—solutions such as religion, superstition, or the threat of violence—prove difficult to employ successfully in online societies characterized by cultural diversity, modernity, and real-world anonymity. This chapter studies how gamers overcome this challenge by making use of the voluntarily adopted legal system called "Dragon Kill Points," which successfully establishes property rights, allocates scarce economic goods, and allows for long-run contractual exchange in an environment utterly different from those examined in most of the law and economics literature.

While Chapter 3 surveys how in-game economies develop complex institutions to encourage social cooperation, Chapter 4 takes things a step further by looking at ways in which virtual worlds such as those of massively multiplayer online role-playing games (MMORPGs) can provide insight into the nature and dynamics of social, economic, and political processes. One very popular MMORPG that shows great promise in this regard is *EVE Online*. Much of the scholarly interest in this game has been inspired by the light it sheds on international relations. Yet it is also a fascinating virtual laboratory for the study of the interplay between economic and political orders. The chapter examines the following features of this virtual world as it has developed since it was first launched: the importance of economic factors as the basis for power within the virtual world of New Eden; the emergence of political orders or coalitions, and the bases for these; the part played by both natural affinity and charismatic leadership in the emergence of these coalitions; the acceleration of innovation in a number of areas as the game and its virtual world have developed and the part played by one key innovation in particular; and the insights to be gained from studying the turbulent and fast-changing economy and politics of New Eden.

Chapter 5 turns to the study of money. Special attention is placed on the way that money, a general medium of exchange, emerges spontaneously in response to the difficulties of direct barter exchange. The chapter closely studies the game mechanics of *Diablo II* and the development of its player community, showing how the technical conditions of the game not only created conditions similar to a barter economy but also facilitated the emergence of a series of currency units that were unplanned by developers. After evaluating the significance of various game mechanics that influenced production and exchange in *Diablo II*'s game environment, the chapter then considers the available evidence regarding the monetary system that prevailed in the game's online community and how it evolved over time. It concludes by contrasting the relative success of emergent institutions like money in *Diablo II* with the eventual abandonment of monetary institutions in *Diablo III*.

After studying the emergence of money in *Diablo II* in Chapter 5, Chapter 6 brings the discussion full circle by explaining the hyperinflation and collapse of the monetary unit in *Diablo III*. Released in May 2012, Blizzard Entertainment's

Diablo III included the introduction of a real money auction house as a central feature of its virtual economy. Yet by allowing players to monetize in-game items, incentives were fostered that encouraged automated play via "bots" and ultimately set in motion a series of events that led to an outbreak of virtual hyperinflation. This chapter applies an Austrian-school theoretical framework to analyze message board comments and publicly available prices that trace the episode from its early stages in the summer of 2012 to the apex of the currency crisis in May 2013. A list of other, lesser-known online currency crises are discussed as well, along with policy recommendations designed to avoid similar incidents in the future.

Part III of the book, "The Political Economy of the Video Game Industry," shifts the focus to the broader business of gaming. Importantly, these final chapters are not a comprehensive account of the global gaming business; instead, their purpose is to look at several key ways in which the economic orders discussed earlier in the book influence the structure and performance of the video game industry and vice versa. With this in mind, Chapter 7 examines business strategies for massively multiplayer online (MMO) game developers. Rather than simply ask how in-game economies work, this study looks at how video game companies manipulate their internal capabilities and their external industrial environment to increase their competitive performance. At the end of the day, a video game company is usually a for-profit firm like any other, looking to increase its financial performance through an effective business strategy. Yet one area scholars have not closely explored involves the best competitive strategies for platform-based firms that face competitive pressures from user-generated content. Sometimes user-generated content increases revenues by increasing overall platform usage, but at other times it can decrease revenues by cannibalizing core product offerings. This chapter thus bridges the gap between discussions of internal game mechanics and the external gaming industry. Specifically, it uses transaction costs theory and research on the informal economy to analyze MMO firm strategy. Three MMO mini case studies, on *Rage of Bahamut*, *Minecraft*, and *Dota 2*, help to explain how MMOs face a "facilitate or acquire" decision when managing user-generated content.

Chapter 8 continues this theme by exploring the entrepreneurial elements inherent in the world of video game "modding" and the interactions between the modding community and game developers. Over the last few years, the practice of creating and distributing user mods has become more popular and prevalent, and this chapter attempts to quantify the sheer scale of the phenomenon while also providing a narrative describing the entrepreneurial impact that mods have had on the industry. In particular, mods allow for the addition of new game mechanics and a wide range of other content that developers are unable or unwilling to include in their products. These user-generated programs even inspire fresh ideas among professional developers. Furthermore, mods come directly from consumers and, therefore, represent a truly emergent and competitive novelty as compared to the more centralized downloadable content offered by developers. Modding represents a unique form of crowdsourced learning that overcomes the weaknesses identified in the literature studying "absorptive capacity" and leads to increased firm performance from innovation, particularly for those firms residing in highly dynamic or entrepreneurial industries. This chapter studies three variations of the modding phenomenon—traditional modding, quasi-modding, and multiuser dungeons (MUDs)—to better understand how the process takes place. These insights can inspire firms (both inside and outside the gaming industry) to consider potentially novel mechanisms that will enhance their learning and overall innovative performance.

Building on the same framework used in Chapter 8, Chapter 9 shifts the focus of study to a specific company: Valve Corporation, one of the leading competitors in the video game industry. Beginning as a fairly traditional game developer, Valve has gone from strength to strength, quickly evolving from its original role as a developer to a publisher and content platform. Its financial success makes it notable in its own right, but it is also fascinating from an economic and organizational perspective. Valve is a "flat" organization with no hierarchy or centralized decision-making structure. Instead of top-down management, decision-making is "democratized," and employees choose the projects they pursue and the collaborative groups in which they work. The company's success thus raises many questions about the costs, benefits, and basic feasibility of nontraditional organizations. This chapter provides some possible answers, including about the interactions between informal management and decision-making, the delegation of authority, firm capabilities, and labor markets. It explains that companies like Valve are best thought of as networks of derived decision-making in which the entrepreneur–owners of the firm delegate authority to employees and sidestep traditional management. Although Valve has enjoyed great success, its unique form of organization also carries costs, costs that are sometimes great enough to prevent the company from pursuing valuable projects. The discussion concludes with a case study of the *Half-Life* franchise and suggests that Valve's organizational design was likely responsible for its failure to take the series forward for many years.

Although most of the chapters in this book focus on specific video games and economic problems, we hope readers will soon see that the ideas and theories we discuss apply across titles and genres. The reason is that economics studies universal aspects of human action and choice; as a result, its lessons are valid in many different contexts. To give one perhaps cheeky example, economics shows how hardcore MMO players, veteran speed runners, or old-school gamers modding or emulating forgotten titles from long-defunct consoles often have more in common than they realize with players of the most casual mobile games. This might be an uncomfortable thought for serious gamers, but that is the (sometimes surprising) beauty of economic order: despite our differences, our interests are still profoundly intertwined and, what is more, we are all the better for it. It is our hope that readers of this book will apply this lesson to their own experiences as gamers, developers, researchers, policymakers, or any other "class" we choose in the game of life.

1

The Economic Meaning of Play

Ludology and Praxeology in Video Game Worlds

Matthew McCaffrey

INTRODUCTION

A common misconception about economics is that it only applies to the business world. For many people, economics is simply irrelevant to other areas of life because it treats people like selfish, robotic decision-makers. In this view, while the assumptions and models of economics might work for studying profit-hungry business executives, they simply will not do for studying humans' complicated social and cultural lives. Economics cannot, for example, explain altruism and charity because economists assume that people are always rational, greedy, and motivated by money. Yet, in reality, claim the critics, human beings are none of these things—checkmate, economists.

Fortunately, this view of economics is quite mistaken. Economics, in fact, offers realistic insights into action and choice in many settings, be they boardrooms or game rooms. The latter are the topic of this chapter, which explores the economic meaning of gameplay. In keeping with the subject of this book, the discussion mainly concerns play in the context of video games but the ideas also apply to other kinds of play or gaming activity that are usually believed to fall outside the scope of economics. As I will show, economics provides a useful framework for thinking about play and its human meaning. I argue two main points: first, economics offers a unique way to analyze play and (video) games, and second, games provoke fascinating questions about economic behavior while also providing unique opportunities to answer them.

The chapter is structured as follows: the second section outlines the scope of video game economics and several different types of research included under this umbrella term. The third section then explores one of these types in more detail by examining the relationship of action, choice, and economics to games and play. It explains that, contrary to popular belief, the two fields of study have much in common. The fourth section builds on this insight by exploring the economics of gameplay, especially how the structure of video games implies a series of economic problems that players solve. The fifth section then discusses virtual worlds and their relation to real-world economies. The last section concludes with some thoughts on the purpose, value, and limitations of video game economics.

What Should Video Game Economists Do?

If we want to understand the economic implications of games and play, we must first ask some basic questions. These include: What does it mean to study games in an economic way? Why should we think video game worlds are good subjects for economic research? Further, is the study of game worlds a field of economics, such as labor economics or monetary economics? Or, is it more like a research method, a kind of laboratory for studying all types of economic questions? This chapter (and the rest of this book) is devoted to answering these questions and to constructing frameworks for using economics to analyze video games in all their uniqueness.

The first task is to explain what we mean when we talk about the economic study of video games because there are several different ways to look at games through an economic lens. Here are three major topics or fields of video games research that interest economists, along with samples of the kinds of questions they tend to ask:

1. *The economics of gameplay*: To what extent do gamers act economically within video game worlds? How can we interpret in-game behavior in economic ways? How does the deliberate construction of game worlds influence economic behavior within them? And, how do real-world economic factors influence the construction of game worlds?

2. *The economics of virtual economies and/or virtual worlds*: How are property rights defined and enforced in a virtual space? How do production and trade occur in virtual economies? How are income and wealth created and distributed? What, if anything, is the real-world monetary value of in-game commodities? How do virtual monetary systems compare to real-world ones? How dynamic are virtual economies in terms of growth or decline? How do we measure these and other kinds of virtual economic activity?

3. *The economics of the video game industry*: How large is the video game industry, and is it growing or declining? How are wages and prices determined in the industry? How are development and publishing firms organized, and how competitive or monopolistic are they? Is the industry innovative or stagnant? How do government regulations relating to labor, taxation, and intellectual property affect the success or failure of game firms?

One of the first things we should notice is that these topics are connected. Virtual economies do not exist in a vacuum: they are influenced by many real-world conditions, from the actions of individual developers to the political institutions that govern the gaming industry to the larger social and cultural norms that shape consumer attitudes and behavior. These, in turn, influence how players act and interact within games and the constraints under which they do so. As a result, fully studying any of these topics requires studying the others as well, and that is generally what this book does throughout its three main parts. This first chapter, in particular, looks at the economic implications of gameplay, while later chapters study complex economic relations in virtual worlds and their connections to the real world. The final chapters come full circle by exploring how the economics of the gaming industry influences the content of games.

Action, Play, and Economics

The last few decades have seen an explosion of academic interest in *ludology*, the study of games. Much of this literature involves trying to precisely define games and distinguish gaming and play from other forms of activity. There are numerous schools of thought, and games are at the center of a thriving academic discipline complete with its own conferences, publications, and professional organizations, and within which the study of video games features prominently (Egenfeldt-Nielsen, Smith, and Tosca, 2016). However, economic analysis plays only a small role in this literature. The majority of scholars in game studies work in the humanities or qualitative social sciences, and research tends to be dominated by methods rooted in critical theory (Deterding, 2017, pp. 532–533). As a result, when economic analysis does appear, it tends to invoke long-refuted doctrines such as the labor theory of value or Marxist theories of exploitation.[1]

[1] See, for example, Taylor (2004), the essays collected in Hart (2017), and the criticism in McCaffrey (2020).

My purpose is not to review this literature,[2] or even the part of it devoted to video games; instead, I mention it to highlight the relative lack of economic research in the field. It is also not my intention to simply replace current theories of games or play with a purely economic approach. The purpose of the chapter is rather to better understand the relationship between play, games, and economic behavior, and the ideas presented here are complements for other work.

Understanding basic theoretical assumptions and their limitations provides a helpful starting point for breaking down barriers between disciplines. The pioneer work of ludology was carried out by the Dutch historian Johan Huizinga in his book *Homo Ludens* (1949 [1944]). Huizinga argued that play is the foundation of culture and is inseparable from it. *Homo ludens*, or Man the Player, uses intuition to create meaningful experiences in contrast with the more rational decision-making of "serious" pursuits such as work and business. Implicitly then, Man the Player clashes sharply with *homo economicus*, the archetype of rational, self-interested behavior commonly associated with economic theory. This abstraction describes ideal or purely "rational" economic behavior, typically the pursuit of maximum benefits with minimum costs, defined in monetary terms. Economic man behaves in a hedonistic way: producing, exchanging, and consuming without regard to cultural or spiritual life. He thus has little or nothing in common with *homo ludens*. If we accept this model of behavior as the starting point of economic analysis, there is indeed little room for applying economic analysis to the study of games.

Fortunately, contrary to popular belief, the idea of *homo economicus* is not necessary in economics; in fact, such unrealistic constructs can actually be misleading. Life is not neatly divided between economic and other behaviors that can be easily studied in isolation. Instead, play, work, and other actions are combined and blended within a complex set of values and preferences (Knight, 1946, p. 91). Moreover, studying these does not require assuming that people are selfish or motivated by the pursuit of money or that they are rational decision-makers. A more realistic and complete view need not be based on any kind of "man," but if we must choose one, it would be *homo agens*, or acting man. The ideas of action and purpose provide better foundations for studying economics and its relevance to games and play.

[2] For a discussion of the current state of research on the general meaning of play, especially in child and animal psychology, see Burghardt (2011). For video games, especially "serious" games, see Rodriguez (2006).

To understand this, we must think further about what it means to play, and how play relates to conventional economics. Long before the first video games were created, economist Frank Knight wrote about the role of play in human social behavior. Knight was asking fundamental moral and political questions, especially about how society should be organized and the importance of democratic discussion in resolving social conflicts. Yet his ideas about play also apply to the specific subject of this book: playing video games and the economic significance of doing so. Knight explored the underlying differences between work and play and how each influences society. He thought the main difference was that work is a kind of action that achieves a specific *outcome*, whereas play is more about engaging in a *process*:

> [T]he good life includes play as well as work. In play … activity is usually directed toward some end [Yet] the end is not 'real' but symbolic and instrumental; it is set up for the purpose of making the activity interesting. The value lies as much in the activity of pursuit as in the enjoyment of the result. (Knight, 1946, p. 81)

In this sense, play is an important alternative to work, and giving each its proper place is crucial for a good life. Knight thought economics was an important lens through which to view society but also that it was not the only one. He believed that studying play could provide vital answers to deep questions about humanity and even claimed that "[M]ore is finally to be learned about life and morality, even in the economic field, from the study of play and of cultural pursuits than from the direct study of economics as ordinarily conceived" (Knight, 1946, p. 82). Even though he was not thinking of video games, Knight's point is well taken: studying playful behavior is necessary for gaining new knowledge about a wide range of human experiences, even the more "serious" behaviors analyzed in economics. The chapters in this book are cases in point: each one examines a different aspect of play and uses it to explain, illustrate, and expand on economic ideas. Knowledge transfer thus runs in both directions: students of games can learn to appreciate the economic meaning and complexity of the game worlds in which they play, while economists can learn to better understand the value and the limits of their theories.

Perhaps the clearest account of play and economics was suggested by the Austrian economist Ludwig von Mises. In Mises's view, economics always begins with human action. Action is simply purposeful behavior: people have ends they want to achieve, and taking action is a way to accomplish them (Mises, 1998 [1949]).[3] As we act, we alter the world around us; in particular, we use scarce time and physical resources (means), and we cooperate with other people to reach our goals (ends). Cooperation takes many forms, but the most significant kind that economists study is the division of labor. Scarcity makes it impossible for us to achieve all of our goals by ourselves, so instead of living solitary lives, we form societies and specialize our work in the most effective ways possible. We then exchange the fruits of our labor with others, thereby benefitting everyone involved. These mutual gains from trade are a cornerstone of complex social relations. And, for writers such as Mises, they are the essence of economics, the study of human action and choice, especially in the context of peaceful social cooperation and trade.

Importantly though, the basic elements of economics are universal: they exist everywhere human purpose exists. This helps to explain why economic ideas are broad enough to discuss games and play: they are also kinds of action, and even though they do not necessarily involve commercial behavior such as buying and selling, they do carry economic implications. For example, there is a purpose to playing games, usually some type of stimulation or diversion, and they require time, effort, and scarce resources (that is, the machines we use to play). Likewise, controlling an in-game avatar is also action, even if it only plays out in digital space. Yet games are not always about entertainment. As Mises explains,

> Embarking upon games can be either an end or a means. It is an end for people who yearn for the stimulation and excitement with which the vicissitudes of a game provide them, or whose vanity is flattered by the display of their skill and superiority in playing a game which requires cunning and expertness. It is a means for professionals who want to make money by winning. (Mises, 1998 [1949], p. 116)

Here, we have at least two ways to study games using economics: as means and as ends. Both are common in video games. For instance, anyone who has ever played an online multiplayer shooter knows the pure enjoyment of playing well (and certainly will be familiar with those players "whose vanity is flattered"

[3] Knight defined work as a purposive activity, whereas for Mises, this is the definition of action in general. Knight's view contrasts work and purpose with play and process, whereas for Mises, work and play are nested within action, and each can serve as either a means or an end.

by competing!). Nevertheless, games that are played as ends in themselves can involve labor that is disagreeable or painful. For example, gamers often engage in repetitive or uninteresting play as one part of a full, enjoyable experience. Fans of role-playing games will be familiar with "grinding" for experience points or loot even when doing so is unnecessary to make progress. This could be compared to athletes for whom physical stress becomes enjoyable because it is part of the challenge of play (Mises, 1998 [1949], pp. 584–585).[4]

Likewise, the enormous growth of esports and professional gaming has created new kinds of employment for gamers around the world: people for whom play is a means to achieving fame and fortune. Yet whether gaming is an end in itself or simply a means to earning a living, it should be clear that

> [p]laying a game can therefore be called an action. But it is not permissible to reverse this statement and to call every action a game or to deal with all actions as if they were games. The immediate aim in playing a game is to defeat the partner according to the rules of the game. This is a peculiar and special case of acting. Most actions do not aim at anybody's defeat or loss. They aim at an improvement in conditions. It can happen that this improvement is attained at some other men's expense. But this is certainly not always the case. It is, to put it mildly, certainly not the case within the regular operation of a social system based on the division of labor. (Mises, 1998 [1949], p. 116)

For Mises, games are defined by a kind of antagonism between people and groups. This rivalry is not the same as either market competition or violent conflict: it is a peaceful and artificial competition that occurs according to generally accepted rules. If it is a zero-sum activity, it is this way by design and by agreement of the players. And, while defeat will likely produce discomfort or disappointment for the losers, serious harm is typically ruled out. Writing before the computer age, Mises limited his definition of games to competitions between people and classified single-player pursuits such as solitaire as "pastimes" rather than as games. However, his approach can be extended to computer-based artificial intelligence (AI) opponents as well, so that only one human player is

---

[4] Mises refers to this kind of activity as "introversive labor," or action that provides disutility but also directly provides its own reward, and is not intended to add to production, national wealth, and so on.

required for a game. In all these cases though, gameplay involves agreeing to a kind of artificial competition in the context of some kind of rules or regulations.

The earlier discussion hints that action can serve as a unifying starting point for studying both economics and games. Rather than distinct parts of human life, work and play are often interwoven and can be described using basic components of action such as means and ends. Mises called this kind of analysis *praxeology*, or the science of action. Praxeology has different branches, as there are specialized problems that appear in different contexts. For example, business entrepreneurs trying to satisfy consumers face different obstacles than gamers working toward reaching a higher level or finding an elusive piece of legendary loot. Yet both activities have common ground in the idea of action: both involve scarcity, uncertainty, means, ends, value, preference, and a host of other concepts economists rely on to explain the world. The next section explores this point further by analyzing just how, within video games, the logic of action and economics is embedded in the structure of gameplay and in the decisions players make.

Gameplay as Economic Behavior

By taking human purpose and action as theoretical foundations, it becomes easier to understand the ways economic ideas can be used to study gameplay. Deciding to play and even play itself involve action just as much as buying and selling for profit in the market do—choice, scarcity, and the quest for improved welfare are at the heart of both cases. This can be clearly seen in a variety of game genres and conventions that create choice problems for players. Games offer such choices as a way to construct and emphasize the unique experience of gaming, often the enjoyment of a special form of control and interaction.[5] These economic decisions could be called the "microfoundations" of gameplay. The following subsections draw on specific games as well as broader genre conventions to explain how gameplay illustrates these economic principles. I focus on a handful of ideas from microeconomics that are summarized in simple lessons.[6] I first examine the

---

5 This claim is the subject of criticism, but the debate over interactivity is not crucial for this chapter. An action framework is compatible with, and complementary to, a wide range of game studies research. It does not matter, for example, whether players experience "real" agency and control or if these are simply illusions created by coders (Stang, 2019). What matters is that games have economic meaning because players value them and choose to play.

6 See the survey in Mankiw (2012, pp. 4–10) and many other principles-level textbooks.

basic concepts of action and decision-making: scarcity, choice, trade-offs, and opportunity cost. These in turn lead to ideas about specialization, division of labor, trade, and entrepreneurship.

Scarcity

Scarcity is the fundamental fact of economics, and artificial scarcity is a fundamental trait of gaming. Creating a video game means crafting obstacles for players to overcome, barriers that reflect the existence of virtual scarcity (Castronova, 2001a, pp. 6, 16–17; 2002, pp. 16–17). Unsurprisingly then, scarcity exists across practically all genres of gaming. For example, in strategy games, players are limited in the raw materials they can use to produce capital goods or battlefield units: think of *Command and Conquer*, *Dota 2*, *Starcraft*, *Total War*, *Warcraft*, and *X-COM*. In survival horror games, medical supplies and weapons must be carefully rationed: think of *Dead Space*, *Resident Evil*, and *Silent Hill*. In many action games, rare loot must be found or created from scratch: think of *Borderlands*, *Dead Rising*, and *Diablo*. And in puzzle games, time is often the scarcest resource: think of mobile puzzle games. Notice too that if a game lacks scarcity, the result is often aimless, too easy, or simply boring.

This fits with what we know about real-world scarcity. If scarcity did not exist, economic activity would not exist. We would simply live in utopia and would never need to consciously act or make choices. Likewise, when playing a game, if all resources could be instantly gathered and used, if there were no danger of loss or failure, then there would be no game to speak of. In both cases, action and scarcity are different sides of the same problem. The goal of a game is to overcome a challenge, and that means coping with scarcity. In fact, this is what it means to *economize*: to use scarce resources in the most satisfying ways we can think of, and to prioritize our most important goals while setting aside less important ones. Anyone who has wandered the post-apocalyptic wasteland of the *Fallout* series knows the dangers of failing to make good use of scarce resources. This is also where the ideas of *means* and *ends* come in: the virtual resources a player uses are (scarce) means, and the satisfaction a player earns by doing well is the end.

Scarcity is also the basis of one of economics' most famous thought experiments: Robinson Crusoe. Economists use this imaginary case to highlight basic choice problems. As in Daniel Defoe's classic novel, we imagine that Crusoe is shipwrecked and faces extreme scarcity in his battle for survival. He must therefore make careful decisions about using time and physical resources to improve his life. The experiment is not intended, as some critics allege, to describe contemporary society; instead, its purpose is to clear away unnecessary details and focus on the actions that matter most to people in their quest to improve their lives. Games offer similar thought experiments: in-game economies can be carefully crafted to impose special limitations (challenges) and ignore irrelevant details, just as Crusoe's example does. In fact, it should come as no surprise that there are many games in which players find themselves in Crusoe-type scenarios and attempt to survive using only their wits and a few key resources. The theme of scarcity and choice plays out across this and countless other genres.

> Lesson: *Scarcity is everywhere in gaming and shapes player experiences just as it shapes the everyday actions of all individuals.*

Choice and Trade-Offs

The first implication of scarcity is that choice is necessary: we are always taking action to find ways to make ourselves better off, and both games and "real" life involve a constant series of choices. In the early days of gaming though—before immersive environments, nuanced storylines, and detailed character development—it was difficult to create decision-making opportunities that genuinely challenged players to reflect on their choices. For the most part, good decisions resulted in high scores, bad ones in "game over." In the past few decades, however, the complexity of choice in games has grown tremendously, particularly as a result of technological improvements and increasing production values. These allow developers more room for artistic expression and sophisticated storytelling that can draw players into the experience and encourage emotional involvement in characters and stories. Increasingly detailed worlds also provide scope for more nuanced moral and economic decision-making in which choices are difficult because they carry consequences for players.

An example of this trend is the *Fallout* series, which allows players to make complex moral decisions without simple, moralistic rewards and punishments for "good" and "bad" choices (Schulzke, 2009). Another is Telltale Games' adaptation of the graphic-novel-turned-television-series *The Walking Dead* (as well as other games from the same developer, including *The Wolf among Us* and *Tales from the Borderlands*[7]). Instead of the usual scenario of pitting players in mortal combat against zombies, *The Walking Dead* confronts them with difficult

[7] I am grateful to Brendan McCaffrey for this example.

choices about how to interact with non-player characters (NPCs). In the zombie apocalypse, resources are scarcer than ever, so players must carefully ration food, weapons, and even trust and compassion among various NPCs. The extreme survival situation obliges players to think about their actions to a greater degree than they do in many far less desperate real-life situations (Stang, 2019). The idea that choices imply trade-offs is especially important. Sharing a water ration with one character means it cannot be given to someone else, and even seemingly small actions have the potential for grave consequences. Decisions therefore need to be weighed carefully, meaning players must try to anticipate the options they will forego by choosing one action over another. Other examples of games that emphasize difficult decisions as core elements of gameplay include the *Deus Ex, Dragon Age, Fable, Knights of the Old Republic, Mass Effect*, and *Witcher* franchises, along with individual titles such as *L.A. Noire* or *Spec Ops: The Line.*

Broader examples of gaming trade-offs can be found in the role playing game (RPG) genre. RPGs incorporate extensive and complex choices between different character classes, specializations, and skills. Often, these in-game attributes can only be developed in a certain order, and many skills and skillsets are mutually exclusive. In addition to forcing choices between different branches of a "skill tree," RPGs also use an experience system to limit the scope and speed of player development (to ensure a certain level of difficulty). Systems vary from game to game, but the fundamental idea is generally the same: taking certain actions or completing objectives rewards players with experience points (XP) to spend on improving in-game abilities, such as an avatar's persuasive skill or proficiency with weapons. The limited amount of XP requires players to ration it carefully among competing uses, thereby forcing a trade-off. Experience thus functions as a kind of budget constraint (Castronova, 2001a, pp. 11–12). Because they must deliberate on which talents to develop, players are painfully aware of other valuable skills they must give up.

Lesson: *Scarcity obliges players to choose and to make difficult trade-offs.*

Opportunity Cost

Trade-offs imply that for everything we choose, we must give something up. The values to us of foregone actions are called *opportunity costs.* Many people think of costs simply as money prices, but the opportunity cost is the true cost of every action. Skill trees and similar RPG conventions help to explain why. What makes choosing a particular skill or specialization difficult is not the fact that it requires spending XP but that the scarcity of XP requires us to give up some other valuable option. The true cost of specializing in one set of skills is not the XP spent to develop them but *the alternative skills that could have been developed instead.* The cost of choosing a warrior class is not XP, but the value that could be gained by specializing in magic. This fits with standard textbook examples: Greg Mankiw, for instance, explains opportunity cost using the case of going to college (Mankiw, 2012, pp. 5–6). RPGs are actually analogous to a college education because both are supposed to develop "human capital": education is supposed to make workers more productive, while leveling up makes gamers more productive. The opportunity cost of investing in additional education is (usually) the wage that could be earned elsewhere, and in gaming, each skillset has its own costs that are different from its XP cost.

> Lesson: *All choices have a cost; the cost of developing a skill, skillset, or specialization is the most valuable skill, skillset, or specialization you give up to get it.*

Specialization and Division of Labor

Specialization drives the player's experience in many games or, at the very least, heavily influences it. Stealth action games provide a simple example. In these titles, such as the *Dishonored* series, players are given options about how to complete objectives. They can either take a direct, combative approach or rely on misdirection and stealth. Each option has unique advantages and disadvantages, and gamers choose the style with which they feel most comfortable. Other examples of specialization between basic play styles are found in the *Assassin's Creed*, *Deus Ex*, *Far Cry*, *Hitman*, *Metal Gear Solid*, and *Thief* franchises. But the idea of specialization is nearly ubiquitous in gaming. It is also a vital component of the RPG genre, especially MMO games such as *World of Warcraft*. In these more complex worlds, before players can develop different skill trees, they must first choose to belong to particular species, races, and classes—each with inherent proficiencies and deficiencies—that determine further specialization options. Because MMORPG players must forgo some skills, they are not ideally suited to complete every possible task. Self-sufficiency is impossible, and the need for cooperation arises. Players must often work collaboratively to complete objectives, as when some players focus on physical combat, others focus on magical powers, healing, defense, or various other supporting roles or combinations thereof.

Even some of the earliest MMORPGs witnessed quick and quite complex trends toward specialization and cooperation (Castronova, 2001a, pp. 12–14). Some scholars argue further that modern multiplayer games imply enormous coordination problems in which players must find ways to cooperate to manage scarce, communal resources (Smith, 2007). Problems of trust and commitment between players in online games are the reason for the emergence of "clans" and similar methods of organizing cooperation and ensuring fair and rewarding play. Other examples of early MMORPGs that emphasized the same themes, sometimes unintentionally, were *EVE Online*, *EverQuest*, *Guild Wars*, *Star Wars: The Old Republic*, and *Ultima Online*.[8]

Once again, these systems exist so that players must make difficult choices: if anyone could master all abilities or play styles simultaneously without any trade-offs, games would not hold much appeal. One important difference though between virtual specialization and specialization in the real world is that in the latter, there is no developer or planner who defines the roles we can take on: specialization exists simply because individuals are separated in time and space, and we thus acquire different experience, knowledge, and skills. Nevertheless, in both virtual and real worlds, people are obliged to cultivate particular skills from a fairly limited range of options in order to achieve their goals.

> Lesson: *Choices between different classes and skillsets are examples of specialization, and cooperative play, teams, and clans are examples of the division of labor.*

Trade

Trade is the type of social cooperation economists tend to be most interested in, and the gains from virtual trade are just as real as those from trade in the physical world. When players trade, each one values what she gains more than what she gives up. As a result, both parties benefit from voluntary transactions. Such exchanges are the basis of complex social interactions that create mutual dependency and enhance the welfare of all people in (virtual) society. Importantly though, even if creating these general benefits is not the intention of anyone, and even if all traders are interested only in their own welfare, each nevertheless

[8] For more on *EVE Online*, see the fourth section of Chapter 4. For *EverQuest*, see Castronova (2001a).

contributes to the common good. To paraphrase Adam Smith, "It is not from the benevolence of the wizard, the paladin, or the rogue that we expect our rare loot drops, but from their regard to their own interest." Some RPGs have even spontaneously developed elaborate markets, and in games such as *Diablo II*, money has emerged out of the barter of in-game goods and services (Salter and Stein, 2015).[9]

However, the notion of working cooperatively goes beyond exchange. Economics does not only study trade but also the wider gains from social cooperation and the division of labor. Ludwig von Mises, for example, spoke of a universal "law of association," which holds that cooperative production is always more productive than isolated production (Mises, 1998 [1949], pp. 158–163). He argued that voluntary association for mutual benefit is the basis of all types of specialization, not just specialization for trade. This view reflects the insight that "cooperative action is more efficient and productive than isolated action of self-sufficient individuals" (Mises, 1998 [1949], p. 158). The principle plays out in game worlds as well. For instance, in MMORPGs, major objectives are often impossible to complete using one or a few players. Instead, completing a quest such as slaying a major boss requires the collaboration of a large number of specialized player types, each supporting the others by enhancing their strengths or offsetting their weaknesses. There is a literal division of labor involved in completing these tasks, which are difficult or impossible if players antagonize or violently expropriate each other.[10]

Lesson: *Specialization, cooperation, and trade make all players better off.*

Entrepreneurship

Finally, using economics to study games reveals how play can be an entrepreneurial activity. In the business world, entrepreneurship is about using good judgment to overcome uncertainty, especially by anticipating what consumers will want in the future and planning how to give it to them (Foss and Klein, 2012). Cases of literal video game entrepreneurship such as this tend to be rare compared

[9] For more on *Diablo II*, see Chapter 5.

[10] This raises the question of what to do with antisocial players who disregard the larger gains from cooperation and disrupt peaceful social interactions. For more on this, see the first section of Chapter 3 and the ninth section of Chapter 4.

to the basic examples of trade or collaboration discussed earlier. Nevertheless, entrepreneurship is involved in gaming in some subtle ways.

It should be easy to see that games involve uncertainty, which in turn is closely tied to challenge, a defining characteristic of games. Not knowing what lies in the next dungeon or if it is possible to survive the next battle or if the next tactic used against a boss will be effective are important parts of exploring game worlds, and they reflect the idea of uncertainty. Not all games include elements of uncertainty, of course, and sometimes we play precisely because we know what will happen. Nevertheless, adventuring, exploring, and discovering are important aspects of play, and they are likewise common aspects of entrepreneurship. In fact, early descriptions of entrepreneurs described them using words such as "adventurer" that are also at home in gaming. As Huizinga put it, "To dare, to take risks, to bear uncertainty, to endure tension—these are the essence of the play spirit" (Huizinga, 1949 [1944], p. 51). Entrepreneurs are likewise often described as creators and innovators (Schumpeter, 1942), traits that will be familiar to players of puzzle games or classic adventure games, genres that require thinking creatively and differently to solve problems. Lastly, games are also used to explain practical entrepreneurship. For instance, educators have used *The Sims: Open for Business* to show how real-world entrepreneurs build a business culture (Green, 2014).

> Lesson: *Entrepreneurial behavior is a significant part of playing games, which requires finding creative and innovative ways to overcome uncertainty to solve problems.*

The principles discussed earlier can all be traced back to the idea of *action*, the foundation of economics. Economic elements are everywhere in gaming and, in many cases, even define the gaming experience. Games tend to revolve around solving virtual economic problems relating to scarcity, trade-offs, opportunity costs, specialization, trade, and entrepreneurship, to name only a few. They thus provide numerous examples of economic logic at work as well as opportunities to teach gamers and students how to see things from "the economic point of view."[11] The next step in exploring the economic meaning of games is to look more closely at the emergence of formal economies in virtual worlds.

[11] Games thus exemplify the idea that a "significant portion of learning economics is simply learning a formal structure which encompasses procedures with which the students are already familiar" (Lockard, 2004, p. 134).

What Is So Virtual about Virtual Worlds?

The previous section explained some fundamental ways in which video games involve economic behavior. Starting from action and choice, games encourage social cooperation and the development of increasingly complex economies. The next step is to consider the implications of the most advanced cases—*virtual worlds*. Virtual worlds potentially include all types of microeconomic and macroeconomic problems, from individual choice all the way to economy-wide problems such as unemployment, money, banking, and the business cycle (Nazir and Lui, 2016). For the purposes of this chapter, a virtual world is a "synchronous, persistent network of people, represented as avatars, facilitated by networked computers" (Bell, 2008, p. 2). The most obvious examples are MMORPGs, which capture each part of the definition. In these games, (*a*) players experience a virtual world in real time, (*b*) the world cannot be paused and continues even when players are absent, (*c*) participants' behavior in the world influences the environment and the experience of other players, (*d*) players are represented through avatars, and (*e*) the world is created and maintained through networked computers (Bell, 2008, pp. 2–3). This definition covers more than games, but other types of virtual world are not relevant for this chapter.[12]

Research on the economics of virtual game worlds has been growing steadily for two decades and has helped greatly to show the "gains from trade" between economics and studying video games. The beginning of this field can be traced to two papers published in the early 2000s by economist Edward Castronova, who is justly considered its founding father. The first article surveyed conditions in the online multiplayer game *EverQuest* and explained how real-world economic indicators could be applied to analyze and interpret economic activity in digital space (Castronova, 2001a). A second paper then proposed a general model of the demand for gameplay and outlined the scope and rationale of the economic study of video games (Castronova, 2002). Together, Castronova's

[12] Messinger, Stroulia, and Lyons (2008) propose a typology of electronic games, social networks, and virtual worlds that excludes most video games, even MMORPGs, from the latter category. Their typology does not change the analysis in this chapter, however. Schroeder (2008, p. 2) further argues that virtual worlds should also have clear social purposes independent of gaming activities and goals. Highlighting the social implications of virtual worlds is indeed important, but it is enough that players have the ability to socialize in a game space if they choose. In fact, this is a central theme in economics: it may not be the intention of any player to engage socially with others; nevertheless, the gains from peacefully cooperating with different players encourage all participants to do so.

articles launched a research agenda around virtual economies and their very real players that persists to this day. For that reason, I frame the following discussion using his contributions, especially the question of what they have to offer twenty years later.

Castronova's work was instrumental in drawing scholarly attention to the growing economic complexity of virtual worlds and in cementing games as worthy objects of economic discussion. As usually happens, academics were slow to acknowledge the significance of gaming even as it was becoming obvious to gamers and developers on the ground. Castronova thus fought an uphill battle trying to convince people of the value of studying video game economics (Castronova, 2002, pp. 12–13). He stressed though that the reason we (researchers) should care about games is that many millions of people already do. Castronova showed clearly that gamers attach value to play, to the point that they become immersed in virtual worlds and start "living" in them. They do this not for simple diversion but because they feel that participation enhances their lives and, in some cases, even substitutes for them by providing avenues for work as well as play (Castronova, 2001a, pp. 2, 10). Games are extraordinarily valuable, and this is what connects them to economic analysis. Modern economics is based on the fact that value is subjective: it does not exist "out there" in the physical world but only in our individual minds. Value is a way of describing how we perceive the world in relation to our own needs. It is the importance we attach to different actions, experiences, or objects. And the importance that so many people attach to games makes them a worthy subject for economic research. "The mere fact that the goods and spaces are digital, and are part of something that has been given the label 'game,' is irrelevant," and no grounds for dismissing their importance (Castronova, 2002, p. 15).

Even in the early days of online multiplayer games, player communities were already developing complex economic relations similar to, but simpler than, those found in real-world societies. In practical terms, Castronova helped demonstrate how conventional indicators of economic activity could be applied in these settings. Using some straightforward calculations, he showed that the economy of *EverQuest* was at the time comparable to real-world developing nations such as Russia and Bulgaria, and that the exchange rate of its in-game currency to the dollar compared favorably to major monetary units such as the Yen (Castronova, 2001a). These results foreshadowed the later, greater successes of games such as *World of Warcraft*, which at its peak boasted 12 million players, all participating in the thriving real economy of a virtual world.

Man, Economy, and the Virtual State

It is easier to see the value of virtual economic activity when it is more closely connected with real-world economic value. For instance, in MMORPGs, it is common to "farm" virtual resources that are then traded for in-game money, which in turn is exchanged for real-world currency and is thus a source of income and employment. Yet even activities that are limited to virtual worlds are genuinely economic—as noted earlier, players use avatars to specialize and trade, even when their only goal is to advance the game or earn purely digital rewards rather than increase their real wealth. In addition, there are also more difficult cases where economic activity is highly abstract and seems more like a metaphor for economic activity than a literal example of it.

One such crucial problem is how to define the limits of virtual economies and other institutions. The most obvious case relates to the boundary between the market economy and the state. In the real world, states are defined by a unique ability to use force to achieve their goals. Yet virtual worlds have no literal states.[13] And if we cannot define what a state looks like in a virtual world, it is difficult to ask questions about government regulation or even to explain what constitutes a policy intervention. This in turn limits the usefulness of studying virtual economies.

Of course, an obvious response is that game developers, especially coders, act like governments because they can unilaterally alter virtual worlds and player experiences and effectively ban certain players or behaviors (Castronova, 2002, p. 4). It is common for instance, for developers to monitor online multiplayer games to punish cheating.[14] Virtual worlds have even been described as profit-maximizing dictatorships (Osborne and Schiller, 2009, pp. 12–13). Yet even though developers sometimes enjoy near-complete control over many aspects of virtual worlds, their interactions with players are bound by mutual agreement and contract, not by

[13] Of course, real-world governments can regulate players, developers, or virtual worlds directly. Such practices are becoming more common: state and national governments are considering a wide range of regulations regarding content censorship, the taxation of virtual assets, restriction of in-game purchasing models, and many others. See Bartle (2006) for more on the contrast between real and virtual governments.

[14] Smith (2007) observes that developer control is also limited to those behaviors which can be "targeted algorithmically in a meaningful way," such as cheating by outright hacking.

threats of fines or imprisonment.[15] A player can always choose not to play or to play something else, whereas there is no option to simply stop engaging with a state (for instance, by not paying taxes), except by moving to another state (sometimes also impossible). In economic terms, players have "voice" and "exit" options (Castronova, 2002, p. 35) that are often absent in real states. As a result, developers' "punishments," such as banning players who violate a game's terms and conditions—or even informal norms—pale in comparison to those meted out by governments.[16]

This suggests a fundamental difference between states and developers, namely, the type of power they wield. It is easy to think coders and governments are similar because coders can change game worlds without the direct consent of players. Yet developers' abilities make them *less* like states, not more: although states can try to force citizens to behave in certain ways, they lack the power to change fundamental facts about the world (Bartle, 2006). Much as they might want to, governments cannot wish away the laws of supply, demand, or comparative advantage, and they cannot do away with scarcity. In fact, this limitation is the basis for a key insight of economic policy: part of the reason government interventions fail is that states cannot simply create scarce resources from thin air; for instance, water cannot be wished into existence to resolve a shortage during a hurricane. Yet coders often can create assets with little or no cost. In virtual worlds then, coders are not like states, more like demigods with extraordinary and arbitrary powers—powers they no doubt relish and of which states are no doubt jealous.

Economic Law in Virtual Worlds

The similarities between virtual and real-world economies raise other difficult questions. Chief among these is the problem of whether virtual economies are governed by the same principles and laws that govern real life. Does the law of comparative advantage still hold in a world of wizards and dragons? Do price ceilings for virtual apartments still cause housing shortages?

---

[15] End-User License Agreements, though often unread by the people who agree to them, define in detail the rights and obligations of players and publishers (Boyd, Pyne, and Kane, 2019, pp. 96–103).

[16] Whether developers are de facto states or not (Castronova, 2002, p. 4), it seems they have one thing in common with real governments: they are unable to stop peaceful economic activity. If people wish to trade, they will find a way, whether inside or outside a virtual world, through black or gray markets. This point was already becoming evident in the early days of online gaming (Castronova, 2001a, p. 19*n*18; 2002, pp. 33–34), and markets have since continued to defeat the best efforts of governments to prevent the trade of digital assets.

Although Castronova has been emphatic that economic principles are valid in synthetic worlds (Castronova, 2006, pp. 171–172), in his early work, he highlighted an apparent difference between the two settings: the ability of virtual worlds to radically alter the supply of goods with little cost.[17] He pointed out that masses of goods can be created or deleted simply by making small changes to a game's code (hence, the comparison of state power to developer power) and, crucially, that this implies that price controls in virtual worlds need not have negative effects. The standard economic analysis of price controls shows that they create shortages and surpluses, but if goods can be created or deleted at the press of a button, scarcity and resource allocation can be managed instantly and exactly (Castronova, 2002, pp. 4, 37–38). If so, this would mean that some basic laws of economics might not hold in virtual reality, or simply might not matter.[18]

However, while Castronova is correct that the digital manipulation of goods and services makes video game economies unique, the problems of price controls involve more than simple scarcity. Price controls are meaningful when they forcibly intervene in the market. Merely raising or lowering a price is not the same as controlling it: the crucial distinction is whether buyers and sellers are permitted to make the exchanges they wish, at prices they agree upon, and whether they can decline to exchange if they cannot agree upon terms. As mentioned earlier, developer power is not the same as state power, and one implication of this fact is that developers' decisions to change prices (say, increasing the price of health potions from 5 silver coins to 10) is not a price control in the same sense as rent control in a real-world city.[19]

Furthermore, even if developer power were equivalent to real-world government price controls, it is not the case that the consequences of controls can

---

[17] Altering games is not perfectly costless for developers though, as Castronova implies (Castronova, 2002, p. 37).

[18] Castronova also observes that some standard economic assumptions fail in virtual worlds. For example, economists often assume that population, tastes, and initial abilities are fixed; in virtual worlds though, these factors are all fluid (Castronova, 2002, p. 38). Yet rather than showing that economics fails to apply in virtual worlds, this merely shows how abstract and unrealistic economists' models can be. It is ironic that by dropping these kinds of assumptions, studies of fantasy worlds can become more realistic than much real-world economic research.

[19] The following discussion focuses exclusively on virtual economies, that is, digital spaces where buyer and seller behavior together determine prices. These prices are distinct from the fixed prices charged in most games, which are basically arbitrary, unchanging, and have no effect on other conditions in the game.

be seamlessly eliminated. The reason is that developers cannot remove all types of scarcity at a whim. When real-world rent control causes a housing shortage, it cannot be remedied by building more housing just anywhere; instead, the shortage is specific to a time and place and to a specific group of renters and landlords. These problems exist in virtual worlds as well. For example, MMOs usually contain finite spaces used by all players simultaneously (or at least, all players on a particular server). The world of *Second Life* makes for an excellent example, as it has a well-developed property and construction market, even though it is not a traditional game (Nazir and Lui, 2016). In *Second Life*, resources such as land are scarce and, therefore, command a price. If rent control keeps the price of virtual land artificially low, then a shortage will result, just as economics predicts. This shortage cannot simply be removed by creating more land somewhere in the game space: developers must somehow know exactly when and where new land is needed, and in what quantities and qualities, and they must be actually capable of creating it to these specifications without disturbing land that already exists. In real-world markets, entrepreneurs figure all this out through the price system, which constantly adjusts in response to changes in supply and demand. It is unclear how developers can solve the same problem using only controlled prices.[20]

The Puzzle of Puzzles

The importance of assumptions arises in another way. According to Castronova, using economics to study games requires solving what he calls "the puzzle of puzzles." This problem applies to different kinds of games but is especially clear in the context of video games. The puzzle is as follows: in most areas of life, people try to avoid constraints on their action and will pay or sacrifice to remove constraints. However, in games, players actively demand constraints and will pay or sacrifice to create them. Games require challenge, and challenge can only be created by making it more difficult to complete a game. A game with no constraints—no challenge—would be rejected by players as uninteresting.[21] In

[20] Mises showed definitively that without a price system, as under socialist central planning, the rational allocation of resources in society is impossible (Mises, 1990; Castronova, 2008, p. 41). Price controls suffer from the same problem on a smaller scale.

[21] In fact, it could be argued that such games are not games at all, but some kind of mildly interactive, or even passive, experience. It is worth noting these distinctions in light of the recent popularity of "walking simulators," visual novels, and other game genres that do not involve conventional challenges.

this part of life, people seek out obstacles that in any other context they would avoid. (The trick from a game design perspective is discovering the optimal level of difficulty, as there are limits to the challenges different people are willing to endure [which is why video games often include several difficulty settings].)

For Castronova, this puzzle is intriguing because it shows that virtual worlds turn standard economic analysis on its head. It implies, for instance, that work causes *disutility* (negative value) in the real world, while in virtual worlds, "it is lack of work that causes disutility" (Castronova, 2002, p. 38). Most people would need to be paid to hunt a boar for food in the real world but are also willing to pay for the privilege of doing so in a virtual world. Why? Is there some unique aspect of playing games that distorts conventional economic decision-making?

I argue no; we can resolve the puzzle using the ideas of action and purpose. People have different ends and use different means to achieve them. They have quite different views about what is satisfying and dissatisfying, and thus what counts as a means or an end. It is not the case that people value work in radically different ways in real and virtual worlds but that they define work and leisure differently depending on context. The confusion arises if we focus too much on the external, physical, or objective qualities of our actions: on what *looks* like work, for instance. Hunting a boar might seem like work, but it can be either a means or an end in both real and virtual worlds. In the real world, the boar is an end for a hunter who enjoys the chase and a means (and work) for someone looking for a meal. In a virtual world, the hunt is an end in itself if the player enjoys the thrill of overcoming a challenge or a means if he aims to earn experience points or loot from the kill. It is even work for those players who spend time farming resources to sell for real-world assets (Castronova, 2002, pp. 21–22; Liboriussen, 2017). The same thing is true of constraints: it is a confusion to say that in the real-world, people want to make things easier on themselves, while in virtual worlds, they want to make things harder. The truth is that people have different ideas about what constraints mean exactly in each case and about what counts as a means or an end. Preferring difficulty in a game is a way of saying that overcoming challenge is an end; preferring a less stressful workday is a way of saying that we prefer to minimize the means we use to achieve an end.

A final difference between virtual and real economies relates to the role of economic growth. Building on his point about constraints, Castronova observes that economic growth in virtual economies tends to undermine gameplay. The idea is that the wealthier people become, the fewer constraints they face and, therefore, the worse off they will be. For example, new skills and better equipment reduce the level of challenge, and as a result, success results in having nothing to do and, eventually, to boredom (Castronova, 2001b, pp. 51–53; 2002, p. 38). It seems then there is an incentive to keep virtual growth low to maintain a higher degree of difficulty and, therefore, satisfaction. Developers respond by increasing difficulty roughly in parallel to increases in player skill and by constantly adding new challenges, rebalancing prices and quantities, or simply ending gameplay before it becomes tiresome. It is also common to encourage repeat play through the option to play as different characters or classes, or complete "new game plus" modes. This is really just another way of observing that constraints never fully disappear in the real world, whereas in virtual worlds, there are a limited number of experiences that can be consciously designed: in a way, even artificial scarcity is a scarce resource!

The earlier discussions show that there are still many open questions about where to draw the line between virtual and real worlds. What is more, the line seems to become blurrier all the time. Yet one implication of this chapter is that we may not need to draw sharp lines between work and play or between games and reality: economics is everywhere, and simple concepts such as action and choice provide a framework for connecting many seemingly different areas of our lives.

The Promise of Virtual Economies as a Field of Research

The discussions in this chapter help underscore the unique problems posed by virtual worlds as well as how they overlap with the real world. This leads naturally to some overarching questions about the purpose of doing economic research in and around video game worlds and virtual economies. At the end of the day, why should we use economics to study video games? What can we learn from them? And why should we treat them as serious subjects for research and not as "mere play"? We have already hinted at several possible answers to these questions.

First, as Frank Knight observed, understanding society means studying more than economic activity. It also means investigating culture and leisure and exploring how these and other aspects of human life fit together. If Huizinga was right, play may be inseparable from culture and, therefore, also from any realistic economics. Given that video games occupy an increasingly large part of our commercial and leisure time, their study should take its rightful place beside other forms of art and media. And given that games provide the setting for new and complex economies, they deserve to be treated as a distinct topic or research context in economics.

Second, virtual worlds drive home the universality of economics. As we have seen, the basic themes of economics do not disappear simply because we trade physical for virtual reality or a business suit for a wizard's robe: as human beings, we constantly take action to overcome scarcity (even contrived scarcity) in order to improve our lives as we think best. Virtual worlds are simply one more setting in which to do that. The fact that the basic principles of economics operate in even the most fantastic worlds, where imagination and creativity are pushed to their limits, is a testament to their power to explain social reality. In that sense, video game economics is also a teaching tool, a way to express our accumulated knowledge in new ways. It is not so much a method for *testing* fundamental theories as a way to *illustrate* them. When we study price fluctuations in Norrath or Azeroth, we are not proving the laws of supply and demand in the real world so much as showing their depth and breadth and revealing the conditions under which they operate.

Third, video games offer a unique setting in which to more actively study economic relations. Real-world economies often change slowly and are far more open-ended and uncertain than even the most advanced virtual worlds, at least for now. This makes it extremely difficult and even impossible to directly study them in all their complexity. Large online games, however, are like petri dishes in which we can directly isolate and observe economic behavior (Castronova, 2006; 2018). Such games provide opportunities for natural experiments, especially in MMORPGs. These typically run on several different servers, each one housing a separate but complete version of the virtual world. This means that at any given time, multiple versions of the same world are operating under the same conditions but with different groups of players. Observing these parallel worlds thus allows social scientists to study the consistency of players' economic behavior. Games also function like laboratories, in the sense that developers can tweak one specification of a game while holding others constant, thereby isolating the effects of specific changes (Castronova, 2001b, pp. 19, 35–38). Such experiments are imperfect,[22] but they make for fascinating comparisons between treatment and control groups. Games that offer players large amounts of freedom to act as they wish are called "sandboxes," a term that applies equally well to games as a

[22] For example, players on different servers can communicate and thereby influence each other's behavior. Castronova (2006, p. 176) overlooks this point, while Castronova and Falk (2009, pp. 403–404) dismiss it. For more on the advantages and limitations of games as experiments, see Atlas (2008) and the literature cited there.

whole when seen from an economist's perspective. Merely set out the sandbox, allow players to step inside, and observe the ensuing social order (or chaos).

Along these lines, there are countless topics for economists to investigate in virtual worlds, including social norms and conventions, poverty, law and economics (Bradley and Froomkin, 2004), and spontaneous order (Castronova, 2001b, pp. 35–38). To these general topics could be added further explorations of value, price, distribution, and other fundamentals of the market process. And there are of course institutional questions: comparative economic systems, markets versus governments, competition versus monopoly, and so on. Each of these takes on unique forms and features in virtual worlds and offers economists new data and insight into economic relations.

Despite the optimism of this research agenda, however, it also carries dangers. Some of these are subtle and methodological, such as the risk of conflating social science with natural science, thereby ignoring the unique problems posed by human choice. Yet perhaps the most important is that treating virtual worlds as laboratories encourages economists to think of real social life in the same terms: as an experiment to be manipulated at will by benevolent planners. The games-as-laboratory perspective can yield useful insights, to be sure, but it can also be technocratic, and an example of what F. A. Hayek called "the engineering type of mind" (Hayek, 1952, pp. 94–102). In other words, it is prone to believing that transforming the real world into utopia requires only the right set of incentives and constraints—to be determined and administered by economists, of course—and that by studying virtual worlds, we can overcome the challenges of large-scale economic planning. It is much more difficult to accept with humility that designing and executing these schemes may be impossible, even for the most enlightened economists.

References

Atlas, S. A. 2008. "Inductive Metanomics: Economic Experiments in Virtual Worlds." *Journal of Virtual Worlds Research* 1 (1): 1–15.

Bartle, R. A. 2006. "Why Governments Aren't Gods and Gods Aren't Governments." *First Monday*. https://journals.uic.edu/ojs/index.php/fm/article/view/1612/1527#author.

Bell, M. W. 2008. "Toward a Definition of 'Virtual Worlds'." *Journal of Virtual Worlds Research* 1 (1): 1–5.

Boyd, S. G., B. Pyne, and S. F. Kane. 2019. *Video Game Law: Everything You Need to Know about Legal and Business Issues in the Game Industry*. London: CRC Press.

Bradley, C., and A. M. Froomkin. 2004. "Virtual Worlds, Real Rules." *New York Law School Law Review* 49 (1): 103–146.

Burghardt, G. M. 2011. "Defining and Recognizing Play." In *The Oxford Handbook of the Development of Play*, edited by P. Nathan and A. D. Pellegrini. Oxford: Oxford University Press, pp. 9–18.

Castronova, E. 2001a. "Virtual Worlds: A First-Hand Account of Market and Society on the Cyberian Frontier." CESifo Working Paper Series No. 618.

———. 2001b. "Virtual Worlds: A First-Hand Account of Market and Society on the Cyberian Frontier." *Gruter Institute Working Papers on Law, Economics, and Evolutionary Biology* 2 (1): 1–66.

———. 2002. "On Virtual Economies." CESifo Working Paper Series No. 752.

———. 2006. "On the Research Value of Large Games: Natural Experiments in Norrath and Camelot." *Games and Culture* 1 (2): 163–186.

———. 2008. *Exodus to the Virtual World: How Online Fun Is Changing Reality*. New York: Palgrave Macmillan.

———. 2018. "Worlds as Experiments." In *The Routledge Companion to Imaginary Worlds*, edited by M. J. P. Wolf. New York: Routledge, pp. 298–304.

Castronova, E., and M. Falk. 2009. "Virtual Worlds: Petri Dishes, Rat Mazes, and Supercolliders." *Games and Culture* 4 (4): 396–407.

Deterding, S. 2017. "The Pyrrhic Victory of Game Studies: Assessing the Past, Present, and Future of Interdisciplinary Game Research." *Games and Culture* 12 (6): 521–543.

Egenfeldt-Nielsen, S., J. H. Smith, and S. P. Tosca. 2016. *Understanding Video Games: The Essential Introduction*. 3rd ed. London: Routledge.

Foss, Nicolai J., and Peter G. Klein. 2012. *Organizing Entrepreneurial Judgment: A New Approach to the Firm*. Cambridge: Cambridge University Press.

Green, P. G. 2014. "Building the Culture of Your Business with *The Sims*." In *Teaching Entrepreneurship: A Practice-Based Approach*, edited by H. M. Neck, P. G. Greene, and C. G. Brush. Cheltenham, UK: Edward Elgar, pp. 110–113.

Hart, C. B., ed. 2017. *The Evolution and Social Impact of Video Game Economics*. London: Lexington Books.

Hayek, F. A. 1952. *The Counter-Revolution of Science*. Glencoe, Ill: The Free Press.

Huizinga, J. 1949 [1944]. *Homo Ludens: A Study of the Play-Element in Culture*. London: Routledge.

Knight, F. H. 1946. "The Sickness of Liberal Society." *Ethics* 56 (2): 79–95.

Liboriussen, Bjarke. 2017. "Gold Farming in China—and in Western Academia, Journalism, and Fiction." In *The Evolution and Social Impact of Video Game Economics*, edited by C. B. Hart. Lanham, MD: Lexington Books, pp. 139–153.

Mankiw, N. Gregory. 2012. *Principles of Microeconomics*. 6th ed. Mason, OH: South-Western Cengage Learning.

McCaffrey, M. 2020. "Review of *the Evolution and Social Impact of Video Game Economics*." *The Information Society* 36 (3): 177–180.

Messinger, P., E. Stroulia, and K. Lyons. 2008. "A Typology of Virtual Worlds: Historical Overview and Future Directions." *Journal of Virtual Worlds Research* 1 (1): 1–18.

Mises, Ludwig von. 1990. *Economic Calculation in the Socialist Commonwealth*. Auburn, AL: Ludwig von Mises Institute.

———. 1998 [1949]. *Human Action: The Scholar's Edition*. Auburn, AL: Ludwig von Mises Institute.

Nazir, M., and C. S. M. Lui. 2016. "A Brief History of Virtual Economy." *Journal of Virtual Worlds Research* 9 (1): 1–24.

Osborne, E. W., and S. Z. Schiller. 2009. "Order and Creativity in Virtual Worlds." *Journal of Virtual Worlds Research* 2 (3): 3–16.

Rodriguez, H. 2006. "The Playful and the Serious: An Approximation to Huizinga's *Homo Ludens*." *Game Studies* 6 (1).

Salter, Alexander W., and Solomon Stein. 2015. "Currency Emergence in Absence of State Influence: The Case of Diablo II." *Cosmos + Taxis* 2 (2): 34–45.

Schroeder, R. 2008. "Defining Virtual Worlds and Virtual Environments." *Journal of Virtual Worlds Research* 1 (1): 1–3.

Schulzke, M. 2009. "Moral Decision Making in *Fallout*." *Game Studies* 9 (2).

Schumpeter, Joseph A. 1942. *Capitalism, Socialism, and Democracy*. New York: Harper and Brothers Publishers.

Smith, J. H. 2007. "Tragedies of the Ludic Commons—Understanding Cooperation in Multiplayer Games." *Game Studies* 7 (1): 1–14.

Stang, S. 2019. "'This Action Will Have Consequences': Interactivity and Player Agency." *Game Studies* 19 (1).

Taylor, L. N. 2004. "Working the System: Economic Models for Video Game Narrative and Play." *Works and Days* 43 (44): 144–153.

2

Spontaneous Order and Video Game Narrative

Zachary Gochenour

> In myth and ritual the great instinctive forces of civilized life have their origin: law and order, commerce and profit, craft and art, poetry, wisdom and science. All are rooted in the primeval soil of play.
>
> —Johan Huizinga, *Homo Ludens: A Study of the Play Element in Culture*

> A game is indeed a clear instance of a process wherein obedience to common rules by elements pursuing different and even conflicting purposes results in overall order.
>
> —F. A. Hayek, *The Fatal Conceit*

Consider the practice of storytelling—a deliberate human contrivance where a storyteller consciously guides the listener through a series of events, introducing characters and places, usually with the intent to convey a moral lesson or elicit certain thoughts and emotions. In many stories, especially in more traditional media such as novels and films, the design of the narrative is paramount because it is the only explicit source of the audience's knowledge. Seen in this light, video games provide a fascinating case study of spontaneous orders in narrative: players possess a unique ability to interact with the game space, the game's creators, and other players, and this can fundamentally change how stories are created and experienced. Even in cases where consciously designed stories exist, the narrative that instead arises out of player actions and interactions is often the more interesting and enduring one for gamers themselves. In this chapter, I explore the idea of spontaneous order in games. I argue that early video games had mostly spontaneous narratives due to hardware and software limitations;

however, this emergent quality was gradually replaced with more structured, on-rails narratives of increasing complexity. Nevertheless, in the past decade especially, there has been a resurgence of interest in the spontaneous generation of narratives, which many argue provides a nearly infinite richness not achievable through conventional story structures. More spontaneous games create "stories" that, as Adam Ferguson said of spontaneous order in general, are the "result of human action, but not the execution of any human design." I also argue that the video game medium is particularly well suited to this kind of interactive storytelling, giving it a unique place among artistic media.

Spontaneous Order?

Among Adam Smith's many contributions to economics is the idea of market participants being led "as if by an invisible hand" to increase the welfare of all members of society (Smith, 1776; Rothschild, 1994). The notion of the invisible hand is an excellent metaphor for what we mean in this book by "spontaneous order": despite the fact that the people participating in the market are not being led by any central authority toward some beneficent social end, they *appear* as if they are. Smith's teacher Adam Ferguson defined this kind of order as the product of *human action* but not of *human design*.

The idea of spontaneous order plays an especially important role in the "Austrian" school of economics, and the concept was developed and refined by Carl Menger, Ludwig von Mises, Friedrich von Hayek, and, more recently, by their modern students (Boettke, 1990; D'Amico, 2015; Beaulier, Smith, and Sutter, 2012). The market is the Austrians' primary example of a spontaneous order: an undesigned and undesignable order that arises out of individuals' pursuit of their own interests and goals.

Political scientist Norman Barry called spontaneous order studies the field "concerned with those regularities in society, or orders of events, which are neither (*a*) the product of deliberate human contrivance (such as a statutory code of law or a *dirigiste* economic plan) nor (*b*) akin to *purely natural* phenomena (such as the weather, which exists quite independently of human intervention)." Spontaneous order research is used in a variety of disciplines, from economics to philosophy to literary studies (Cantor and Cox, 2009; Boettke, 1990; see also Barry, 1982, for a comprehensive list of examples).

This chapter is not the first attempt to explore the nature of spontaneous order in video games, although it does aim to provide a general foundation and touchstone for such research. Salter and Stein (2015), for example, examine the spontaneous nature of currency formation in the game *Diablo II*.[1] Among many features of its virtual economy was the fact that players created their own currency-based alternative to the game's intended monetary system, which was rife with inflation. In addition, Miller (2018) provides a fascinating account of spontaneous order in the game *Destiny* that raises similar themes to those developed in this chapter. More generally, the discussion later also fits within a broader literature studying the relationship between spontaneous order and cultural products, especially narrative art such as literature and storytelling (as explored, in detail, in Cantor and Cox's 2009 collection of essays).

One reason video games provide fertile ground for social science researchers is because behavioral conditions in games are similar to those in laboratory experiments: the game designers first establish a framework for interaction, and we can then observe in-game behavior and analyze its meaning for human actions more generally (Castronova, 2006).[2] We can see, for instance, the interplay between the design intentions of game developers and the behavior of the players. Games are thus also an especially useful setting in which to study spontaneous order. In his book *The Fatal Conceit*, for example, Hayek wrote that "a game is indeed a clear instance of a process wherein obedience to common rules by elements pursuing different and even conflicting purposes results in overall order." Although he was not speaking of video games, his logic applies just as well to virtual worlds as it does to the real one.

In the remainder of this chapter, I will make the case that spontaneous (also called emergent) order is a useful framework for understanding the evolution of narrative structure in video games. I contend that in video games, the narratives that most motivate players are frequently the result of human action but are not, or only partially, the result of human design. Sometimes this spontaneity results from subverting the designers' goals, whereas sometimes (particularly in more recent years) there is a conscious effort on the part of the game development community to cultivate this type of player interaction.

Older Games: Limitations Encouraged Spontaneity (1971–1991)

Many early video games intended to tell stories, but hardware and software limitations meant that results were quite simplistic (Heide Smith, Tosco, and Egenfeldt-Nielsen, 2008). As a result, players were obliged to create their own

1 See also the discussion in Chapters 5 and 6.

2 See also the discussion in Chapter 1.

narratives or, as emphasized in this chapter, to fill large gaps in existing stories by inventing and pursuing their own goals in the game—often goals that were unforeseen by designers. These narratives were necessarily created based on "the particular circumstances of time and place": the creativity of the player working within the boundaries of the game to create her own story. Although the structure of a game is roughly the same for everyone, no individual player's experience is exactly like another's, thus allowing for an open-ended narrative to emerge.

Early video game design was heavily constrained by the available hardware. The central processing unit (CPU) was invented in 1971 and, by the late 1970s, had become an affordable option for creating interactive games; games with rudimentary stories used to explain and motivate the player's actions followed as core technologies developed. *Pong*, one of the earliest popular arcade games, was released in 1972. It relied on discrete circuitry that severely limited the possible complexity of the game. In 1980, Japanese company Namco released *Pac-Man*, the now-famous yellow circle who tries to eat all of the dots inside a maze while evading ghosts try to stop him. To make the game more interesting, the ghosts were given unique artificial "personalities" (each moved according to a pattern) and behaved in predictable ways. Unlike games of later generations, there was no way to complete *Pac-Man*: levels simply increased in difficulty as they were cleared, with players chasing after a high score. Eventually, skilled players could find a way to "win" by getting the 256th level, where the game crashed due to a lack of memory. In 1999, gamer Billy Mitchell allegedly played the first recorded "perfect" game of *Pac-Man*, playing flawlessly over five hours, even circumventing the memory error to continue to increase his score (Ramsey, 2006). His quest to play the perfect game thus allowed for an experience that the original developers of *Pac-Man* did not anticipate.

One way to understand the role of spontaneous order is to consider a sport such as baseball. The original creators of the game merely set the initial rules: where the foul lines should be drawn, how many players are allowed on the field, how they may interact with the ball, and so on. In this sense, the number of possibilities for how play can occur seems limited. Yet once you put real humans into the positions and commence play, the number of "stories" that can be told is essentially infinite. The designers of baseball could not have predicted the myriad narratives that would emerge from their simple game rules. And just as no two games of baseball are exactly alike, no two games of *Pac-Man* are either. The element of interactivity by a human player enables these stories to emerge organically, as they did in Billy Mitchell's quest to play the perfect game of

Pac-Man. Even the flaws of the game, like the 256th level integer overflow error, become a part of the tapestry of the game's larger story when played out in real-world competitions.

After the "golden age" of video games, which ended in the mid-1980s, games started to become moderately more complex. The popularity of home gaming systems allowed developers to consider creating different sorts of games that might appeal to players interested in more complex designs than were practical for the arcade. *Super Mario Bros.* (1985), one of the most well-known and best-selling games of all time, uses a simple fantasy narrative where the hero searches after and saves a princess. Yet the enduring appeal of the game, as well as the community that has emerged around it, is not based on its written story but its underlying game mechanics that have allowed players to craft unique experiences for themselves and others. For decades, players have created their own challenges in these kinds of games, competing with each other for high scores (which were originally sent to video game magazines where they could be compared) or by trying to finish the game in the least amount of time.[3] Creating these kinds of experiences and even subcultures was not the intention of game developers: in some cases, the kinds of activities and communities that now exist around classic games were not even technically possible when the games were first created.[4] These challenges rather *emerge* from communities of players who, through their individual actions, created a new sort of game with goals never imagined by the developers.

Despite the growing interest in video games during the 1980s, the potential market value of the industry seemed to be in decline over the same period: in 1986, the video game industry was generating only half the revenue it had in 1981.[5] But by the 1990s, the technology available on home gaming systems had improved a great deal and designers began to explore more complicated designs and longer, more curated narrative experiences for players. Games such as *Dragon*

[3] This sort of competition is now called "speedrunning," and players still compete for the best times in the classic titles, with performances often broadcast through online platforms like Twitch and YouTube.

[4] One type of speedrunning, called "tool assisted," makes use of modern technology to find optimal ways of completing old games in times that are literally impossible for humans.

[5] From about 1983 to 1985, there was a worldwide crash in the video game industry, with some estimates claiming a loss of 97 per cent of revenue during that period. See Ernkvist (2008) for more details.

Quest (1986) and *Final Fantasy* (1987) defined a new role-playing genre that saw players working through epic stories taking tens of hours to complete. The popularity of these games, along with ever-improving technology, took game design down a road of increasing linearity.

The Rise of Linearity and Planned Orders in Video Games (c. 1992–2009)

As video games increased in technical complexity, game designers were able to craft far more elaborate narratives. Player experimentation was not always encouraged, as it could detract from the preestablished narrative developers had in mind. Too much player autonomy could even break the game. Game studios began to employ large staffs of quality assurance testers who tried to anticipate player actions that would subvert their intended designs; when oversights were discovered, these teams would try to find ways to limit or restrict unconventional player behaviors. Developers have recognized clearly that there is a trade-off between the ability to provide a well-crafted experience and the ability of players to do whatever they want in a game world.

This trade-off and transition between design styles can be seen in the early games of the *Final Fantasy* series, created by Square Inc., starting in 1987. In this series, players formed parties of hero characters comprised of different roles (healer, fighter, thief, and so forth), and the number of potential gameplay combinations was quite high. Playing with particularly strange and unbalanced combinations (such as a party of all healers) is still popular today among players who like a challenge. The first game's characters had no dialogue and no preset personalities, which would have been quite difficult to create given the technical limitations of its time. By 1996 though, *Final Fantasy* was a mega-franchise and the new capabilities of the Sony PlayStation meant that the series' 7th installment was filled with full-motion video cutscenes and tens of hours of scripted dialogue. The composition of the player's party was preset to fit with the game experience the designers envisioned. This meant a more consistent gameplay experience, but opportunities for spontaneous play were extremely limited.

Released in 1992, *Myst* was a surprise hit that went on to become the best-selling personal computer (PC) game of the decade. It put the player in the middle of an expansive fantasy world where one could interact with many different objects in an effort to solve puzzles and progress through the narrative—

but each puzzle had only one solution, making the game completely linear.[6] Of course, by limiting the types of responses the player can expect from elements in the game, designers are able to deliver a more curated experience. Another point in favor of this approach is that it limits the possibility of game-breaking bugs that occur when players interact with the game environment in unanticipated ways. Designers thus face a trade-off between offering predictable but highly designed experiences and giving players the freedom necessary for spontaneous play to emerge. Consider an example such as *Metal Gear Solid*, or many Japanese RPGs, which favor cinematic storytelling that often removes control from the player entirely for long periods of time. In Nintendo's wildly popular *Legend of Zelda* series, designers opted against the free-form nature of the original *Zelda* game when they designed 1998's *The Ocarina of Time*. The latter favored a more scripted experience where players were guided from one objective to the next. The general trend of games in the 1990s especially was toward completely linear gameplay and designed set pieces.

Yet not every game in this era embraced highly linear gameplay. The international mega-hit *Starcraft*, for instance, with its focus on competitive multiplayer, operates in a similar way to traditional sports: the designers set the rules for the game and curate it as players find creative ways to play, and developer interventions exist only to make sure the game stays competitive and interesting to fans: the real stories all emerge from the competitive gameplay. *The Sims* (2002), which replaced *Myst* as the best-selling PC game of its era, is likewise a game where the stories arise from design decisions the player makes for artificially intelligent agents in the game world (the sims). And, of course, we should recognize that the best-selling franchise of the 2000s, *Madden NFL*, also tells stories such as most sports or sim games: spontaneously.

Despite these notable exceptions though, this middle period in game history was the era of maximal design and the smallest amount of emergent gameplay. The success of franchises such as *Call of Duty* and *Uncharted* was possible because of the incredible leaps in technology and development budgets that drove their design. In an effort to design an experience similar to novels and films, designers limited the kind of emergent and imaginative gameplay that had drawn so many

6 This style of game, called a point-and-click adventure, was popular during the 1990s and saw great success with games like *Day of the Tentacle*, *Grim Fandango*, and the *Monkey Island* and *Sam and Max* franchises, all produced by LucasArts, and the *King's Quest*, *Space Quest*, and *Leisure Suit Larry* franchises produced by Sierra.

people to video games in the past. Yet following the lead of the more spontaneous kinds of titles, designers in recent years have embraced the role of spontaneous order in games in various ways.

The Ascendance of Spontaneity (2009–Present)

Recently, the world of video games has seen a return to a style of design less focused on tightly designed narratives. Linear-style games still exist, of course, with cinematic set pieces backed by massive budgets, but their popularity is nowhere near universal, and perhaps even in steep decline. Instead, games such as *World of Warcraft* and other MMO games have tried to foster a sense of community, cooperation, and competition with other players as the basis for an emergent narrative that is merely curated by the developers, not designed with such a heavy hand. In these games, players create their own economies (Castronova, 2003; Salter and Stein, 2015) and their own complex systems of goals and rewards (Miller, 2018). The multiplayer aspects of these games create spontaneity—each player is different and affects the players around him. Furthermore, in recent years, independent developers with relatively small budgets have entered the industry in large numbers. Their limited resources in many cases necessitate a less structured approach to development that allows for more spontaneity.

On the far end of the spectrum are games such as Mojang's *Minecraft*, first released in 2009, and now one of the highest-selling games of all time. *Minecraft* has no predetermined goal and provides players with little guidance regarding how to navigate and interact with its world. In *Minecraft*, the player must manipulate the environment to find resources needed to survive, and after securing their survival can look for additional resources to continue to explore the game world and modify it to suit their needs. There was initially no narrative and no ultimate objective: only limitations. Finding ways to overcome these limitations (or setting your own to make things even more restrictive) becomes the fun of the game, not following a pre-written script. The number of possible stories that can be told in this world is practically limitless.

Another example of increasing spontaneity in games is the adoption of "open world" mechanics in games alongside other more or less predetermined stories. The goal of this more minimal form of design is to increase the perception of player choice so that the individual player feels more in control of their own narrative. The open world format increases the feeling of agency the player has even if the story is still mostly linear, as in the *Assassin's Creed* or *Far Cry* franchises.

Games such as *Minecraft* close the narrative circle, bringing video games back to an earlier era where narratives were emergent rather than prescribed. Because each player and play-through is different (worlds are procedurally generated such that each one is unique), the possibilities for new narratives are inexhaustible. Furthermore, game designers today actually react to games' evolutionary progress by further curating the experience and responding to player demands. In some cases, spontaneous play may be detracting from the overall game experience, such as when exploits are found in fighting games that give unfair advantages. In other cases, designers are responding to the players by expanding the types of play that players want, especially by offering expansion content in response to customer requests.

Conclusion

The concept of spontaneous order is not limited to economics: it is applicable in biology, physics, ecology, and any field where we observe self-organization. It is especially valuable to any field in which there is an element of human behavior: humans do not simply follow simplistic, designed paths like automatons but adjust their behavior in light of the particular circumstances of time and place. Video games are a perfect opportunity to observe such emergent behaviors because, for many of us, part of the fun—or perhaps all of it—comes from exploring new types of play and subverting the intentions of game designers. We can see this from the earliest periods of video game development, when resources did not exist to create the types of highly designed experiences that came later. Early video gamers frequently behaved in ways that designers never intended, such as finding ways to set new high scores (or "perfect" games) in *Pac-Man*. Simulators set rules for gameplay but they could not have dreamed of what stories would be created in those simulations. While advancements in computing technology opened up many avenues for more overtly designed, curated experiences, games that allowed for spontaneous play have remained popular, with some of the best-selling games of all time such as *The Sims* keeping the tradition alive. In recent years, an element of spontaneous play has become standard in many popular games, with some of the most popular, such as *Minecraft*, catering specifically to this style of play. Ultimately, there is a fine line between over- and under-designing games, and developers would be wise to keep this aspect of human behavior in mind while deciding how to craft compelling experiences. And since video games are more popular than ever, with all sorts of demographics and interests to cater to, we will doubtless see a continual flowering of spontaneous order in the games of the future.

References

Barry, Norman. 1982. "The Tradition of Spontaneous Order." *Literature of Liberty* 5 (2): 7–58.

Beaulier, S. A., D. J. Smith, and D. Sutter. 2012. "Technology and the Architecture of Emergent Orders." *Studies in Emergent Order* 5: 157–176.

Boettke, Peter. 1990. "The Theory of Spontaneous Order and Cultural Evolution in the Social Theory of FA Hayek." *Cultural Dynamics* 3 (1): 61–83.

Cantor, Paul, and Steven Cox, eds. 2009. *Literature and the Economics of Liberty: Spontaneous Order in Culture*. Auburn, AL: Ludwig von Mises Institute.

Castronova, Edward. 2003. "On Virtual Economies." *The International Journal of Computer Game Research* 3 (2).

———. 2006. "On the Research Value of Large Games: Natural Experiments in Norrath and Camelot." *Games and Culture* 1 (2): 163–186.

D'Amico, Dan. 2015. "Spontaneous Order." In *The Oxford Handbook of Austrian Economics*, edited by Christopher Coyne and Peter Boettke. Oxford: Oxford University Press.

Ernkvist, Mirko. 2008. "Down Many Times, but Still Playing the Game: Creative Destruction and Industry Crashes in the Early Video Game Industry 1971–1986." In *History of Insolvency and Bankruptcy*, edited by Karl Gratzer and Dieter Stiefel. Södertörns högskola, pp. 161–191.

———. 1991. *The Fatal Conceit: The Errors of Socialism*. Chicago: University of Chicago Press.

Heide Smith, J., S. P. Tosca, and S. Egenfeldt-Nielsen. 2008. *Understanding Video Games: The Essential Introduction*. New York, London: Routledge.

Miller, William. 2018. "The Role of Spontaneous Order and Choice in Video Games: A Case Study of Destiny." *Cosmos + Taxis* 5 (3): 63–72.

Ramsey, David. 2006. "The Perfect Man." *Oxford American* no. 53 (Spring 2006).

Rothschild, E. 1994. "Adam Smith and the Invisible Hand." *American Economic Review* 84 (2): 319–322.

Salter, Alexander William, and Solomon M. Stein. 2015. "Currency Emergence in Absence of State Influence: The Case of Diablo II." *Cosmos + Taxis* 2 (2): 34–45.

Smith, Adam. 1776. *An Inquiry into the Nature and Causes of the Wealth of Nations (Book I)*. London: W. Strahan.

3

Law and Economics in a World of Dragons

Robert S. Cavender

Introduction

Nobel Prize-winning economist Elinor Ostrom's seminal thesis was that even when placed in an environment without government, individuals are nevertheless capable of developing alternative institutions that successfully turn conflict into cooperation. In her book *Governing the Commons,* Ostrom writes, "The central question in this study is how a group of principals who are in an interdependent situation can organize and govern themselves to obtain continuing joint benefits when all face temptations to free-ride, shirk, or otherwise act opportunistically" (Ostrom, 1990). She goes on to detail several real-world examples of such self-organization, including the self-governance of communally owned lands in Törbel, Switzerland, dating back to the 1500s, irrigation practices near Valencia that have survived for hundreds of years, and similar institutions in the Philippines dating back to at least the seventeenth century, among others. Following Ostrom, a number of authors have since contributed to a broader strand of the literature on self-governance (Milgrom, North, and Weingast, 1990; Ellickson, 1991; Bernstein, 1992; Greif, 1993; Clay, 1997; Zerbe and Anderson, 2001; Anderson and Hill, 2004; Dixit, 2004; Skarbek, 2011; Fike, 2012; Leeson, 2007, 2012).

This literature is relevant wherever government-enforced law and order are largely absent, for example, for a large part of human history (see, for instance, Benson, 1988; Leeson and Stringham, 2005; Posner, 1980), on the fringes of society (Ellickson, 1991; Leeson, 2007, 2012; Skarbek, 2011, 2012), and everywhere a "new frontier" emerges before the government has had a chance to get involved (for example, Anderson and Hill, 2004). Counterintuitively, this latter category is perhaps most relevant today, where a rapidly expanding new frontier has so far gone mostly unnoticed in the law and economics literature: the world of virtual online societies.[1] This chapter contributes to the earlier literature by providing a modern case study of the emergence of cooperative rules for self-governance to solve economic problems in virtual online environments. In particular, I examine the emergence and subsequent employment of the set of commonly understood and privately generated rules known collectively as "Dragon Kill Points," or "DKP," in MMO games and which were first introduced to economists in 2007 through an appreciative paper by Castronova and Fairfield (2007).

This setting is particularly interesting because of the methods that would *not* work to induce cooperation. For example, in many examples of reliable self-governance, individuals are able to rely on "simple" ostracism (Leeson and Coyne, 2012). In the relatively large but anonymous world of online virtual societies, however, such a mechanism is not as effective. Leeson (2012) does discuss a special real-world case of just such a limitation, where gypsies who also cannot rely on simple ostracism instead leverage superstition to enforce collective punishment of defectors and reward cooperation. However, since virtual online societies usually involve modern, highly educated, technologically savvy individuals, superstition is not a feasible recourse. These characteristics also tend to obstruct the ability of these persons to rely on religion for similar purposes (Iannaccone, 1992). Examining an altogether different case with a similar theme, Skarbek discusses how members of prison gangs create cooperation through strict monitoring and violent enforcement of gang codes. But since the economic interactions dealt with in this chapter occur online, often in environments where violence is strictly *impossible* (due to hard-coded virtual mechanics), a similar solution is out of the question.

What the legal system to be examined here does share with these cases and others like them is a more general thesis, to wit, that where simple ostracism is ineffective, private institutions can emerge that *reinforce* otherwise simple ostracism by making ostracism more costly until the point at which it proves effective. This sort of solution prevalent throughout the literature on self-governance seems to be sufficient, if not necessary, for the private establishment

[1] The most notable exception to this is Edward Castronova, who has published several works on virtual worlds, including an informal piece on the case examined in this chapter. See Castronova (2004), Castronova et al. (2009), and Castronova and Wagner (2011).

of effective property rights, and thus for self-governance to work. In Leeson's "Gypsy Law," this is the very role that superstition serves. In Skarbek (2010, 2011, 2012), racially segregated gangs who tattoo themselves with difficult-to-remove identifying markings make ostracism, and thus defection, more costly. The same goes for Greif's Maghribi Traders' coalition (Greif, 1993) which both increases in-group profits (raising the relative opportunity cost of being ostracized), and simultaneously reinforces the reputation mechanism by lowering the cost of monitoring. Likewise also the champagne fairs of Milgrom, North, and Weingast (1990) as well as the religions, communes, and cults Iannaccone investigates (Iannaccone, 1992), and so on.

In the case examined here, individuals must innovate a legal system utterly different from any of the earlier cases in that it cannot rely on the usual mechanisms of simple ostracism, religion, superstition, or violence. Moreover, these virtual online societies are characterized by anonymity, often the ability to change one's name and appearance at will, a relatively young population, and the absence of government intervention of any kind. All of these factors combined make this case a particularly challenging one for the emergence of law and property rights. And yet, in a variety of online virtual societies characterized by these very features, individuals rely on a privately adopted legal system of DKP to effectively establish and protect property rights, allocate economic goods, and engage in long-run contractual exchange. The rest of this chapter will explore how it is that the various systems of DKP employed throughout these virtual societies go about doing just that.

To that end, this chapter is divided up into the following sections: the second section begins by arguing for the relevance of the case to be examined, the next section examines the legal system of DKP as it emerged and is employed today in virtual societies, the fourth section discusses how the properties of DKP described in the previous section serve to establish property rights and long-run contractual exchange, and the final section offers avenues for further research, and concludes.

Virtual Worlds as Empirical Platforms

What Are Virtual Worlds, and Why Do They Matter?

The virtual environment examined in this chapter belongs to a particular subset of virtual online games called "massively multiplayer online role-playing games" or "MMORPGs." These are video games wherein individuals login to an online server or set of servers, which allow(s) them to play with other individuals who login to the same server(s) to play the same game. In MMORPGs, in particular, these are games where individuals create a virtual avatar and essentially go on adventures with said avatar: slaying virtual monsters, going on virtual quests, and so on, all in a *persistent* online virtual world. Importantly, "persistent" here means that the virtual world, including the economy therein, continues unabated even when any individual character is logged off—indeed, even when all persons might be (temporarily) logged off.

And unlike most laboratory experiments, the sheer size of these virtual reality worlds allows us to examine not just micro but *macro* phenomena.[2] This is important since most economic phenomena we are concerned with in the real world (like, for example, the outcomes of multiple simultaneous market processes) belong in the latter category. Second, virtual worlds often have economies that have persisted for long periods of time.[3] This is what has allowed the most interesting observable macro phenomena in these worlds the time needed to come about in the first place, as well as to evolve and become realistically complex. This is extremely important for economic research since, again, most analogous real-world institutions also emerge only after lengths of time that usually extend beyond the scope of a normal laboratory experiment.[4]

While demonstrably further to the right on the simplicity–complexity scale than laboratory experiments, virtual economies are nevertheless far simpler and easier to observe than the real world. In addition, virtual economies allow programmers full control over the technological possibilities in the virtual world, enabling them to create simple environments that encapsulate whatever payoff structures are desired. And unlike agent-based modeling, virtual economies are made up of real people dealing with real economic goods. Finally, unlike both laboratory experiments and agent-based modeling, virtual economies take place in long-term dynamic environments capable of supporting man-made

---

[2] The population of players for some of the more popular online games can grow remarkably large. *World of Warcraft*, for example, reportedly peaked in late 2010 with a total population of about 12 million players—more than many real-world countries (Holisky, 2010).

[3] *EverQuest*, another popular MMORPG, has had persistent, continuous economies since 1999.

[4] In no way is this meant to disparage laboratory experiments. Quite the contrary. What laboratory experiments accomplish, and intentionally so, is a clear empirical distinction between control groups and treatment groups. The same goes for field experiments, to a slightly lesser degree. Virtual worlds lie somewhere in between.

institutions for solving economic problems not unlike those we observe in the far messier real world.

The Stakes

It is worth briefly discussing the stakes of this research, since at this point, it remains unclear just how relevant virtual worlds are in the grand scheme of things. Yes, they are persistent; yes, they are big; but why should they otherwise matter to economists? The answer is that virtual worlds are important for the same reason as any other economic phenomena: because they matter to the individuals involved.[5]

First, the economic goods created in these virtual worlds serve as status symbols within their respective online communities. Most of these goods are immediately visible to those who observe their owners within these environments and confer upon their owners a conspicuous wealth apparent to everyone around them. This is, perhaps, enough of an incentive for people to care a great deal about these goods. Indeed, goods produced in these economies are often worth a hefty sum of real-world cash via online (gray) markets. Single spaceships in *EVE Online* have sold for thousands of real-world dollars.[6] Virtual real estate was reportedly sold for hundreds of thousands of real-world dollars in the online game of *Entropia.* As of the writing of this chapter in 2019, one may purchase a "blue partyhat"—literally a blue-colored party hat, albeit virtual—for $3,400 online for an avatar to wear in *RuneScape*. As economists, we do not have to agree with said buyers and sellers in order to recognize that clearly these goods mean a great deal to them. In 2005, for example, a Chinese gamer named Qiu Chengwei stabbed another player, Zhu Caoyuan, to death (in real life) for selling a sword in *Legends of Mir 3* worth about $650. And while a real-world murder over virtual goods is rare, selling them for real-world cash is not.

Moreover, time and effort spent producing virtual goods in online environments nevertheless has real opportunity costs, and we can examine some averages to get a sense of what those are. Williams, Yee, and Caplan (2008) conducted a survey of the online game *EverQuest 2,* the sequel to the original *EverQuest* that is to be examined in more detail in the third section. They found that the average male subscriber played about 25.03 hours per week, while the average female played about 29.31 hours. Having found 80 per cent

---

5 See also Chapter 1.

6 See also Chapter 4.

of the subscribers to be male, this put the weighted average at 25.886 hours per week, or 1,345.072 hours per year per player. They also found that the average *EverQuest 2* player tended to be more educated than the average US citizen, with an average income of $84,715 per year per household. Dividing this generously by the average household size in 2008 of 2.56 (United States Census Bureau) suggests an average income of roughly $33,091.80 per year per player. At an average rate of 1,791 hours worked per year in the United States in 2008 (Organisation for Economic Co-operation and Development 2015), this puts the average hourly wage of *EverQuest 2* players at $18.48 that year. Finally, multiplying the weighted average number of hours played per year times the average hourly wage of *EverQuest 2* players puts the average opportunity cost *per player* at $24,852.51 of wages "lost" in 2008 by playing *EverQuest 2* instead. This is in addition to the (typical) $15 subscription fee per month per player!

Neither is this result atypical nor idiosyncratic to this virtual world. In fact, *EverQuest 2* was not even among the top five most popular MMO games by market share as of April 2008, those spots being taken by *World of Warcraft*, *RuneScape*, *Lineage*, *Lineage 2*, and *Final Fantasy XI*.[7] Nor was MMORPG gaming a short-lived product of the times. Where a population of hundreds of thousands of players was once considered remarkable, as of 2019, several top online games have active populations numbering in the millions (MMO Populations, 2019), and the trend shows no sign of letting up (McGonigal, 2011; Aguiar et al., 2018). Indeed, when one considers the tens of millions of players who continue to play these sorts of games on a yearly basis, the aggregate opportunity cost in terms of foregone real-world wages within these virtual worlds easily exceeds the gross domestic product (GDP) of most countries. These environments at the very least matter to those who act within them, for at least the time that they act within them. Add to this the fact that producing certain virtual goods often takes many consecutive hours per night at several nights per week—not to mention the skill and upfront time investment usually required to enable said production in the first place—and it becomes clear that, though virtual, these economic goods are very real.

It is in the production of virtual goods that law and economics comes into play. Notably for this chapter, the production of virtual goods in most MMORPGs is perhaps best captured by the payoffs associated with what economists would

[7] Other competitors included *Dofus*, *EVE Online*, *The Lord of the Rings Online*, and *City of Heroes/Villains*. See Woodcock (2008).

call a *stag hunt*, where productive cooperation is mutually beneficial *but not otherwise assured*—a feature characteristic of many of Elinor Ostrom's real-world case studies. Lo and behold, just as Ostrom demonstrated took place in reality, it turns out that virtual societies have evolved an analogous set of privately ordered institutions that not only serve to incentivize cooperative outcomes within firms in MMORPGs but also simultaneously act to strengthen the use of ostracism as a mechanism of private enforcement of contracts.[8] The most commonly known set of these institutions belongs under the heading of Dragon Kill Points, or DKP.[9] Investigating how and why it is that DKP came to be initially created, as well as how the system acts to incentivize cooperation and increase the costliness of ostracism absent government intervention, is the task of the rest of this chapter.

"Dragon Kill Points"

The Economic Problem

Naturally, the ultimate goal of any game is to have fun, but in a role-playing game, this most often entails developing the abilities of one's avatar. Online role-playing games are no different, and in many of these (much like the real world), one's status within the game world corresponds roughly to how good one's *stuff* is. Take, as an example, the virtual world of *EverQuest* circa 1999. In this case, judging the quality of one's stuff amounted to asking how tough was their armor, how sharp were their swords, how powerful were their spells, and so on. The best of these pieces of equipment were obtainable only by teaming up with a large number of other players to kill a big virtual monster, like a dragon. Most of the time the way it worked was that upon slaying said dragon, a semi-random piece of equipment, or perhaps several pieces of equipment, would appear as a reward.[10] This sort of cooperative production process came to be known informally as a "raid."

---

[8] Although the first version of the system was consciously *designed* for private use, it has since come to have a life of its own. See the section "A Private Solution."

[9] While other similar types of institutions, not necessarily colloquially referred to merely as "DKP," also exist and will be briefly discussed, it is important to recognize that most or all of them have evolved in some way from or alongside the original DKP system, and so are also referred to more generally here for the sake of brevity. For another excellent (though less formal) economics paper on DKP, see Castronova and Fairfield (2007).

[10] By semi-random, it is meant that most of the time, upon slaying a particular monster, a small number of items would be produced randomly but from a predetermined (and consistent) larger list of *possible* items, akin to randomly drawing a name from a finite hat.

However, the numbers of goods rewarded from these "raids" were never as many as the number of people it took to engage in the process itself. For instance, often monsters which required twenty or more people to kill would only drop something like one or two goods as a reward. This created a kind of temporary scarcity.[11] Both of these points together, that individuals were dealing with a cooperative production process that also involved scarce economic goods, are related to real-world concerns, both of providing adequate reward to incentivize participation in the first place and, importantly, ensuring long-term cooperation (that is, in the language of game theory, incentivizing "cooperate-cooperate" and disincentivizing "shirk-shirk"), all in a world of relative anonymity. Whether individuals can manage to solve these two problems without the government is not only a relevant question for its own sake but also for real-world concerns over our ability to do the same.

In addition, these rewards were very much like capital goods in the real-world economy in two broad ways. First, they were heterogeneous and multi-specific in that certain goods could only be used by certain types of player avatars, and not at all by others. Second, equipping enough player avatars in the group with good enough equipment from slaying mid-sized monsters was often a prerequisite for the group to slay ever-larger monsters for even better treasure, making much of the equipment that dropped from the midsized monsters resemble a sort of intermediate capital good. Thus, we have here the usual economic problems associated with the efficient distribution of intermediate goods—in many ways, a more integral yet complex question than those involving the production of consumer goods—as well as problems related to the creation of public goods and how to prevent free riding thereon.

Therefore, here were real people coordinating their actions in a production process to create scarce, heterogeneous, multi-specific final as well as intermediate goods, which somehow had to be allocated postproduction. Furthermore, given the built-in semi-random nature of the reward process, this had to be done in such a way that players could be credibly ensured that they would eventually be rewarded (read: paid) so that they were willing to cooperate in these production

[11] Moreover, often it was the case that monsters would not be slayable again for long periods of time. In *World of Warcraft*, any one specific group of avatars could only slay certain large monsters once per week. In *EverQuest*, if anyone at all on any particular server slew certain monsters, this would prevent *everyone else* on the server from being eligible to slay said monsters for upwards of half a week in some cases.

processes multiple times eventually reaching into the long run,[12] with otherwise no guarantee for a reward any particular time.

Finally, it is important to point out that this was not the only way in which players could obtain economic goods within the game. Players could instead quest for equipment alone or in very small groups—but such equipment was typically vastly inferior. Therefore, this was a perfect example of a *stag hunt*, just like most production processes in any real-world economy. For those familiar with game theory, the corresponding payoffs are illustrated in Figure 3.1, where $a > b \geq c > d$:

Figure 3.1

	Raid	Don't Raid
Raid	A, a	D, b
Don't Raid	B, d	C, c

Since both "raid-raid" and "don't-don't" are stable equilibria in this game, this means that if all players, for whatever reason, simply default to "raid" every single time, or if everyone at least has good enough reason to expect everyone else to contribute every time, then there will be no problems at all. But since a successful raid requires most potential raiders to actually contribute all at the *same time*, this means that if enough players have no particular reason to expect others to play "raid," or if enough players simply default to playing "don't," then basic game theory predicts it will be difficult or even impossible for the best outcomes to emerge.[13] In other words, all it takes is a handful of players to play "don't" for the entire raid group to fall apart, whereas it takes *all* players playing "raid"

[12] The usual expectation for the best equipment is at least a number of weeks' or months' worth of effort.

[13] Skyrms (1996, p. 21) writes explicitly that the "fundamental question of the social contract" is: "[How] can you get from the noncooperative hare hunting equilibrium to the cooperative stag hunting equilibrium?" He draws our attention, too, to Hume's *Treatise*, in which he pointed out using the meadow-draining example that the mutual expectations of trust necessary for cooperation in a stag hunt are all the more difficult to achieve when the players involved are more numerous than a mere pair (Hume, 1896 [1739]).

simultaneously in order for it to be successful. Unfortunately, this means that "don't-don't" appears to be not only a stable equilibrium but in fact a *particularly* stable one compared to "raid-raid." In such an environment, we expect relatively few groups to engage in successful raids—and that makes for a whole lot of fun *not* being had.

However, as the new institutional economics literature has demonstrated time and again, if living, breathing persons are unhappy with a "don't-don't"-type outcome, and especially if said outcome exists in a perpetual environment, there is good reason to expect individuals to attempt to change the stakes (and, therewith, the expectations) of the game itself. Theoretically, all that was needed to ensure "raid-raid" in *EverQuest* in 1999 was some sort of institution capable of generating both initial as well as continued mutual expectations of cooperation for all players involved. In the real world with a functional government, the solution to this sort of dilemma would be simple: a legally binding contract promising payment to all participating players who agree to continually engage in this production process enough times. That is, essentially, all that was really needed was an employment contract. This is the typical proposed solution to the problem of reinforcing cooperative outcomes in real-world stag hunts—for example, production within a firm. But in these virtual online worlds, no outside legal entity existed to enforce such contracts.[14] A private institution needed to emerge to solve these problems. And that is precisely what happened.

A Private Solution

The most commonly known set of these privately adopted institutions is DKP, the original version of which was created by an *EverQuest* player by the name of Thott in 1999 to solve the very sorts of problems mentioned earlier. But DKP has since been adopted for use in numerous other online virtual worlds, many of which contain "raids" of the sort necessitating DKP's initial creation.

In Thott's original instantiation of DKP, which he developed for an *EverQuest* guild[15] called Afterlife, players were allotted a quasi-currency (more like coupons

---

[14] Blizzard (2010), the company that produces *World of Warcraft*, even specifically included in its Terms of Use agreement that players "shall have no ownership or other property interest in any account stored or hosted on a Blizzard system," including any presumed property rights over items acquired therein. *EverQuest*, and almost all other popular MMORPGs, include similar clauses.

[15] Most often, these systems were and are run and kept track of by the leaders of so-called "guilds"—the official designation for in-game groups who consistently raid together. These guilds essentially act as *firms* in the production process of virtual goods.

or points) for successfully taking part in a raid. These were the "Dragon Kill Points" (DKPs) after which the system itself came to be named. Players attended these raids and earned these DKPs for assisting in the production process. These points were then accumulated by individual players to spend on loot rights to rewards.[16] It is important to note that accumulation here does not refer to any in-game sort of collection of digital points. Since players were unable to alter the overarching rules of the environment itself (since those were hard-coded into the game's mechanics), DKP had to be entirely created and kept track of privately by individual players.[17]

As far as purchasing the rights to loot treasure, the rules were relatively simple. Every time an individual helped to slay one of several particular monsters, that player received a single DKP. When an item would drop that a player desired, he or she would enter into a lottery to win the item alongside every other qualified player who wanted it.[18] Each player would essentially get one "ticket" in the lottery for every DKP that that player had accumulated over time, so that players who routinely contributed to the raid would receive more chances to win each time. However, in the event that a player won an item, he or she would lose DKPs equal to the "value" of the item, where the value was a set price agreed to beforehand by the guild.

Finally, if a player had more than one avatar capable of attending the raid and that might have benefited from the dropped item, but that player chose to bring a different avatar for the sake of helping the raid *and* said player announced his or her intent beforehand, he or she could roll for the item to win it for the alternate avatar instead. Then, after an item was won, even if it was technically tradable according to the official hard-coded game mechanics, it was deemed impermissible to trade the item away to someone outside of the guild. Even trading within the guild had to go through the lottery system again, although

---

16 More modern systems of DKP often feature a kind of price catalogue instead, where the player must purchase their desired loot at a set "market" price that has been agreed to by the group beforehand. In reality, there are a great number of complex incarnations of this system depending on the circumstances. See the section "DKP Today."

17 The use of the word "privately" rather than "informally" or "unofficially" is intentional here, because while these points were kept track of outside of the game mechanics themselves, they nevertheless were often tallied within highly formalized systems of rules by predesignated scorekeepers.

18 Being "qualified" to purchase the item produced during the raid could involve a complex list of prerequisites not necessarily relevant for the general story here. For a more in-depth explanation, see anonymous (n.d.).

"selling" an item in this way earned back the DKP the seller had spent on the item. Additionally, any items won outside the system (for instance, by a guild member who happened to attend a raid led by an outsider) could be "sold" into the system in this way, but the seller received only half the normal DKP value.

The Role of DKP in Reinforcing Cooperative Outcomes

Reinforcing Long-Term Cooperation

The basic system of DKP described earlier was cleverly constructed and employed precisely to increase the payoffs to cooperative play and decrease those to shirking. To understand how, let us consider first the problem the DKP system addressed most directly, that is, the problem of adequate reward.

Prior to the introduction of DKP, the way loot was often distributed was by simple lottery, even within guilds.[19] When a useful item was "dropped," any individual who desired that item and who engaged in the production process of the raid was allowed to roll a 100-sided die against any other individual who also desired said item, regardless of how many times each individual was present in previous raids. Whomever rolled the highest number would win the good. This meant that every raid was a mere roll of the die in terms of whether one would receive any actual payment for assisting. Even if one were fortunate enough to belong to a powerful guild (and especially if not), one could spend days or weeks waiting on the preferred monster to be generated within the world, spend hours organizing a large enough group of individuals,[20] undertake the often daunting task of getting everyone safely to the monster and, finally, (hopefully) slay it, only to lose the desired item to another lucky individual in the raid. This assumes the desired item even dropped, of which there was no guarantee. If one did not receive the hoped-for reward on any particular raid, then it was essentially a complete waste of time for that person.[21] A single individual could repeatedly participate in the same daily or weekly raid slaying the same monster for months hoping to receive a particular item only to lose it (when it finally dropped) to someone participating for the first time; or an individual whose entire virtual

[19] Or else by simple agreement or decree.

[20] Upward of twenty to forty people were often required for raids in earlier MMORPGs, while some raids in later games could require up to seventy-two coordinated individuals.

[21] Except, of course, for the fun of it. It is, after all, a game. It should be noted, however, that many if not most players took these raids very seriously. See the sections "The Economic Problem" and "A Private Solution."

character depended on receiving a particular item could lose it to someone who had only minor uses for it. These situations were commonly referred to as "bad lottos." The easy possibility of bad lottos meant that for many, despite the allure of potentially receiving the very best rewards in their respective virtual world, even the best players would often abstain from raiding or even quit altogether. Due merely to the consequence of inadequate (or uncertain) reward, players ended up having not only less loot but also, perhaps even more tragically, less fun.

Enter DKP. By being paid DKP regardless of whether one received more direct rewards, individuals could rightly feel that they were progressing. Some payment was given regardless of luck, so long as a player cooperated. Even otherwise fruitless raids accrued some payment to those who participated. This was an important step in the history of online gaming guilds, as it allowed guild members to receive for the first time something akin to hourly wages. At the very least, for risk-averse individuals (read: most people), this meant an increase in the expected return to raiding—psychologically speaking, a literal raise in their wage—resulting in more production.

It is important to point out here, then, that the relative dearth in production prior to DKP was due not necessarily to the lack of *opportunity* to be productive. Rewards were there for the taking. It was, rather, a problem of long-term contracting. It was true that a player's desired item may not have been generated from successfully slaying a particular monster one time, but even without DKP, it was still mathematically the case that repeat attempts would have granted additional chances for said item to appear. However, due to the random nature of rolling dice against other players for items *even after* the desired item was generated, it was quite conceivable for a player to (within a reasonable time frame) *never* receive their desired reward from the monster in question, no matter how much that player contributed to the production process, and no matter how many times that player helped other players to receive their just dues. Theoretically, a simple incentive-compatible way of getting players to voluntarily contribute to raids would have been to gradually raise their chances of receiving their desired items as they contributed more often to the production of such equipment, but such a solution required the ability to contract with other players *over the long term*. Notably, in this case, that needed to occur absent any sort of government. And once again, that's exactly what happened. Essentially, in game-theoretic terms, this new means of payment could be characterized as having produced an increase in the expected payoff to playing "raid" for all players involved. But that was not the only problem DKP had to solve.

Disincentivizing Free Riding

Another problem confronting individuals in these production processes was the issue of free riding. Almost always, in these virtual worlds, players were allowed to create multiple avatars per server but were restricted by the game mechanics to playing one avatar at a time.[22] Thus, players often had various avatars with correspondingly varying degrees of powerful equipment. In one common form, free riding would thus involve a player purposely bringing his or her avatar with the worst equipment to raids in order to receive the greatest potential marginal benefit from item drops. Such players would necessarily rely to a greater extent on the rest of the individuals in the raid to do more of the work. Although different from not cooperating at all, free riding in this way is most properly characterized as similar to playing "hare" in the usual stag hunt framework.

In other words, players who intentionally brought their weakest avatars to a raid as a result of the incentive to free ride were thus imposing a negative externality on the rest of the raid group by forcing everyone else to pick up the slack when it came time to slay those dragons.[23] In fact, prior to the adoption of DKP, since loot was only distributed to active raid participants, and because most loot had such rapidly diminishing marginal returns, lucky players who had already won all of the most powerful loot on their "main" avatars were naturally discouraged from bringing said "main" avatars to any further raids, since there was very little loot those avatars could possibly need from slaying those same monsters again. Therefore, since raids required a significant number of powerful avatars (contributors), but only the weakest avatars (free riders) were willing to attend raids, there arose the familiar economic problem of private under-provision of public goods (Samuelson, 1954; Olson, 1971 [1965]; Smith, 1980). Indeed, one of the biggest concerns in any serious discussion of law and order absent government is this very question of how to prevent free riding. And in this case, even though it occurred in a virtual world, it nevertheless involved real individuals coming up with a solution to what is often thought of as the raison d'être for government intervention in the real world.

---

[22] Some individuals did manage to play more than one at a time, a practice known as "multi-boxing," but they often had to use special computer setups and pay for multiple accounts simultaneously, since only one avatar was usually allowed to be played per account at any one moment.

[23] Or the occasional orcs, goblins, cyclopes, demons, bugbears, beholders, giant spiders, werewolves, or armies of the undead—whatever needed slaying at the time. Adventurers rarely discriminate.

Once again, the system of DKP assisted in doing just that. Since one player's DKP was tied not to any specific avatar but rather to their entire collection of avatars on any given server, this private system of receipt-keeping allowed players to roll for non-present avatars rather than only for the one they happened to have brought. Thus, in order to maximize the chances of succeeding at slaying a monster, after adopting DKP, each player would be incentivized instead to bring his or her most powerful avatar, simultaneously providing the maximum social benefit to the rest of the raid even while winning equipment for their neediest avatars.

Counterintuitively, this also had the unfortunate side effect of generating additional uncertainty for some players regarding adequate reward for their participation in any given raid. That is, where before if a player had the only avatar present who needed a particular piece of loot, under a system of DKP, this player found herself potentially having to roll against avatars who were not even present during the raid. But it turns out the solution for that pickle was already built into one of the restrictions described at the end of the section "A Private Solution." Namely, DKP required participants to state any intention to roll for a non-present avatar ahead of time. Thus, the problem of free riding was addressed without any additional uncertainty, again without the need for government intervention. And once again, the ultimate consequence was another increase in the payoff to playing "raid."

Internal Enforcement

However, while ostensibly the DKP system was designed to solve the issues outlined earlier, the fact that the rules of the system still had to be *enforced* somehow without recourse to a third-party contractual institution like the government meant that in order to work properly, some means of internal enforcement had to be devised. This is perhaps the primary problem facing the implementation of any otherwise desirable set of rules where the government is absent or ineffective. This held especially true in the case of MMORPG raiding, since there in fact existed an even more furtive form of free riding that occasionally took place wherein an individual would attend a raid (with their very best avatar!) but nevertheless employ very little effort in the guild-wide attempt to down a monster. In a classic display of free riding, such individuals would hide among the large numbers of players and on-screen graphical effects, thereby concealing the fact that they themselves were doing very little work. Instead, these despicable deadbeats would rely on the rest of the group to do most of the dirty work. Of course, a close observation of each individual present could *sometimes* confirm whether this method of free riding was taking place, particularly when later third-party programs were written to determine how much each individual player contributed.[24]

But still, there was the problem of how to punish such players. If it was noticed by the end of the raid that certain individuals were free riding in this way, they could potentially be denied loot rights by the leader of the raid. But sometimes such free riders could go several raids before being noticed, giving them at least a chance to win loot with minimal effort. Even if such players were kicked out of their respective guilds (supposing they were in one), if they managed to get their loot beforehand, it would hardly have mattered. They got what they came for, and nothing more could be done to punish them.

This is the familiar problem of defection that economists originally thought proved the complete infeasibility of law and order without government intervention. This consensus was renewed at a scholarly workshop entitled *Explorations in the Theory of Anarchy*, which took place during the early 1970s at the Center for the Study of Public Choice. However, more recent work has suggested ways in which ostracism in particular can be used to overcome such difficulties (Clay, 1997; Milgom, North, and Weingast, 1990; Leeson, 2012; Klein and Leffler, 1981; Klein, 1992; Leeson 2006), although the consensus in the literature is generally that such mechanisms work only in small, close-knit communities (Zerbe and Anderson, 2001; Greif, 2002; Dixit, 2004). Virtual economies, however, often involve large numbers of anonymous individuals—exactly the sorts of situations in which ostracism is ordinarily considered least effective. Yet reputation and ostracism are the main sources of order that DKP exploits.

Indeed, the use of the "guild" system itself already assisted in turning otherwise large numbers of individuals into comparatively smaller groups in which group name reputation could have an increased effect. However, in addition, by tying DKP crucially into membership of the guild (as per the rule prohibiting selling items outside the guild as well as the discount with which items could be brought in), the very system itself strengthened the use of simple ostracism as a private mechanism of enforcement without the need to make use of any third parties. In fact, in guilds that made subsequent use of amended versions of the

---

[24] Although such programs (often known simply as "DPS meters") were not flawless since they had to focus on semi-arbitrary quantitative statistics for the sake of measurability, which were not always the best indicators of a potentially diverse production process involving many potential ways of contributing.

original DKP system, often a player first had to go through several raids before even qualifying to receive DKP. This gave guilds more time to detect free riding before doling out loot to new members.

Second, by inventing and keeping track of a system of points that a player accrued while in the guild (and *only* while in the guild), making use of a DKP system of accounting served to effectively increase the cost of being kicked out of the guild after accumulating said points. This is the primary way in which DKP served to increase the payoffs to cooperation and the opportunity cost to noncooperation, again absent any sort of external government. Since a player's DKP was kept track of only within the guild and was only considered legitimate by members who voluntarily accepted that player as a member of the guild itself, such points were only accrued to the player so long as he or she remained in good standing with the entire guild. This actually allowed for the enforcement of all sorts of other socially beneficial rules as well.[25] Just as handily, this particular means of strengthening the enforcement mechanism of ostracism by increasing its relative cost could impact even the leaders of guilds, functionally preventing them from manipulating loot drops to serve their own needs, such as by looting all of the gear for themselves or for their closest friends at the expense of the rest of the group. It was entirely possible for the entire guild to leave, choosing to keep their own DKP but disallowing the leader from joining ever again (effectively eliminating his or her entire collection of DKP wealth, not to mention power). By both adding a direct cost to noncooperation and increasing the opportunity cost of continued refusal to cooperate, DKP thus also served to decrease the expected payoff to "don't raid."

Game-Theoretic Implications[26]

Sections "Reinforcing Long-Term Cooperation" and "Disincentivizing Free Riding" may be understood as a description of the means with which DKP increased the expected payoffs to cooperation ("raid"), while the section "Internal

---

[25] For example, the *World of Warcraft* guild known as Ignorance had clearly outlined rules posted on their guild website prohibiting disrespectful chat, bullying behavior, raiding with an outside guild, being late to raids, being unprepared, looting items out of turn, and so on. Specific DKP penalties were imposed according to a formally ordered list.

[26] For any reader new to game theory and interested in learning more about it, check out *The Evolution of Cooperation* by Robert Axelrod (1984) and/or *The Stag Hunt and the Evolution of Social Structure* by Brian Skyrms (2003).

Enforcement" describes the ways in which DKP lowered the expected payoffs to noncooperation ("don't raid"). And although the payoffs change as constantly as the player-base, the newly adjusted post-DKP stag hunt payoffs associated with raiding may be roughly represented by the following table, where $a > b \geq c > d$, and where x and y are greater than zero and represent the reward and penalty provided by the adopted system of DKP to "raid" and "don't raid," respectively:

Figure 3.2

	Raid	Don't Raid
Raid	A + X, a + x	D + X, b – y
Don't Raid	B – Y, d + x	C – Y, c – y

After adopting DKP, the "raid-raid" outcome was more promising than before, while the "don't-don't" outcome became less promising. Indeed, if the consequences of ostracism were great enough (for instance, if y were greater than both b and c), then playing raid became *always* desirable—in fact, serving to change the game from a stag hunt to a pure cooperation game where "raid raid" was the *only* stable outcome. Most importantly, however, even with only a minor punishment to playing "don't raid" and/or a minor reward to playing "raid" compared to before (that is, if y and/or x were relatively small), *expectations* about what others would do were still effected in the direction of "raid" within a guild making use of DKP compared to one operating without. The bigger the stakes to "raid" were relative to "don't raid," the more cooperation became the focal point of the game.

Thus, just as Elinor Ostrom demonstrated took place in so many real-world cases, here DKP generated a working example of individuals voluntarily coming together to develop a set of institutions that successfully established lasting property rights over the products of their labor, helped allocate scarce economic goods, and enabled coproducers to engage in long-run contractual exchange—all taking place in an environment utterly different from those examined in the literature so far, and all without government intervention of any kind.

DKP Today

Like any system for coordinating the activities of large numbers of people, DKP has since been confronted with new problems, some of which are unintended consequences of the system itself. An important question for any system of self-governance is how it responds to such pressure, whether positively or negatively, and DKP is no exception. However, since its inception, DKP and its offshoots *have* in fact successfully evolved, branching into a number of different forms of loot distribution systems depending on relative price signals. Some have primarily emerged to deal with unforeseen consequences of the standard model described earlier. Others have evolved to better negotiate trade-offs between equitability and fairness, or between thoroughness and parsimony, and so on.

For example, while the use of DKP in this way often served to better enforce social cooperation and coordination within guilds, the biggest undesirable and unforeseen consequence of the standard DKP model was a steady "inflation" of DKP. This occurred when more DKP were flowing into the system than out, as was particularly likely in guilds that had been raiding for a long time, wherein raid monsters were slain at an ever-increasing pace and more and more members' inventories became saturated with desirable loot. Indeed, DKP inflation could and did occur even when DKPs were only handed out for successfully slaying particularly *big* monsters, and the problem was even worse for guilds that did so on a regular basis. Typical solutions to this common problem have since generally taken the form of some sort of redistribution of DKP wealth from veteran guild members to newer members, to name just one example, by artificially imposing diminishing marginal returns to DKP accumulation in the so-called "Relational DKP" system.

These sorts of solutions have engendered even further variance in rule structures. For instance, if a guild is brand new and does not have veteran members to worry about, its members may choose to adopt a simple, standard DKP system. That is, unless it is trying to poach members away from other guilds full of players who are fed up with DKP inflation elsewhere. Old guilds with a few veterans trying desperately to attract new members may opt for a more equitable loot system. Guilds with strong player bases but weak or lazy guild leaders, officers, or a meager player pool to draw from may opt for systems which require very little effort in terms of tracking or calculating DKP, like a so-called "Spend-All" or "Suicide" system, where instead of keeping track of DKP, purchasing an item involves sacrificing one's position on a mere ordered list. Small enough guilds may choose to use no DKP system at all, opting instead for simple arbitration and friendly agreement between relatively few members. All of these concerns, as well as which sorts of DKP systems are deemed acceptable or adequate, are affected by the ever-changing culture and expectations of the player-base on any given game server.[27]

Innumerable subtypes of the earlier rule-sets are employed to this day by various guilds in popular online games like *World of Warcraft*, *Rift*, *EverQuest*, *EverQuest 2*, and *The Lord of the Rings Online*, among many others. Indeed, the auspicious evolution of DKP is itself testament to the very point Elinor Ostrom was making when she argued that in order to get good institutions, it is often pivotal that those who are involved in their design and implementation are the same individuals who would benefit most from the success of those institutions. Even where government is completely absent, whenever people have a stake in the game, it pays to try to achieve cooperation—and at least sometimes, apparently, they manage to succeed.

Concluding Remarks

This chapter began with a brief discussion of the literature on the institutions of self-governance. In the introduction, I drew attention to some of the mechanisms that have proven successful in inducing economic cooperation absent government intervention in past cases, namely simple ostracism, superstition, religion, and violence. Next, I identified virtual online societies as a particularly challenging case where these mechanisms are unreliable at best. Finally, I examined the privately developed legal system known as DKPs and described how that system established property rights, helped allocate scarce economic goods, and allowed for long-run contractual exchange in online virtual societies despite the aforementioned challenges, as well as how the system has evolved in various ways since.

Further avenues for research include an investigation of whether any sort of order emerges in virtual worlds where (virtual) violent coercion, rather than being impossible, is commonplace and encouraged—a subject explored

[27] Other popular variants include the "Zero-Sum" set of DKP rules, where players must literally "buy" the rights to loot from the rest of the guild to ensure equivalence between DKP "entering" and DKP "leaving" the system, and "bidding" DKP systems where auction-style mechanisms are used instead of fixed prices. Each system has its own relative trade-offs. Numerous guides now exist to assist guilds in negotiating between these systems, given their respective constraints. For example, see Caraway (2011).

elsewhere in this book. Other future work might include investigations of other emergent economic phenomena in virtual worlds that have so far not been discussed. Chapter 5 of this book is an exploration of emergent money but other empirical examples abound. The relative price stability of almost completely unfettered markets is demonstrated on a daily basis in many virtual online economies, for example. These worlds also provide a chance to observe macro-level effects from unregulated, "pure" entrepreneurship.[28] Studies might also be done on the incentives and consequences of what are essentially the purest of monopolies in said worlds, where players for all intents and purposes control entire streams of resources.[29] Also observable are the effects of various changes in game mechanics (sometimes analogous to changes in economic policies) on virtual economies, including the effects of "bannable" offenses like selling in-game currency for real-world cash and the demand-driven gray markets these policies generate. All of these and more are potential areas of future research.

This chapter has also provided some empirical evidence that real people facing real problems of coordination and cooperation that resemble in many important ways the problems all societies face on a daily basis are indeed capable of developing and successfully implementing private institutional solutions without government, and even without resorting to simple ostracism, superstition, religion, or violence. The primary real-world implication, beyond the contribution to game theory, is that we should be more optimistic about our human ability to solve problems without relying on an external savior. Where this implication plays out in more specific instances of domestic and international politics is fruit for further picking. But without a doubt, the institutions examined in this chapter are at the very least relevant to virtual worlds—which are, for better or worse, clearly on the rise.

---

[28] Where the archetypal "entrepreneur" is, according to economist Israel Kirzner, "a decision-maker whose entire role arises out of his alertness to hitherto unnoticed opportunities," who "starts out without any means whatsoever" and essentially arbitrages his way to profit, acting as an equilibrator in the market process. That we have clear examples of individuals doing naught but typing into their computers and ending up with digital items often worth hefty sums of real-world money is astounding, and perhaps an excellent example of this type of phenomenon (Kirzner, 1973).

[29] An example of this would be guilds staking claim to sole ownership of all the spots where a rare monster spawns, an activity commonly known as "camping."

References

Aguiar, Mark, Mark Bils, Kerwin Kofi Charles, and Erik Hurst. 2018. "Leisure Luxuries and the Labor Supply of Young Men." NBER Working Paper Series. Working paper no. 23552. DOI: 10.3386/w23552. Revised February 2018.

Anderson, T. L., and P. J. Hill. 2004. *The Not So Wild, Wild West: Property Rights on the Frontier*. Stanford: Stanford University Press.

Anonymous. n.d. "DKP Explanation (Historical)." *Afterlife*. Accessed on January 20, 2021. https://web.archive.org/web/20200805130240/http://afterlifeguild.org/dkplist/dkp-explanation-historical/.

Axelrod, Robert. 1984. *The Evolution of Cooperation*. New York: Basic Books.

Benson, Bruce L. 1988. "Legal Evolution in Primitive Societies." *Journal of Institutional and Theoretical Economics* 144 (5): 772–788.

Bernstein, Lisa. 1992. "Opting Out of the Legal System: Extralegal Contractual Relations in the Diamond Industry." *Journal of Legal Studies* 21 (1): 115–157.

Blizzard Entertainment. 2010. "World of Warcraft End User License Agreement." *Blizzard Entertainment*. Accessed on September 2, 2012. http://us.blizzard.com/en-us/company/legal/wow_tou.html.

Caraway, Tyler. 2011. "Ready Check: Looking into DKP Loot Systems." *Joystiq.com*. Accessed on January 9, 2021. http://wow.joystiq.com/2011/09/23/ready-check-looking-into-dkp-loot-systems.

Castronova, Edward. 2004. "The Right to Play." *New York Law School Law Review* 49 (1): 185–210.

Castronova, Edward, and Gert G. Wagner. 2011. "Virtual Life Satisfaction." *Kyklos* 64 (3): 313–328.

Castronova, Edward, and Joshua Fairfield. 2007. "Dragon Kill Points: A Summary Whitepaper." Prepared for the Rational Models Seminar, University of Chicago, October 16, 2006.

Castronova, Edward, Dmitri Williams, Cuihua Shen, Rabindra Ratan, Li Xiong, Yun Huang, and Brian Keegan. 2009. "As Real as Real? Macroeconomic Behavior in a Large-Scale Virtual World." *New Media & Society* 11 (5): 685–707.

Clay, K. 1997. "Trade Without Law: Private-Order Institutions in Mexican California." *Journal of Law, Economics, and Organization* 13 (1): 202–231.

Dixit, A. 2004. *Lawlessness and Economics: Alternative Modes of Governance*. Princeton: Princeton University Press.

Ellickson, R. 1991. *Order without Law: How Neighbors Settle Disputes*. Cambridge, MA: Harvard University Press.

Fike, R. 2012. "Is Anarchy without Coercion Possible? Lessons from the Old Order Amish and Their Exemptions from the Federal Government." Mimeo.

Greif, A. 1993. "Contract Enforceability and Economic Institutions in Early Trade: The Maghribi Traders' Coalition." *American Economic Review* 83 (3): 525–548.

———. 2002. "Institutions and Impersonal Exchange: From Communal to Individual Responsibility." *Journal of Institutional and Theoretical Economics* 158 (1): 168–204.

Holisky, Adam. 2010. "World of Warcraft Reaches 12 Million Players." *WoW Insider*, October 7, 2010. Accessed on June 18, 2013. http://wow.joystiq.com/2010/10/07/world-of-warcraft-reaches-12-million-players/.

Hume, David. 1896 [1739]. *A Treatise of Human Nature by David Hume. Reprinted from the Original Edition in three volumes and edited, with an analytical index, by L. A. Selby-Bigge, M.A.* Oxford: Clarendon Press.

Iannaccone, Laurence R. 1992. "Sacrifice and Stigma: Reducing Free-Riding in Cults, Communes, and Other Collectives." *Journal of Political Economy* 100 (2): 271–291.

Kirzner, Israel M. 1973. *Competition and Entrepreneurship*. Chicago: University of Chicago Press.

Klein, B., and K. Leffler. 1981. "The Role of Market Forces in Assuring Contractual Performance." *Journal of Political Economy* 89 (4): 615–641.

Klein, D. 1992. "Promise Keeping in the Great Society: A Model of Credit Information Sharing." *Economics and Politics* 4 (2): 117–136.

Leeson, Peter T. 2006. "Efficient Anarchy." *Public Choice* 130 (1–2): 41–53.

———. 2007. "An-arrgh-chy: The Law and Economics of Pirate Organization." *Journal of Political Economy* 115 (6): 1049–1094.

———. 2012. "Gypsy Law." *Public Choice* 155 (2013): 273–292.

Leeson, Peter T., and Christopher J. Coyne. 2012. "Conflict-Inhibiting Norms." In *The Oxford Handbook of the Economics of Peace and* Conflict, edited by Michelle Garfinkel and Stergios Skaperdas. Oxford: Oxford University Press, 840–860.

Leeson, Peter T., and Edward P. Stringham. 2005. "Is Government Inevitable?" *Independent Review* 9 (4): 543–549.

McGonigal, Jane. 2011. *Reality is Broken: Why Games Make Us Better and How They Can Change the World.* New York: The Penguin Press.

Milgrom, Paul R., Douglass C. North, and Barry R. Weingast. 1990. "The Role of Institutions in the Revival of Trade: The Law Merchant, Private Judges, and the Champagne Fairs." *Economics & Politics* 2 (1): 1–23.

MMO Populations. 2019. "Top MMOs in 2019." MMO Populations. Accessed on December 2, 2019. https://mmo-population.com/top/2019.

Olson, Mancur. 1971 [1965]. *The Logic of Collective Action: Public Goods and the Theory of Groups*. Rev. ed. London, England: Harvard University Press.

Ostrom, E. 1990. *Governing the Commons: The Evolution of Institutions for Collective Action.* New York: Cambridge University Press.

Organisation for Economic Co-operation and Development. 2015. "Average Annual Hours Actually Worked per Worker." *Organisation for Economic Co-operation and Development.* Accessed on April 17, 2015. http://stats.oecd.org/index.aspx?DataSetCode=ANHRS.

Posner, Richard A. 1980. "A Theory of Primitive Society, with Special Reference to Law." *Journal of Law and Economics* 23 (1): 1–53.

Samuelson, P. 1954. "The Pure Theory of Public Expenditure." *The Review of Economics and Statistics* 36 (4): 387–389.

Skarbek, David. 2010. "Putting the 'Con' into Constitutions: The Economics of Prison Gangs." *Journal of Law, Economics, & Organization* 26 (2): 183–211.

———. 2011. "Governance and Prison Gangs." *American Political Science Review* 105 (4): 702–716.

———. 2012. "Prison Gangs, Norms, and Organizations." *Journal of Economic Behavior and Organization* 82 (1): 96–109.

Skyrms, Brian. 1996. *Evolution of the Social Contract.* Cambridge: Cambridge University Press.

———. 2003. *The Stag Hunt and the Evolution of Social Structure.* Cambridge, UK: Cambridge University Press.

Smith, Vernon L. 1980. "Experiments with a Decentralized Mechanism for Public Good Decisions." *American Economic Review* 70 (4): 584–599.

United States Census Bureau. "Average Population Per Household and Family: 1940 to Present." Accessed on January 20, 2021. https://www2.census.gov/programs-surveys/demo/tables/families/time-series/households/hh6.xls.

Williams, Dmitri, Nick Yee, and Scott E. Caplan. 2008. "Who Plays, How Much, and Why? Debunking the Stereotypical Gamer Profile." *Journal of Computer-Mediated Communication* 13 (4): 993–1018.

Woodcock, Bruce. 2008. "MMOG Subscriptions Market Share - April 2008." *Wayback Machine*, March 2, 2008. Accessed on November 1, 2019. https://web.archive.org/web/20080302182111/http://www.mmogchart.com/Chart7.html.

Zerbe, R., and L. Anderson. 2001. "Culture and Fairness in the Development of Institutions in the California Gold Fields." *Journal of Economic History* 61 (1): 114–143.

4

Minerals, Titans, and Connections

The Political Economy of Empire in the World of *EVE Online*

Stephen Davies

The online game *EVE Online* is of interest to scholars from a wide range of academic disciplines in addition to those concerned with the specific topic of video games as such. That is because the nature of the game and its setup, together with the deliberate policy of its creators, CCP Games, has brought about a complex and evolving emergent order. The phenomenon of emergent or spontaneous order is very important for several disciplines but in this case, the details of the order and the paths the evolution has taken are relevant for several important debates in a number of disciplines.[1] In particular, *EVE Online* casts light on questions about the ability of rational choice to give a convincing account of the evolution of political orders, the value of Hobbesian state of nature models, and questions about the dynamics and stability or otherwise of interstate systems—to mention just three.

EVE Online is perhaps the best known and most widely discussed example of the genre of massively multiplayer online games (MMOGs) (Achterbosch, Pierce, and Simmons, 2008). This is despite its having far fewer subscribers and active players than some other MMOGs, such as *World of Warcraft* for example. *EVE* has appeared on major mainstream news outlets such as the BBC and has already become the topic of a scholarly literature (BBC, 2013; Carter, Bergstrom, and Woodford, 2016). Interest from mainstream media reflects distinctive features of the game, such as its single server and the lack of prohibitions against conduct that would be considered "grieving" and lead to barring in almost all other games

[1] See the discussion in Chapter 2.

(Evans, 2010). This results in spectacular scams and acts of betrayal and, most notably, massive armed conflicts in the virtual world of *EVE*, the best known of which destroyed capital assets worth $300,000 in real money (Moore, 2014). The scale of these events is what attracts the popular attention. The scholarly interest has two foci. One is the way in which the game is different from others in terms of its organization and the degree of control exerted by the designers as well as in other ways. It is thus an example of a different kind of online game to the normal or typical models. It is therefore of interest to those concerned with the internal logic, nature, and development of the genre of virtual worlds. In terms of business models, you would have to say it has been highly successful: it is still going on seventeen years after it was launched, despite requiring a subscription fee (which most other games do not). (One interesting question is that of why there have not been many attempts to imitate the model.) The other source of academic interest is in the internal nature of the game and the way it has developed over time. This is, as is widely acknowledged, an example of an emergent order. As such, it can cast light on a range of major issues in political theory and political science, history, and international relations.

Distinctive Features of the Game

The distinctive features of the *EVE* game are well known but it is worth briefly setting out the ones that are relevant for the discussion here because they explain or lead to the reality of an emergent order where complex relations and institutions arise from the interactions of players in an almost totally unscripted way. The first is that *EVE* is a sandbox game in which the developers provide a framework and certain raw materials, but it is the players who do what they want in that setting with those materials and the further products they have created using those raw materials (CCP Games, n.d.). Thus, there is not a script or prescribed set of options for players at decision points (as is the case in what are commonly called theme park games). In addition, although role-playing of a prescribed and defined character, of the kind that is a central feature of many online games, is possible, relatively few players chose that option. They choose instead to become simple players and the role they have in the game is something they create themselves through their actions and interactions with other players.

Second, there is a single persistent server that all worldwide *EVE* players log onto, unlike all other games where there are typically multiple servers each in a different time zone (Khaw, 2013). This means that even though other games have more players, the number on any one server is much smaller than on *EVE*'s main server. You can only interact with the players on your own server and so the number of players available for interaction is far less than the total number involved in the game. In addition, they will all be from the same group of time zones and therefore (typically) fairly homogeneous in terms of language and background. In *EVE*, you can interact with all of the other players of the game (apart from China) in a single shared universe and time, and because of the literally global scope of the server, these will come from a very wide variety of backgrounds. This means that the number of people any one player will interact with is much larger and more varied than in other games. This, combined with other features of the game, makes it possible for a far more elaborate spontaneous order to emerge from the interactions of the players. This is because the number and variety of connections and interactions leads to more complex and elaborate higher-level organizations appearing than would be possible with fewer. By analogy, if you have a larger number of Lego bricks and many more types and shapes of brick, the range and complexity of the structures that can be created is larger. For the metaphor to work completely, however, we have to imagine that the bricks are not inanimate but can communicate with each other and get together to form complex structures. This is only possible because of the large number of interactions made possible by a single server. (The qualification to the above is that there is a separate server in China, for Chinese players, because of Chinese government internet regulations, but this has created a fascinating natural experiment that enables us to answer certain questions, such as the degree to which the behavior of the agents [players] is culturally influenced or determined.)

Third, the developers (CCP Games) have pursued an explicitly hands-off policy in terms of limiting or restricting what players can do. Simply put, there are almost no rules. Actions and activities such as killing another player's character or destroying her property, conspiracy, theft, murder, and betrayal are all allowed (de Zwart and Humphreys, 2014). In one part of the fictional world of *EVE*, there are prohibitions on attacking other players or their assets in the shape of an automated police force that will respond almost instantly to any violation by appearing and destroying the perpetrator, but the great bulk of the fictional world ("zero security space" or "null sec space") has no such restrictions. Moreover, even in the so-called high security region, the automated police force (CONCORD) only responds to attacks, it does not take proactive steps to prevent them. The literal laissez-faire policy of the developers was best illustrated when one of the game's most fascinating and notorious characters, The Mittani, orchestrated an attack on one of the key commercial hubs of the supposedly protected sector by having large numbers of ships that could deliver a devastating strike in the short moment before the arrival of CONCORD mount a suicide mission: the point was that although the participating ships were destroyed with their pilots, other ships could then come in and pick up lots of valuable assets, because CONCORD would not act against them (EVE Community, 2013).[2] This was described by one of the senior developers as "fucking brilliant" (Yin-Poole, 2012). So, in *EVE Online,* or at the very least in large parts of it, there are no limitations on what players can do: actions that would get you banned or blocked in any other game, and in many cases incur a severe criminal sanction in the real world, are permissible (Dibbell, 2008; Hammer, 2007a, 2007b, 2007c, 2007d).

Fourth, a number of distinctive features make the game more difficult to play for newcomers and add considerably to the costs that new players can face (and indeed, even established ones) (Paul, 2016; Drain, 2012). Unlike the typical industry model where the more often you interact with the game, the greater your skill and capacity regardless of the time you take doing this, in *EVE Online,* training and skills acquisition takes place in real time and can often take a long time. Several of the foundational activities of the game, particularly mining and manufacturing, also take place in real time; building a large ship can take several weeks so if it is destroyed, a significant amount of time and effort is written off and lost (Stigg, 2010). An important consequence of this real-time training is that no matter how long you play for, you will not catch up with more established players who have remained active. This again is different from most other games, where catching up by acquiring skill points or abilities is possible, in fact, a design feature. In addition, death in this virtual world is far more costly than it is in other ones. In most online games, if your character is killed you come back to life with all of the skills and capacities you had at the moment of death intact. In *EVE,* although in extremis your consciousness will be relocated to a prepared clone kept in a safe location, you will lose all of your recently acquired skills and training, which represent a considerable expense of real time and money. All of this means that the penalties for mistakes made by players are very high. To make it worse, the game is notoriously hard to play for the new entrant, with what has been described as a concave learning curve (Egan, 2009). The developers have actually made things even more difficult (almost certainly by design) by

---

[2] This strategy of using suicide attacks to get around the rules, known as "ganking," is a recurrent feature of *EVE* play, having been developed by enterprising players.

providing introductory tutorials that are themselves hard to understand, and which often leave out crucial information or tips (CrazyKinux, 2008, 2010; CCP Games, 2010b; CCP Greyscale, 2013).

This final point is partly a matter of marketing because it means that casual players are scared off and only the most hard-core fans stick out the initial learning process, producing a body of people who are highly committed to the product (Bergstrom et al., 2013). The experience of adapting to the way the game works acts like a form of hazing and has the same function that that activity does in organizations such as the military and team sports: building identification with, and loyalty to, the product (Cimino, 2011). However, it also has effects on the dynamics of the virtual world. The acute difficulty of adapting to the game on the part of new entrants and the harsh and brutal virtual world created by the no-actions-barred practice of the developers means that for many new subscribers, the only course of action is to associate with and get advice and support from established players, thus building chosen links within the game and making them a feature of its dynamics (CCP Phantom, 2014).

Incentives and the Spontaneous Order of *EVE Online*

All of these distinctive features of the virtual world create a series of incentives for the players which they naturally respond to. In this world, the ultimate decision-makers are individual persons (the players) who can interact with each other in a very wide variety of ways because of the sandbox nature of the game, the large number of players on the single server, and the lack of inbuilt constraints put in by developers. These interactions produce a complex outcome that is not reducible to the individual choices that produce it and underlie it—the outcome has qualities that are not found at the individual level and only become apparent when the system as a whole is examined. In other words, the distinctive features of *EVE* make possible an emergent order. In this complex order, initial conditions are enormously important, maybe even determinative, in two ways. There are many examples of cascade effects or butterfly effects as they are sometimes called, where a trivial initial choice leads directly but step-by-step to massive unforeseen and unintended consequences (CCP Games, 2009a). Secondly, the course of many of the game's complex evolutionary processes was set in the early period after the game was formally launched in 2003, with players who had participated in the development or beta phase playing a key part in setting the initial direction of development. However, the importance of initial conditions should not hide the most striking feature of this emergent order which is its unpredictability. Although there is an order and a pattern to the society of the fictional universe of New Eden, the form that pattern takes at any point in time was not and could not be foreseen, much less designed, and is not fully or even substantially predictable on the basis of past events.

One obvious conclusion to draw from the descriptions and accounts of *EVE*, and the structural principle of there being no built-in limitations on the actions of players, is that in this world you cannot trust anyone (Schaefer, 2010). Indeed, this is a message drummed into newbie players that betrayal is always possible and you should not trust anyone. (There is one exception to this, a player called Chribba who is trusted by everyone and for a while was a very important economic actor as a result, as he became the essential middleman for the buying and selling of the massive supercapital Titan ships) (Chribba, 2016). Such a complete lack of trust should, according to much economic and social theory, make complex institutions and elaborated cooperation impossible. In fact, though, despite the many scams and betrayals and widespread predatory behavior such as piracy that happen constantly in New Eden, a complex economic and political order has emerged.

The Nature and Features of the Spontaneous Order: Economy

What are the main features of this emergent order that has come into being over the last sixteen years? In the first and foundational place, a complex economy has come about. Market economic systems are a feature of several MMOGs and arise when a game has an internal money (which may or may not be convertible to real-world money), allows trades and exchanges, and is set up so that scarcity and variable supply and demand are features of the virtual world (Castronova, 2001). In the case of *EVE*, the additional elements are ones brought about by the design features listed earlier, which together mean that economic exchange has a much more diverse and unscripted quality than in other games. This accounts for the greater complexity of the economic aspect of the virtual world. There is much debate about the nature of the economic systems of virtual worlds. In many cases, they are clearly more like gift exchange than market exchange, and Yannis Varoufakis has argued that this is the normal state of affairs in virtual worlds (as well as related platforms such as STEAM), with little or no true market exchange taking place (Varoufakis, 2012). As other authors have argued, this is clearly not the case because of the presence of scarcity and fluctuations in both demand and supply for commodities and services, which together produce exchange prices and opportunities for arbitrage (buying low and selling high in other words).[3]

Varoufakis, however, has argued with specific reference to *EVE* that it does not have a full-fledged market economy (as he puts it). He suggests two reasons for this. The first is that standard microeconomics is not applicable because of the prevalence of violence and predation—as he puts it, "The whole point about *Eve Online* is to corner markets, to forge cartels, to maximise one's power over price. And unlike Adam Smith's fiction, where such aspirations cancel each other out, leaving everyone with zero market power, and thus enabling the 'invisible hand' to perform its magic, in *Eve Online* power rules OK" (Varoufakis, 2014). The second is that standard macroeconomics is simply irrelevant because the economy of *EVE* lacks two key features of a modern capitalist economy: a labor market and an endogenous money supply. Leaving aside the misrepresentation of Smith (Varoufakis is projecting post-Walras neoclassical economics back onto classical economics), the first argument is beside the point. In *EVE*, you have economic relations between players—they mine minerals then refine them, turn them into manufactured products, and buy and sell goods between each other at every stage of the productive process. These relations are conducted using the game's in-house money ISK (Interstellar Credits) and are entirely unscripted (Dibbell, 2006; Edwards, 2011). The result is a pattern of prices that behaves according to the principles of supply and demand, with arbitrageurs acting to equalize prices between trade hubs, subject to time lags and actors seeking out profit opportunities (Mark, 2017–2018). There has been a growth in economic complexity, with many specialized economic occupations appearing and being offered, often by relative newcomers to the game. A complex division of labor has developed in other words, alongside an increasingly extensive and elaborate trade system, complete with a superstructure of things such as credit, insurance, and investment markets. The point is that there is a recognizable system of complex economic relations that has emerged, with widely understood rules and norms (even if many, while understanding them, proceed to flout them). The role of exchange and flexible pricing means that this is clearly a market- or exchange-based economic system. That it does not conform to the abstract models of neoclassical economics actually makes it more interesting because it makes the economy that has emerged in *EVE* more like a real-world historical example of a market economic system, where power and its misuse and constant efforts to establish and keep supernormal profits were and are a regular part of things.

[3] See the discussion in Chapter 1.

One thing that is not allowed in *EVE*, but is in other MMOGs, is converting in-game currency directly to real-world money, in either direction. However, there is an indirect way around this as there is a product you can use in the game called a Pilot License Extension (PLEX) that can be bought with real money from CCP. Once bought, it can be traded and sold within the game for, among other things, the in-game currency of ISKs. This enables players to indirectly invest real-world money in the game (it also allows players to pay their subscriptions indirectly with in-game money as one of the things the PLEX can be exchanged for once bought is playing time). What it also does is to establish a means of calculating prices of *EVE* assets such as ships, expressed in ISKs, in real-world equivalents.

Varoufakis's second point is well taken, however. Although the economy that has arisen is a market or exchange economy, it is not a capitalist one in any meaningful sense of that term (that is, one that refers to specific instances of a certain kind of economic order rather than market exchange throughout history) (Goody, 2004). One of the striking features of the economic order that has emerged is that there is no employment as such (Butler et al., 2002). There is a great deal of labor that is paid, but the payment is contractual, for a product or service, rather than being a wage that buys a certain amount of a person's time, so the central economic and social relationship of capitalism is absent (but see Taylor et al., 2015; see also Terranova, 2013). Another striking absence is centralized and integrated mass production, with goods then being distributed. There is some of this for large capital items, but most of the manufacturing and the foundational activities such as mining are still distributed geographically and connected and held together by contracts. Yet another is large complex firms—where such entities are found they are actually an aspect of the emergent political order of *EVE* and should be thought of as political organizations as much as commercial ones, mainly because their economic goals are subordinated to political ones, as we shall see. There is entrepreneurship in abundance, much of it displaying the classic quality of "alertness" identified by Israel Kirzner, but what is not found is the combination of entrepreneurship and technical invention that is such a prominent feature of contemporary capitalism (Kirzner, 2015). This last does derive from one of the structural features of the game—complex products are produced from blueprints sold to players by NPCs and these (so far) cannot be amended and major technological innovations such as the introduction of massive ship classes such as Titans are done by the developers, which makes them exogenous to the order produced by player interaction. If we were to try and find a real-world analogy for the economy of *EVE*, it would be not modern capitalism but some example of premodern exchange economy. The best match is probably the economic order of the early modern world, which is interesting because the current political order of *EVE* is also similar to that of Europe at that time.

It is the political order that has emerged in *EVE* since 2003 that has attracted the most attention, not least because this aspect of the game's development is the one that has produced the massive wars and space battles that pique the interest of the mainstream media (Pronger, 2014; Purchese, 2013; Groen, 2016). From the account of the game's basic parameters given earlier, we might imagine that what would emerge would be an order of radical individualism, of every (individual) man for himself, but in fact this is not so. Instead, there is a political order that is institutionally complex and elaborate and marked by strong cooperation as well as competition. Certainly, many players do participate in the game on a purely individual basis. (This is common among those who chose to play mainly as miners and manufacturers and avoid the player-versus-player [PvP] style of play that most favor.) However, to achieve almost any complex task (or mission in the language of games), players have to cooperate. In addition, the steep learning curve for new players makes being part of a cooperative group a near imperative for them, particularly if they have any idea of venturing from the high-security regions of New Eden to the low security or null-security regions. The result is the appearance of what are called corporations, associations of players who cooperate to achieve shared goals, watch out for each other and protect each other, and pool some or all of their resources. This is found in most other MMOGs under the name of guilds, but what has happened in *EVE Online* is that the political organization of the game has gone two or three stages beyond that.

Most corporations in *EVE* initially had fewer members than Dunbar's number of 150—the number of close social connections that the average human mind can keep track of at any time. As such, they corresponded to the kinds of band or small tribal groups that were the dominant social unit during the Paleolithic or Neolithic periods or social groups such as gangs that form in the contemporary real world. With time though, many *EVE* corporations have grown beyond Dunbar's number with some of the largest such as Goonwaffe or Dreddit having several thousand. Very often, the first large corporations and alliances were formed by people who had some kind of real-world affinity, such as speaking the same language or who knew each other already from another game or from some kind of social association in the world outside *EVE*. For example, both Goonwaffe and Dreddit consist of people who were already acquainted through preexisting and non-*EVE* related online chat sites (in the case of Goonwaffe, the Something Awful comedy chat board, for Dreddit the Reddit boards). The other is that one particular ethnicity of players, the "Russians" (actually, a combination of Russians, Ukrainians, and others) do tend to stick together (partly because of using a different typeface). In economic or sociological terms, such preformed groups have higher levels of social capital (bonding capital, to be precise) and this makes them more effective as group actors in the early phase of the internal evolution of *EVE*. In some cases, such as the Goons from Something Awful, there was a preexisting identity or outlook that led them to approach the game and its dynamics in a particular way, which turned out to be advantageous to them.

However, this did not last and one of the most noticeable features of the order that has emerged in *EVE* is the way that the social bonds of corporations and alliances have come to develop beyond their starting point in groups with an already formed connection. One main reason for this is the single server. This means that to prosecute war successfully in New Eden, you have to be allied to players from many parts of the world or have members from many parts of the world in your own corporation, so that there will always be some of your "team" awake and logged on around the clock (otherwise, your opponents will attack when it is 2 a.m. your time and you are probably asleep). This, in turn, means reaching out beyond natural, real-world links. It also means actively recruiting new members that you do not have any personal knowledge of, or connections to, to build up your numbers. As explained, new members also have strong incentives to join a group of more experienced players because of the hazards and difficulties of the game for newcomers. Moreover, unlike in the real world, there are no natural affinities such as kinship or proximity to ease the formation of corporations in the first place other than the initial ones already mentioned, so they are purely a matter of individuals combining on the basis of mutual interest. There are two main qualifications to that, however. Today, and for some time, the bulk of new memberships for corporations is acquired through recruitment. This has developed rapidly and has gone from word of mouth to highly professional marketing, complete with glossy websites and recruitment advertising. The actual game, as well as support sites, provides links to advertising and recruiting pages where the new player can study the offers made by recruiting corporations. For their part, established corporations have a wide range of recruiting policies, which reflect their strategies and current status.

As corporations became larger and passed Dunbar's number, they came to need a management structure with a team with defined roles. They also became more complex and structured in other ways, with a more elaborate internal division of labor, and came to be more like tribes or clans. From a very early date in the evolution of the game, corporations came together to form alliances which marked a further step upward in size and internal complexity. The largest alliances in *EVE*, such as Test Alliance Please Ignore, Goonswarm, and Pandemic Horde are very large and truly complex organizations—Goonswarm has just over 30,000 members, for example. This makes running one of them as demanding in terms of time and effort as administering a company of the same size, but with a global reach and workforce (thanks to the global server principle) (The Mittani, 2016). As political entities, alliances correspond to something like states and have most of the definitive characteristics of a state. They tax their members to fund shared or common interest activities, they settle disputes among members, punish "defectors" and rule breakers, operate a welfare system to compensate members for losses incurred during collective activities such as wars, and provide a range of services and assistance to members. Above all, they engage in the key enterprise of states—they make war.

The Spontaneous Order: Politics

It is the need and desire to engage in warfare to expand territory and control or to merely protect what one already has that leads to the escalating increase in organizational size and complexity. Coordinating the actions of an assembled fleet of hundreds or even thousands of individual players is a demanding task and requires massive logistical back up and organization. All of this requires an enormous coordinated effort in terms of time, much of which is not "fun" but clearly work. Because of the mechanics of space warfare in *EVE*, individual players engaged in a battle have little or no idea of what is going on. That is reserved for the alliance's leadership and fleet commanders and they in turn have to be able to give orders and expect that hundreds or thousands of people will follow them immediately and unquestioningly. (Actions are frequently time-critical, which makes immediate compliance essential.) So, the demands of warfare not only increased the size of corporations and led to the appearance of alliances but also produced a complex military and political hierarchy of a kind that would be recognizable to anyone with experience of a real-world military, large business firm, political party, or government bureaucracy. Nor does it end there. From an early date, propaganda has played a key part in conflict in *EVE* and most alliances now have a separate propaganda corporation as one of the member corporations (Carter, 2014). These work to bolster the loyalty and enthusiasm of the alliance's members while undermining that of its opponents, as well as spreading disinformation and performing the other typical functions of a propaganda or psychological warfare department. They will also have a diplomatic corps, which has exactly the same role and function as its real-world counterpart, of negotiating and smoothing relations with other alliances, whether friend, foe, or neutral. Alliances also have intelligence services, again carrying out all of the functions one would expect a real-world service to engage in, from intelligence gathering, to recruiting, training and placing agents, to countering the "other side's" activities, to black ops and assassinations (although these may be contracted out), to subversion and psychological warfare. Again, these can be very large organizations, with hundreds of members and thousands of informants (Harrison, 2016).

More recently, there has been an advance beyond even the level of the alliance to less integrated groupings called coalitions. These are analogous to institutional arrangements such as NATO or the formal alliances of Renaissance and Baroque Europe. The dominant alliance within the coalition will provide the leadership and organizational infrastructure, as well as the actual people and material. This means that you have a nested or layered structure in which the same elite group are in the decision-making positions at every level, as far as the core group is concerned. Thus, The Mittani is simultaneously the CEO of the Goonwaffe corporation, of the Goonswarm alliance (of which Goonwaffe is the key component), and of the Clusterfuck Coalition (CFC, aka The Imperium), which is built around Goonswarm. The point though is that a complex and hierarchical political order has emerged, without anyone having designed it as part of the game's architecture, and with the organizational structure of the scripted legendarium of the game (the four active interstellar empires that together make up the high security zone of New Eden) having no influence on the structure that has grown up in the bulk of New Eden (null sec space) (CCP Games, 2009b, 2010a; Kelly et al., 2008). Moreover, this has happened in an environment that according to many models and theories of contemporary philosophy and social science should not be conducive to that kind of development. What has happened also does not reflect the plans or intentions of the actors in the system (the players), other than in the general sense of being the product of their purposive choices and interactions. In the politics of *EVE*, the best laid plans of players seldom work out as they expect.

War and International Relations in *EVE Online*

The central feature of the politics of *EVE* is war and it is wars between organized groups of players that have driven the emergence of a complex political order. This might not seem inevitable: economic competition, trade, and production might well have become the dominant activities instead. This might seem plausible and likely, given that in *EVE*, as in the real world, activities such as trade, mining, and manufacturing provide the sinews of war—an alliance or coalition that cannot produce the ships and material it needs will lose out in any large conflict, and many of the largest battles in *EVE*'s history have been fought over control of production facilities such as shipyards. In the very early stages of *EVE*, it did seem as though the structure of the game was going to develop on those lines, as a producer-driven system, but that was not how things worked out. From a very early stage, war fighting alliances such as Band of Brothers became the key actors (Groen, 2016). What this means is that the productive activities of players in the game, such as mining and manufacturing, are subordinated to and driven by the competition between war-making factions as well as purely predatory groups such as pirates and professional assassins. Most of the other organized and structured activities in the virtual world are also ultimately driven by war and politics (the continuation of war by other means, in *EVE* as much as Sun Tzu or Clausewitz). It is a game of thrones (or at least alliances) that produces and drives the overall emergent order of the game and shapes it, as opposed to other kinds of game. This means that one of the principal parts of the emergent order is something akin to a system of international relations or politics.

At first sight, this may seem a strange claim: there is no overarching authority or leviathan in most of New Eden. As a result, there is nothing like the rule-bound political order that exists in a modern state, much less the kind of transnational order of regulations and treaties that has been built up in the real world since 1945. What you do have is the kind of order that would be familiar to any historical practitioner of realpolitik or student of the internal politics of most medieval monarchies. There is a system of evolved conventions and understandings that has emerged from regular wars and competition, rules that exist because of mutual self-interest on the part of the players but subject at all times to the understanding that people will break those rules if the potential gains are large enough (Carter and Gibbs, 2013). In terms of historical comparisons, this is very like the international system that grew out of the breakdown of the old medieval order of empire and papacy, before it was formalized via the treaty of Westphalia (although *EVE* is getting close to that). Other obvious historical comparisons are with China during the Warring States period or Renaissance Italy, and *The Prince* does in fact give good advice for would-be galactic overlords in the game. The point is that there are stable expectations as to how people will behave and react, even if it does pay to present yourself as a complete sociopath (which is how medieval monarchy also worked)—even in that case there will be predictability and regularity to behavior.

The Meta-Order of *EVE Online*

One of the most striking features of the spontaneous or emergent order of *EVE*, which many leading players have commented on, is the existence of a significant meta-order, a network of communications and connections that is about the game and driven by its internal developments, but which takes place outside it, in the real world. The way the game's interface works means that it is very difficult to near impossible for the large-scale coordination of the actions of thousands of players over long periods of time that is required for conflicts and other activities to be done by someone actually logged in to the game. As a result, the leading figures in *EVE*, the senior managers if you will, hardly ever actually log in to the game itself. Instead, they communicate with each other in real time using chat boards or conversation software applications such as Jabber (The Mittani, 2016). There is also a whole infrastructure of sites and pages online but not within the game, which are used to build solidarity among the members of an alliance, pass on messages and propaganda, and share information of all kinds. Things such as this have appeared with other games but the extent and degree of development is much greater in the case of *EVE*, because the need for it is greater within the game.

Over the years, a clear social order, and even a social hierarchy of sorts, has emerged in *EVE*. The striking thing about this is that it is not built into the game (as is the case in role-playing games based on historical eras or fantasy worlds based on real historical experiences): it has arisen as a side effect of the way the political order of the virtual world has developed. There are certain "natural" divisions, which reflect the kinds of styles of play available (Pearce, 2009). Over time, the players who take part mainly in the economic and productive activities such as mining and trading (carebears in the lingo of the game) have become a distinct class or type of players, with their own consciousness of the role they have and the kind of character they are portraying. Alongside them is another group of players who act as middlemen or service providers to the organized groups, sometimes in close association with them, but frequently on an independent basis. If the carebears are the working or productive classes of *EVE*, these are the professional or service classes.

Over and above both are the players who are mainly interested in PvP activity, above all war, but also scams, piracy, bounty hunting, and subversion and assassination. These are the players whose activities and interactions tend to drive the evolution of the complex political order. This class of players can be subdivided into those who are part of an organized political structure within the game and those who are in some sense freelancers. From a very early stage, the first subtype has developed a clear hierarchy, with recognized leaders at the top, clearly identifiable high-level subordinates and decision and policy making core groups, down a graded level of responsibility. This does not mean there is no social mobility, quite the contrary, as the rise and fall of particular individuals is one of the main features of the game, but the structure is persistent. One notable feature, which the Mitanni among others has noted, is that the internal organization of corporations and alliances is typically that of an apparent autocracy in which one leader is the ultimate decision-maker, even if those decisions are arrived at after discussion and then cascaded through levels of management. There have been attempts to try democratic or discursive decision-making but these have always proved ineffective to disastrous in the context of *EVE*. The autocracy though is apparent because disaffected individual players (in the case of corporations) or corporations (in the case of alliances) can leave at any time they please. In terms of Hirschman's model of politics, the social and political order that has emerged in *EVE* has very high levels of exit but almost no voice. (The third part of Hirschman's trilogy, loyalty, is also important and, as in his model, is something that develops over time and depends upon reciprocal relations and experience.)

Technology and Order

The most difficult aspect of the emergent order is technology. As already mentioned, this is in some sense exogenous to the game's spontaneous dynamics, as major technological innovations are introduced by CCP Games rather than developing from within the game. An example was the introduction of supercapital ships, Titans, and carriers, which could not be docked at a station (for many years until a new type of station was introduced by CCP Games that made this possible—that was what wiped out Chribba's brokerage function mentioned earlier) and were therefore vulnerable to attack at all times while being immensely powerful and, for some time, capable of determining the outcome of a battle on their own. This had a dramatic effect on the incentives and hence the dynamics of political competition, because Titans were enormously valuable because of their capacity to determine the outcome of conflict, but also so valuable that they had to be protected at almost any cost and only used sparingly (Groen, 2016). The way that technological innovations are introduced into the game by the developers mimics the effects of natural events such as major epidemics or natural disasters in human history and also the way that in real-world history, political order has been repeatedly transformed by technological innovation, such as the advent of gunpowder or the transformation of the ancient Middle East by the invention of the chariot. In the real world, these innovations are of course produced by historically situated human beings; but even so, it suits both historical and economic analysis to treat them as actually exogenous, as they are in *EVE*. What the setup in *EVE* does is to speed up the real-world process of the adoption and impact of transformative technologies. What is spontaneous in *EVE* (as in the real world) is the use made of these technologies by actors and the effects they have as a result. It is this social aspect of technology that is an important aspect of the emergent order we can see in New Eden.

The Reality of *EVE* and What It Tells Us: The Nature of Emergent Orders

So, given that the way *EVE Online* is set up and run has allowed or even encouraged the emergence of a complex order that is not designed or intended by either the designers (CCP Games) or any individual player or group of players, what does that order tell us? Does it have anything to say about some of the key questions of political science and philosophy, for example? Before considering that, there is an obvious question that must be addressed. Can you derive any meaningful insights from the artificial environment of a virtual world, a persistent video game? Another underlying question is: Is this virtual world real, and if so, in what sense? If not, does this unreal construct have anything pertinent or informative to tell us about major intellectual questions?

Leaving aside technical questions of ontology, the answer to the first question is that the world of New Eden and *EVE Online* is real, in a significant sense of that word (Carter et al., 2015; Lehdonvirta, 2010). Clearly, New Eden does not physically exist as an actual star cluster with thousands of planets: its physical existence is as code and electrical impulses in a computer system. Similarly, the supposed physical characters that the players act through while logged on are not physically real in any sense that most philosophers would recognize. However, they are real in another very important sense. What undoubtedly exist in the real world are the actual players and the relations they have with each other in this world through contacts (the meta-order described earlier). These players in turn have characters that they control in the game and the things that those characters do and create and the relations between them are therefore real, albeit in a secondary or derivative sense. New Eden is not just the imaginary but persistent and nonarbitrary physical world created by the designers, it is the social world created by the characters and their interactions, which in turn is driven by the decisions, action, and interactions of real physically existing people. In terms of the analytical (and theological) category developed by J. R. R. Tolkien, *EVE Online* is a secondary world or creation (Tolkien, 1997). When Tolkien came up with this concept, he used it to explain and make sense of literary creations such as his own and the many imitations of it that followed. In the case of a literary secondary world, such as Middle Earth or Earthsea, the characters within it have no will of their own—they only do what the author (designer and secondary creator) wills (although many authors actually have doubts about that). In MMOGs, the characters in the world created by the designers have an actual will of their own, which is the will of the human being animating them. In a game with *EVE*'s distinctive qualities, the degree of free will that the characters in the game have and scope for its exercise is much greater than in other MMOGs. Consequently, we can say that the emergent order of the secondary creation that is New Eden is not only undesigned and unplanned, it is also real in a very important sense, as real as many social phenomena that sociologists and political scientists study in the primary world we inhabit.

That means that what we have here is a real social world or secondary world that can therefore tell us something useful. In addition, even if you deny this and think of virtual worlds as merely a kind of scenario or experiment, with a high degree of randomness built in, it would still be useful, in the way that simulations of things such as epidemics or social crazes and panics can be useful (van Lent, 2008). Here though, because of the reality of actual human beings making choices, acting and interacting, in a secondary world with specific qualities and characteristics, we can gain important and clear insights. To the degree that the conditions of life and interaction in New Eden are similar in important respects to those of the primary or real world, those lessons will be applicable, sometimes to the present day, more often to the historical past, and certainly to the kinds of models and theories that scholars in various disciplines have created. As several authors have commented, including Yannis Varoufakis, *EVE Online* is a kind of natural laboratory of social interaction that is a paradise or godsend for economists, sociologists, and political scientists and theorists—not to mention historians (Varoufakis, 2012). What we can observe over the seventeen years of the game's existence is a kind of accelerated social evolution. Things that took hundreds of years in the real world happen in a matter of a few years or even months in New Eden. To take one main example, warfare and politics in *EVE* were transformed in a matter of two or three years by the introduction of Titans and carriers, whereas it took at least a century for the chariot to transform warfare in the ancient Middle East. The polarization of Europe to the point where a chance event could trigger a catastrophic war took about thirty years before 1914 but less than a year in *EVE Onlin*e (Groen, 2016).

The first insight that we can gain from *EVE Online* is into the phenomenon of emergence itself, of spontaneous order. In this virtual world, we can see several of the features of such orders in the real world, as theorized by complexity theory and people such as Friedrich Hayek and Michael Polanyi (Hayek, 1945; Polanyi, 1998). What players face in *EVE* is a knowledge problem of the kind that Hayek and Polanyi identified. Even in the earliest days of the game, the knowledge that would be needed to plan, control, and foresee all of the possible actions that could take place in the virtual world, and their outcomes, was too much for any one player or group of players, or even, crucially, for the designers at CCP Games. Even worse, they face a Hayekian knowledge problem: the critical knowledge is dispersed among the hundreds of thousands of active players and is often tacit—players cannot communicate it in explicit form even if they wished to. This knowledge problem becomes more acute the longer the virtual world persists and the more complex its emergent internal social and political order becomes. In the economic aspect of the game, the market economy that has developed, this means reliance on free exchange and the prices that generates, and the entrepreneurial acts of self-interested actors moved by the profit motive and alertness to opportunities for super-normal profits, such as arbitrage. If this followed the rules of standard neoclassical economics, then the activities of the entrepreneurs would wipe out and eliminate profit opportunities and produce an equilibrium.

This is not what we see, to put it mildly. There are two reasons why it does not happen. First is the reason Varoufakis cites, the widespread and unchecked (by neutral law) existence of predatory activity such as theft and piracy, fraud and scams, collusion and market fixing, and predatory taxation by political entrepreneurs (Martuk, 2011; Geere, 2010; Drain, 2010a, 2010b, 2010c). He believes this is the primary reason but, although it has an undoubted and often dramatic effect, it is not the main cause for the failure of the neoclassical model to work in *EVE*, because the effects while ongoing as a process are not permanent in any specific place: the people engaged in these activities are not able to capture the windfall gains they get on a persistent and continuing basis. The second, more important reason is the simple and inescapable element of randomness and unpredictability in complex human interactions. (It is this that produces the "butterfly effects" mentioned earlier.) This is endogenous to the social, economic, and political order of the secondary world because it arises from the choices and actions of the players and their responses to the choices and actions of other players. The result of both of these is that any equilibrium is evanescent and unstable and the actual reality is constant ferment. All of this is much closer to the world we observe in reality, both historically and in the present day, than the abstract models of contemporary economists, however useful they are for clarifying thought. There is bad news here for devotees of both planned economies and a naïve view of self-correcting free markets. For the first, *EVE* confirms the evidence of the real world, that to control and plan or even understand and make accurate predictions about, a complex social and economic order is impossible. For the second, the strong conclusion to draw is that a world of completely apolitical market exchange is a mirage: in reality there will always be collusive and predatory behavior, and this together with genuine uncertainty, will make any kind of order temporary, and often not self-correcting.

Another aspect of the emergence process in *EVE* is that it illustrates the way complexity works in the political and social spheres, as set out with regard to the political order by authors such as Hilton Root, Claudio Cioffi-Revilla, and Michael McCullough. We can see the importance of initial conditions, something that Root emphasizes, along with the resulting tendency for the process of emergent order to produce quite different outcomes in different places rather than convergence on a particular norm (Root, 2013). The evolution of political order toward greater complexity and hierarchy and a complex system of relations between political actors that produces a stable meta-order or international relations system, which is described earlier, is very close to the classic model set out by Cioffi-Revilla in 2010 (Cioffi-Revilla, 2010). Over the sixteen-year history of the virtual world, we can see clearly the process of growing complexity and interconnectivity, increased hierarchy and specialization, and the emergence of trust or substitutes for it (such as credible mutual deterrence) in a structurally low-trust environment. One of the most important insights that *EVE* gives us here relates to the argument made by McCullough in a recent (2018) paper. He is concerned with the distinction made in studies of power between relations of domination and relations of collaboration. He argues that the former is ultimately destructive while the latter is constructive and leads to larger, more complex orders (McCullough, 2018). In his terms, domination produces disorganized complexity while collaboration produces self-organized complexity. We can see this clearly in *EVE Online*. The internally complex and self-sustaining order of the larger and more successful alliances such as Goonswarm or Test Alliance is clearly connected to a collaborative form of power relations whereas attempts to build structures based on domination or a simple spoil-sharing model, such as the one pioneered by Band of Brothers, produce short-lived orders that are unstable and brittle, and ultimately disordered (not least in their susceptibility and vulnerability to betrayals by key individuals) (see the account of this in Groen, 2016).

However, *EVE* also suggests two caveats or further elaborations of this model. The first is that while it explains the way to stable and self-organizing complexity in individual political units (alliances and coalitions in *EVE*), it does not show how this can be achieved at the level of the system as a whole (the whole of New Eden or, in our case, the world as a whole). Here the model does not work in a sustained way because the incentive for collaboration is always to cooperate and collaborate against a competitor. For the system as a whole, there is no competitor. This suggests that any apparently collaborative order in the system as a whole will be fragile and temporary and subject to sudden disruption. The only way to achieve long-lasting order in the system as a whole is if one cohesive group achieves a hegemonic position. The problem of course is that the relations of the hegemon with the rest of the system are of the domination type and therefore ultimately destructive of stable complexity. This shows the second insight that *EVE* provides, which is that beyond a certain level of size and complexity it becomes necessary to rely upon domination to an ever-greater extent to hold the system together, rather than collaborative relations. This though undermines the long-term coherence of the system and makes it more fragile, which in turn means that even more explicit power and domination has to be used to keep it going, which in turn undermines its self-sustaining order even further. There is, in other words, what one science fiction work called a "principle of social entropy" that limits the growth of stable complex orders (Spinrad, 2013 [1967]). *EVE Online* shows both of these at work over its history and continues to do so.

EVE Online, State-of-Nature Theory, and Rational Choice

EVE also has obvious implications for one of the central theories of modern political philosophy and thinking about government and political order, which is state-of-nature theory. As formulated by Thomas Hobbes, the idea of a state of nature is a concept that clarifies our understanding of both the nature of political order and the way it either came about or is sustained (assuming that a state of nature as Hobbes conceives it is a realistic possibility). Several commentators have noted or argued that the world of *EVE* is a Hobbesian state of nature, one in which there are no limits on what one person can do to another other than relative power, and that therefore there is at least implicitly a war of all against all, with the ever-present fear of violent death (Varoufakis, 2014). Certainly, the world of *EVE* is like this account. It is indeed a world of zero trust, where any kind of predatory action can be taken with no fear of any sovereign power "to keep men in awe" as Hobbes puts it (Combs, 2007; Carter, 2015). It is in fact quite a close approximation to his idea of a state of nature (more so than the milder version described by Locke). In addition, the kind of character adopted by many of the players conforms to Hobbes's model of human psychology as predatory, competitive but also fearful, and therefore always assuming the worst of others for prudential reasons and getting retaliation in first (Schaefer, 2010). (It is important to realize that for Hobbes's model to work or be consistent, we do not have to accept that everyone is like this, only that some, and a not insignificant number, are.) Certainly, there are enough characters in *EVE Online* who fit Hobbes's description for his model to apply.

The result of the spontaneous order process though is not what Hobbes predicted. We see no sign of people collectively acting to surrender their independence and almost all of their rights to a leviathan, as he argued. The obvious response is that this is because in New Eden, as opposed to real world, death, while costly and annoying, is not permanent. The incentives are therefore not as intense. However, even allowing for that we see a different pattern of development from the one hypothesized in *Leviathan* and other works influenced by it. The key difference is that in Hobbes, the actors are individuals (radical methodological individualism is a central feature of his argument). In *EVE*, the effective agents are small groups that correspond to bands, gangs, or clans in the real world. This is much closer to what we observe in real-world situations where there has been a collapse of political order, such as Somalia. There are pre-political bonds and units that exist in the state of nature and it is the groups formed by those bonds that are the actual actors, rather than solitary individuals. Even when people start off as Hobbesian individuals, *EVE* suggests that the incentive is to establish strong relations with and cooperate closely with a small number of other individuals, to form a social unit that then becomes the actor.

The reason why this happens is obvious to an economist and can be seen both in *EVE* and in real-world situations such as the formation of gangs—transactions costs, information costs, and the costs of large-scale coordination. To establish relations with a large number of people, most of whom are not known to you, is difficult and costly in terms of time and effort. There is a level of cost that makes cooperation and bonding worthwhile because the benefits (such as mutual support and protection) exceed the transaction and coordination costs, but because the costs escalate with numbers and geographical dispersion, this cooperation will initially take place on a small scale (Fiorentini and Pelzman, 2008). Movement to large-scale cooperation will take place between these smaller groups and will always reflect the nature of the complex system in which they are operating. All this means that a state of nature is a temporary phenomenon. Even when the rules seem to explicitly create a state of nature, as in *EVE*, you will find that cooperation and a complex but stable order will arise. This will not take the form or path described in Hobbes and much other literature, however. Arguments for the emergence of political order based on methodological individualism and the actions of rational and self-interested individuals are wide of the mark. The driving dynamic is actually tribalism and small-scale group identity and the way these gradually make a stable complex order possible at higher and higher levels—up to a point.

This brings us to a second way in which the experience of *EVE Online* can be informative, which is the uses and implications of rational choice theory. The Mittani has observed that the evolution of *EVE* and the way it has developed are a nightmare for rational choice and he is undoubtedly right (as well as being unusually well-placed to make that judgment) (The Mittani, 2016). In rational choice theory, agents make decisions based on a rational judgment as to what course of action will best serve their self-interest or maximize their utility. Utility in this context is often assumed, whether explicitly or implicitly to mean material benefit, but this is not necessary—it is perfectly possible to combine the model of rational decision-making with a subjectivist way of thinking about utility, although doing this weakens the explanatory power of the analysis and runs the danger of making it a tautology. That is why most rational choice theorists do assume material self-interest to be the foundation of utility. This is a very powerful type of analysis and can be used to explain social phenomena from crime to divorce to the emergence of ethics. *EVE Online*, however, shows its limitations, at least in a virtual world. It is clear that for many of the players the motives for their actions are not reducible to rational self-interest, unless we go down the route of tautology and make all actions self-interested by definition (what we may call the Joey Tribbiani way of thinking). For the Goons who play the game (and not only the ones in Goonswarm), the main motives are playfulness and the desire to prank or wind up other people. The obvious problem with rational choice in a MMOG is precisely that it is a game and therefore other kinds of motive than rational self-interest play a major part which can range from acting in a way that conforms to a role or character type to simply the desire to be a complete asshole (which is common!). This does not mean that the choices made by players in *EVE* are random and unpredictable—we are not dealing with the dice man here—just that they cannot be understood or predicted straightforwardly using the frame of rational choice. Given other understandings of motivation and behavior, player actions are highly predictable.

The obvious response is that this shows the problems of extrapolating from behavior in the specific and unusual context of a game to behavior in human society in general. Several disciplines suggest that this is overconfident. There is an influential school of psychology (transactional analysis) that explains human behavior in terms of games and role-play—something captured in the title of the most famous work of that school (Berne, 2016). A lot of human behavior in the real world can be understood in this way. History and politics also suggest that rational choice has severe limits as a tool for understanding the world and that much of human experience historically should be understood using the model of a complex game and the kinds of motives for actions that it encourages. This makes *EVE Online* reflective of what we actually observe in such areas of human life as war, international relations, and politics, and even the internal life of the academy. For most of human history (and still today in the view of many people), these kinds of human activity and interaction are the prerogative of a distinct class, who view them in some sense as a game or sport they are competing in. We can say the same of other areas of human life as well, such as fashion or the higher levels of commerce (Kucklich, 2009; Voorhees, 2009). That is why people talk of international relations and diplomacy as "the game of nations" and George R. R. Martin captured the very bloody and competitive world of medieval politics in the title "A Game of Thrones." In *EVE*, the higher-level players of the player versus player mode (people such as The Mittani) correspond to the ruling classes or elites of both history and the contemporary world. The way they act reflects not rational choice but the other kinds of incentives mentioned and is best captured using something such as transactional analysis. If we accept, *pro arguendo*, that this is also the case for large numbers of historical and contemporary actors in the real world, then we can understand much of what goes on historically (such as the collapse of Europe into war in 1914) much better, and the parallels with the world of *EVE* become striking.

The Implications of *EVE* for IR and History

Perhaps the best example of this and the way in which *EVE* (and other MMOGs) acts as a natural experiment is in the area of international relations and the development of interstate systems. The political order of *EVE* mimics several real-world examples of a highly competitive state system that is systemically stable but turbulent and changing in detail. Several obvious examples spring to mind: the ancient Middle East at various points in its history, the Mediterranean between the death of Alexander and the rise of Rome, the Warring States period in Chinese history, the Sengoku Period in Japan, and the world of Greek city states before their conquest by Macedonia. The best known for most would be Renaissance Italy and Renaissance and Baroque Europe more generally. What *EVE* can do is cast light on the different evolutionary routes we can observe in actual history and help us with the question of how much those routes are predetermined or the product of contingency. If we look at the real-life cases mentioned, and others, there are several paths of development, which reflect the dynamics of conflict and choice in systems of this kind. The first is for the age of conflict and competition to end with the unification of the system under a single authority. This happened, for example, with China, Japan, and the ancient Greek world. In these cases, the unification is often brought about by a party that is initially a peripheral power (Ch'in in the Chinese case, Macedonia in the Greek, for instance). The dynamic is that one power gains an advantage that becomes self-reinforcing so that after a relatively short time, it has become hegemonic or an actual empire. Sometimes the unification is long-lasting and we may even see it as permanent (in the Chinese case, for example, despite several episodes of decomposition). In others the imperial phase is short-lived and the empire then collapses and a period of competition resumes—this is a recurring pattern in Indian history, for instance. The third route is for no imperial power to emerge: instead, there develops a stable multipolar system in which there is competition between actors but no individual competitor ever achieves hegemonic status.

This is what we observe in Europe from the gunpowder revolution onward. The mechanism appears to be that a blocking coalition will arise to check any power that seems to be on the verge of establishing itself as a hegemon.

EVE has clearly gone down the third route so far. At one point, it did seem that it was going to follow the first, as Band of Brothers (BoB) was close to achieving hegemonic status, which was the explicit goal of BoB as articulated by its charismatic leader SirMolle. However, this did not happen because the success of BoB led to the formation of a blocking coalition (between Goonswarm and the Russians essentially) that was able to defeat and ultimately destroy BoB, after two enormous wars. The victorious coalition was unable to become a hegemonic power in turn because of the rapid appearance of new alliances that were able to block it (such as Test Alliance and Pandemic). Right now, the politics and "international relations" of *EVE* are rather like those of mid-seventeenth century Europe, before they were formalized by the Treaty of Westphalia. Why though was this the outcome? It was not because of inherent design features of the game (which would correspond to geography in the physical world), with one exception. Apart from that, current conditions resulted from the internal dynamics of the game and as such must result to a great degree from contingent events and outcomes that could have gone a different way.

In the first place, no player group was able to gain a decisive military advantage that would prove to be self-reinforcing. At the point where Titans were introduced, it seemed that this would be the case and that this new technology would give a clear advantage to the then-ascendant Band of Brothers. In the event, BoB's opponents developed tactics to defeat the enormous firepower and sheer size of Titans (most strikingly in the destruction of one of the early Titans piloted by Shrike, one of the characters of BoB leader, SirMolle). They also rapidly developed their own production capacity so that the initial advantage of having a Titan was soon wiped out.

Second, no coalition or alliance was ever able to get control of enough of the production capacity of New Eden to have an overwhelming economic advantage. This was firstly because of a design feature of the game (although it seems that was not CCP Games' original intention) which determined that although key minerals and other resources were distributed unevenly (making certain systems particularly valuable and important), there was no single region that would give whoever controlled it a significant advantage, much less an overwhelming one.

Third, it is clear from looking at the history and development of the world of *EVE* that networks and connections are of huge importance. The larger and more varied a network and its connections (in terms of talents and distribution across time zones), the more powerful and effective it will be. As we have already seen though, there are limits to this, which derive from the nature of interactions among large numbers of human beings, most of whom do not know each other, whether in the physical world or a virtual one. As a network becomes larger, the marginal benefit of adding new members diminishes while the costs rise. In particular, adding new members undermines the cohesion and group identity or the corporation of alliance, which is what enables it to act effectively as though it were a single entity. There are ways of mitigating this problem but they in turn also have limits. The alternative model would be to eschew expansion beyond a certain point so as to strengthen and thicken the connections between the members of a group so that the group becomes more united and effective. This was the strategy pursued by BoB but in the test of virtual war it proved unable to cope with the flexibility and adaptability of the looser opposing coalitions and it also proved to be highly susceptible to subversion—it was actually wound up when a member of its inner circle was subverted and turned by The Mittani (Chalk, 2010). This shows the fundamental problem with cohesion and solidarity models of cooperation—they work as long as everyone in the leadership is indeed aligned with the collective purpose, but it only takes a small number of defectors from that core to destroy the whole structure. The looser model by contrast can survive defections of this kind and is more adaptable.

Finally, nobody was able to gain a clear-cut or decisive advantage in military organization and the ability to mobilize resources (which was what enabled the Roman republic to unite the Mediterranean world) (Scheidel, 2019). The reason was the adaptability of the player coalitions and their ability to either emulate and copy the breakthroughs made by their opponents or to come up with ways of neutralizing them. This is analogous to the way that tactical innovation in organized sports only ever brings about an advantage for a few seasons at most, because other teams and coaches develop effective responses or adopt the innovation themselves.

The way this process has worked in *EVE* has clear parallels with the actual world but also interesting divergences. To take the second point, China's history of persistent imperial rule can partly be explained by the way that control of the Yangtse Yellow River valleys and the plains of North China give the power of a strategically and economically dominant position relative to the rest of Greater China: by contrast, controlling the Ganges and Indus valleys in India does not confer such an advantage because of the barrier of the Deccan. The different effects of the gunpowder revolution in different parts of the world can be understood using the prism of *EVE* as being due to the different degrees to which knowledge could be circulated and innovations copied rapidly. The tension between expanding the size of a network and its internal cohesion and effectiveness is reflected in the continuing debate in the European Union (EU) between widening and deepening of the organization and its institutions while the collapse of BoB has interesting parallels with the collapse of the Soviet Union (ironically, given the key role of Russian players in the process in *EVE*). What *EVE* does is to act as an accelerated social experiment that can tell us about what has happened historically in different parts of the world and the differing dynamics of interstate cooperation and competition, given certain factors as a starting point.

Another important question where *EVE* can bring insight is that of the role and importance of individuals. Here it gives very clear evidence that individuals and their particular personalities, quirks, and obsessions are of enormous importance. Although structural factors obviously play a part and limit the range of possibilities within *EVE* at any given time that still leaves a wide range of possible outcomes, and the key factor in determining which ones happen has been individual players and their qualities. Repeatedly it has been the case that charismatic and effective leaders are essential to the success and even survival of alliances and coalitions—in many cases when leaders have left the game, coalitions have disintegrated. Decisions made by leaders and fleet commanders or by major economic players have proved to be critical in determining the outcome of major conflicts and competitions. This will come as no surprise to students of the history of politics or military affairs but it is something of a shock to economists or sociologists. This should make all of us reflect about how the polarity often asserted between structural explanations and ones that emphasize individual agency is misleading—we should rather distinguish between areas of human life and experience where one way of thinking is more important as opposed to others where the other way is more appropriate. The big question of course is whether one of these areas is determinative of the other, making the other in some sense an epiphenomenon. The social evolution of New Eden suggests that there at least it is politics that is the dominant or determinative activity and area and this has interesting implications for how we think about our world, to say the least.

What this does in fact is tell us something about the nature of complex social orders, empires, and ruling classes. These are not designed but spontaneous orders but that does not mean that conscious purpose and deliberate choice are not important. Empires and elaborate social and political orders rest upon and cannot survive without an economic and productive "base" and this is as true in *EVE* as in the physical world. What *EVE* shows though is what we may call the primacy of politics, the degree to which politics, the competition for power, and the actions of those engaged in that competition, drive other areas of human life and are not reducible to an epiphenomenon of the underlying productive relations. In the modern world, a large part of social life has become independent of politics and power and there is a persistent effort to increase this and consolidate it. In *EVE*, that has not happened but its history and development so far suggest that this will not happen, at least not anytime soon. The implication of that for the real world, to the extent that we think of *EVE* as both real and close enough to the physical world to tell us useful things about it, is that the domination of life by power and politics is not going to end soon and may well be undergoing one of its periodic resurgences. The political economy of empire, founded on military technology, control of resources and production, and the size, nature, and effectiveness of social networks, is still a key to understanding human affairs both in *EVE Online* and the actual world.

References

Achterbosch, Leigh, Robyn Pierce, and Gregory Simmons. 2008. "Massively Multiplayer Online Role-Playing Games: The Past, Present, and Future." *Computers in Entertainment* 5 (4): 1–33.

BBC. 2013. "Eve Players Stage Giant Online Space Battle." *BBC*, July 29, 2013. Accessed on January 5, 2021. http://www.bbc.com/news/technology-23489293.

Bergstrom, Kelly, Marcus Carter, Darryl Woodford, and Christopher A. Paul. 2013. "Constructing the Ideal EVE Online Player." Paper presented at DeFragging Games Studies, Atlanta, Ga.

Berne, Eric. 2016. *Games People Play: The Psychology of Human Relationships*. London: Penguin.

Butler, Brian, Lee Sproull, Sara Kiesler, and Robert Kraut. 2002. "Community Effort in Online Groups: Who Does the Work and Why?" http://repository.cmu.edu/hcii/90

Carter, Marcus. 2014. "Emitexts and Paratexts: Propaganda in EVE Online." *Games and Culture* 10 (4): 311–342.

———. 2015. "Massively Multiplayer Dark Play: Treacherous Play in EVE Online." In *The Dark Side of Game Play: Controversial Issues in Playful Environments*, edited by Torill Elvira Mortensen, Jonas Linderoth, and Ashley M. L. Brown. London: Routledge, pp. 191–209.

Carter, Marcus, Kelly Bergstrom, and Darryl Woodford, eds. 2016. *Internet Spaceships Are Serious Business: An EVE Online Reader*. Minneapolis: University of Minnesota Press.

Carter, Marcus, and Martin Gibbs. 2013. "eSports in EVE Online: Skullduggery, Fair Play and Acceptability in an Unbounded Competition." In *Proceedings of the Eighth International Conference on the Foundations of Digital Games*. Chania, Greece: SASDG, pp. 47–54.

Carter, Marcus, Kelly Bergstrom, Nick Webber, and Oskar Milik. 2015. "EVE Is Real." Paper presented at the Digital Games Research Association Conference: Diversity of Play, Luneberg, Germany, May.

Castronova, E. 2001. "Virtual Worlds: A First-Hand Account of Market and Society on the Cyberian Frontier." *The Gruter Institute Working Papers on Law, Economics, and Evolutionary Biology* 2 (1). http://papers.ssrn.com/sol3/Papers.cfm?abstract_id=294828.

CCP Games. 2009a. "EVE Online: The Butterfly Effect." *CCP Games*, July 29, 2009. YouTube video, 2:38. https://www.youtube.com/watch?v=08hmqyejCYU.

———. 2009b. "EVE Online: Old Storyline Intro." *CCP Games*, March 6, 2009. YouTube video, 4:48. https://www.youtube.com/watch?v=T84nrp08MWo.

———. n.d. "Find Your Path in the Sandbox." *EVE Online*. Accessed on February 8, 2020. http://www.eveonline.com/sandbox/.

———. 2010a. "EVE Online: Backstory." *EVE Community*. Accessed on January 5, 2021. http://community.eveonline.com/backstory/.

———. 2010b. "EVE Online: FAQ." *EVE Online*. Accessed on January 5, 2021. http://www.eveonline.com/faq/faq_01.asp.

CCP Greyscale. 2013. "Upcoming Tutorial Revisions." *Eve Community*, July 25, 2013. Accessed on February 8, 2020. http://community.eveonline.com/news/dev-blogs/73075.

CCP Phantom. 2014. "Community Spotlight—Brave Newbies Inc." *Eve Community*, December 2, 2014. Accessed on January 5, 2021. http://community.eveonline.com/news/dev-blogs/74260.

Chalk, Andy. 2010. "More EVE Online Shenanigans: GoonSwarm Ganks Band of Brothers." *The Escapist*, February 5, 2010. Accessed on January 5, 2021. http://www.escapistmagazine.com/news/view/89219-More-EVE-Online-Shenanigans-GoonSwarm-Ganks-Band-Of-Brothers.

Chribba (Crister Enberg). 2016. "The Art of Selling Trust." In *Internet Spaceships Are Serious Business: An EVE Online Reader*, edited by Marcus Carter, Kelly Bergstrom, and Darryl Woodford. Minneapolis: University of Minnesota Press.

Cimino, Aldo. 2011. "The Evolution of Hazing: Motivational Mechanisms and the Abuse of Newcomers." *Journal of Cognition and Culture* 11 (3–4): 241–267.

Cioffi-Revilla, Claudio. 2010. "A Methodology for Complex Social Simulations." *Journal of Artificial Societies and Social Simulations* 13 (1): 7.

Combs, Nick. 2007. "A Culture of Mistrust in EVE-Online." *TerraNova*, November 11, 2007. Accessed on February 6, 2020. http://terranova.blogs.com/terra_nova/2007/11/culture-of-mist.html.

CrazyKinux. 2008. "10 Posts for the Eve Newbie." CrazyKinux's Musing (blog), August 20, 2008. Accessed on January 5, 2021. http://www.crazykinux.ca/2008/08/10-posts-for-eve-online-newbie.html.

———. 2010. "EVE Blog Banter #16: The Three Pillars of Wisdom." CrazyKinux's Musing (blog), March 15, 2010. Accessed on January 5, 2021. http://www.crazykinux.ca/2010/03/eve-blog-banter-16-three-pillars-of.html.

de Zwart, Melissa, and Sal Humphreys. 2014. "The Lawless Frontier of Deep Space: Code as Law in EVE Online." *Cultural Studies Review* 20 (1): 77–99.

Drain, Brendan. 2010a. "EVE Gambling Website SOMER. Blink Is the Target of 125 Billion ISK Theft." Massively (blog), November 16, 2010. Accessed on January 5, 2021. http://massively.joystiq.com/2010/11/16/eve-gambling-website-somer-blink-is-the-target-of-125-billion-is/.

———. 2010b. "EVE Online Player Steals $45,000 Worth of ISK in Massive Investment Scam." Massively (blog), September 11, 2010. Accessed on January 5, 2021. http://massively.joystiq.com/2010/09/11/eve-online-player-steals-45–000-worth-of-isk-in-massive-investm/.

———. 2010c. "Questionable EVE Attack Deals 30 Billion ISK in Damage." Massively (blog), October 10, 2010. Accessed on January 5, 2021. http://massively.joystiq.com/2010/10/10/questionable-eve-attack-deals-30-billion-isk-in-damage/.

———. 2012. "EVE Evolved: EVE Online's New Tutorial." Massively (blog), August 19, 2012. Accessed on January 5, 2021. http://massively.joystiq.com/2012/08/19/eve-evolved-eve-onlines-new-tutorial/.

Dibbell, J. 2006. *Play Money, or, How I Quit My Day Job and Made Millions Trading Virtual Loot* (Reprint ed.). New York: Basic Books.

———. 2008. "Mutilated Furries, Flying Phalluses: Put the Blame on Griefers, the Sociopaths of the Virtual World." *Wired*, January 18, 2008.

Edwards, T. 2011. "Eve Online Players Protest against Monocle Prices/ Microtransactions. Lasers Involved." *PC Gamer*, June 25, 2011. Accessed on January 5, 2021. http://www.pcgamer.com/2011/06/25/eve-online-players-protest-against-monocle-pricesmicrotransactions-lasers-involved/.

Egan, James. 2009. "The Lowdown on EVE Online's New Player Experience." Massively (blog), February 18, 2009. Accessed on February 1, 2020. http://massively.joystiq.com/2009/02/18/the-lowdown-on-eve-onlines-new-player-experience/.

Evans, Monica. 2010. "Murder, Ransom, Theft, and Grief: Understanding Digital Ethics in Games." In *Videogame Cultures and the Future of Interactive Entertainment*, edited by Daniel Riha. Oxford: Inter-Disciplinary Press, pp. 81–89.

EVE Community. 2013. "Observing the Burn Jita Player Event." *EVE Community*, May 2, 2013. Accessed on February 8, 2020. http://community.eveonline.com/news/dev-blogs/28640.

Fiorentini, Gianluca, and Samuel Pelzman. 2008. *The Economics of Organised Crime*. Cambridge: Cambridge University Press.

Geere, Duncan. 2010. "EVE Online Fraud Nets 'Bad Bobby' £42,000." *Wired*, September 14, 2010. http://www.wired.co.uk/news/archive/2010–09/14/eve-online-heist.

Goody, Jack. 2004. *Capitalism and Modernity: The Great Debate*. Cambridge: Polity Press.

Groen, Andrew. 2016. *Empires of Eve: A History of the Great Wars of EVE Online*. Milwaukee, WI: Lightburn Industries.

Hammer. 2007a. "About Hammer's Guide." Hammer's Eve (blog), May 2007. Accessed on January 5, 2021. http://hammer-eve.blogspot.com/2007/05/about-my-guide.html.

———. 2007b. "Death and Clones." Hammer's Eve (blog), May 2007. Accessed on January 5, 2021. http://hammer-eve.blogspot.com/2007/05/death-and-clones.html.

———. 2007c. "Eve: For Experienced Gamers." Hammer's Eve (blog), May 2007. Accessed on January 5, 2021. http://hammer-eve.blogspot.com/2007/05/eve-for-wow-gamers.html/.

———. 2007d. "Eve Is Harsh: You Get Ganked." Hammer's Eve (blog), June 2007. Accessed on January 5, 2021. http://hammer-eve.blogspot.com/2007/06/eve-is-harsh-you-get-ganked.html.

Harrison, Keith. 2016. “The Accidental Spymaster.” In *Internet Spaceships Are Serious Business: An EVE Online Reader,* edited by Marcus Carter, Kelly Bergstrom, and Darryl Woodford. Minneapolis: University of Minnesota Press.

Hayek, Friedrich. 1945. “The Uses of Knowledge in Society.” *American Economic Review* 35 (4): 519–530.

Kelly, Erika, Blake Davis, Jessica Nelson, and Jorge Mendoza. 2008. “Leader Emergence in an Internet Environment.” *Computers in Human Behavior* 24: 2372–2383.

Khaw, Cassandra. 2013. “Meet Tranquility, the Military-Grade 2,500GHZ Monster That Powers EVE Online.” *PC Gamer*, June 15, 2013. Accessed on February 8, 2020. http://www.pcgamer.com/au/2013/06/15/eve-online/.

Kirzner, Israel M. 2015. *Competition and Entrepreneurship*. Chicago, IL: University of Chicago Press.

Kock, Marcus. 2014. “CFC vs Black Legion.” https://www.youtube.com/watch?v=F9YoeaMGwdA.

Kucklich, Julian. 2009. “Virtual Worlds and Their Discontents: Precarious Sovereignty, Govern Mentality, and the Ideology of Play.” *Games and Culture* 4 (4): 340–352.

Lehdonvirta, Villi. 2010. “Virtual Worlds Don’t Exist: Questioning the Dichotomous Approach in MMO Studies.” *Game Studies* 10 (1).

Mark, Mogul Eve Online Trading Series. 2017–2018. Vol. I: *Hotspot Trading: The Secrets Pro Eve Online Traders Don’t Want You to Know*. Vol. II: *Interhub Training: A Step-By-Step Eve Trading Guide to Making ‘Billions’ by Dominating the Market Hubs*. Vol III: *How to Destroy Your Eve Trading Competition*. Self-published.

Moore, Bo. 2014. “Inside the Epic Online Space Battle that Cost Gamers $333,000.” *Wired*, February 8, 2014.

McCullogh, Michael F. 2018. “A Complexity Theory of Power.” Paper at Second International Conference on Complexity and Policy Studies, George Mason University.

The Mittani (Alexander Gianturco). 2016. “The Evolution of Player Organizations: A Goonswarm Perspective.” In *Internet Spaceships Are Serious Business: An EVE Online Reader*, edited by Marcus Carter, Kelly Bergstrom, and Darryl Woodford. Minneapolis: University of Minnesota Press.

Martuk. 2011. “EVE Online Ponzi Scheme Claims over 1 Trillion ISK from Players.” *Ten Ton Hammer*, August 12, 2011. Accessed on January 5, 2021. http://www.tentonhammer.com/eve/news/eve-online-ponzi-scheme-claims-over-1-trillion-isk-from-players.

Paul, Christopher. 2016. "EVE Online Is Hard and It Matters." In *Internet Spaceships Are Serious Business: An EVE Online Reader*, edited by Marcus Carter, Kelly Bergstrom, and Darryl Woodford. Minneapolis: University of Minnesota Press.

Pearce, C. 2009. *Communities of Play: Emergent Cultures in Multiplayer Games and Virtual Worlds*. Illustrated ed. Cambridge, Mass.: MIT Press.

Polanyi, Michael. 1998. *Personal Knowledge: Towards a Post-Critical Philosophy*. London: Routledge.

Purchese, Robert. 2013. "EVE Online: When 3000 Players Collide." *Eurogamer*, January 28, 2013. Accessed on January 21, 2020. http://www.eurogamer.net/articles/2013-01-28-eve-online-when-3000-players-collide.

Root, Hilton. 2013. *Dynamics among Nations: The Evolution of Legitimacy and Development in Modern States*. Cambridge, Mass: MIT Press.

Scheidel, Walter. 2019. *Escape from Rome*. Princeton, NJ: Princeton University Press.

Schaefer, Beowolf. 2010. "Trust No One! Zen and the Art of Internet Spaceship Management." March 19, 2010. http://eve-zen.info/blog/?p=699.

Spinrad, Norman. 2013 [1967]. *Agent of Chaos*. Scott's Valley, CA: CreateSpace.

Stigg. 2010. "Eve: Ship Costs, USD, Time Spent." The Black Temple (blog), February 10, 2010. Accessed on December 2019. http://www.knightly-slumber.com/worldofwarcraft/node/2860.

Taylor, Nicholas, Kelly Bergstrom, Jennifer Jenson, and Suzanne de Castell. 2015. "Alienated Playbour: Relations of Production in EVE Online." *Games and Culture* 10 (4): 365–388.

Terranova, Tiziana. 2013. "Free Labor." In *Digital Labor: The Internet as Playground and Factory*, edited by Trebor Scholz. New York: Routledge, pp. 33–57.

Tolkien, John Ronald Ruel. 1997. "On Fairy-Stories." In *The Monsters and the Critics and Other Essays*. London: Harper Collins.

Yin-Poole, Wesley. 2012. "CCP: Players' Attempt to Destroy Eve Online Economy Is 'F***ing Brilliant'." *Eurogamer*, April 27, 2012. Accessed on January 5, 2021. http://www.eurogamer.net/articles/2012-04-27-ccp-players-attempt-to-destroy-eve-online-economy-is-f-ing-brilliant.

van Lent, Michael. 2008. "The Future Is Virtually Here." *IEEE Computer* 41 (8): 87–89.

Varoufakis, Yanis. 2012. "To Truck, Barter, and Exchange? On the Nature of our Digital Economies." *Valvesoftware*, July 1, 2012. Accessed on October 2020. http://blogs.valvesoftware.com/economics/to-truck-barter-and-exchange-on-the-nature-of-valves-social-economies/.

———. 2014. "War Spikes in the Eve Online Universe: A Political Economist's Account." *Yanis Varoufakis*, January 30, 2014. Accessed on January 5, 2021. https://www.yanisvaroufakis.eu/2014/01/30/war-spikes-in-the-eve-online-universe-a-political-economists-account/.

Voorhees, Gerald A. 2009. "I Play Therefore I Am: Sid Meier's Civilization, Turn-Based Strategy Games, and the Cogito." *Games and Culture* 4 (3): 254–275.

5

The Origins of Money in *Diablo II*

Solomon M. Stein

Diablo II is a noteworthy game for a variety of reasons: it was a tremendous commercial success, one of the bestselling titles of its era, and along with contemporaneous MMORPGs, its online mode was among the first game environments to generate gray markets for in-game goods and the associated commercialization of "gold farming" (although in *Diablo II*'s case, this is quite a misnomer).[1] When it comes to political economy, however, it deserves a place of particular distinction because its virtual economy evolved in a distinct (and far more interesting) fashion than many of those in MMOs—a process related only indirectly to its associated gray-market item sales denominated in "real-world" currency. As became quickly evident to individuals joining the online player base, *Diablo II*'s nominal in-game monetary unit did not function effectively as a medium of exchange for player transactions. With this default option proving nonviable, and no obvious alternative available, players looked to barter one item for another rather than acting as buyers and sellers of goods valued in monetary terms. From this initial situation in which, in the absence of a monetary unit, players fell back on barter transactions, the course of the game's history shows a gradual transition toward the use of an increasingly sophisticated system of commodity money. *Diablo II*'s monetary standard is one remembered with sufficient fondness that the economy in one of its present descendants (*Path of Exile*) was designed to replicate it.

[1] For further discussions of early virtual economies, see Chapter 4.

Diablo II is a case study of great interest for monetary theory, first of all because it provides a set of observable circumstances in which monetary exchange emerged from a barter economy. We can therefore use it to assess competing claims regarding what preconditions, if any, are required for the emergence of monetary exchange, and of the degree of correspondence between the properties expected of an emergent monetary commodity and their mapping into the game's environment. This allows us to evaluate the accuracy of theories regarding the mechanisms at work in the process of monetary emergence. More general questions can be asked as well regarding the institutional environment in which exchange in *Diablo II* took place and the relationship between these institutional features and the successes—and shortcomings—of the game's economic interactions. Building on previous work focused on the exchange institutions found in *Diablo II's* online mode (Salter and Stein, 2015, 2016; Stein, 2015), this chapter provides an overview of *Diablo II's* economic environment and the development of its monetary institutions. In the second section, I consider the nature of the social problems raised by the emergence of a monetary system and the significance of Carl Menger's solution to them, which is borne out in *Diablo II*. The next section then describes the nature of "production" and the exchange environment found within *Diablo II* and its online community, followed by a description of the evolution of its monetary system in the fourth section. The last section concludes by briefly considering the experience of *Diablo II* in light of *Diablo III* and suggests some potential factors in the divergent trajectories taken by their exchange institutions.

The Basic Problem of Money and Menger's Solution

Although (as Adam Smith recognized) not money *per se* but exchange is the essential wellspring of economic phenomena, as systems of exchange become increasingly sophisticated, money of some form generally plays a role. (The wide range of possible forms of money is reflected in the diversity found in the historical record.) Money's historical ubiquity is all the more remarkable given that the basic premise of monetary exchange seems implausible, that is, why exchanging anything of value—time, effort, and potential consumption goods—for something such as a coin, or fancy paper, or scribbles in an account book could possibly reflect prudent decision-making. That is, it would seem implausible were it not such a routine feature of everyday life in commercial society that we simply take for granted. A partial solution to this "mystery" comes with recognition of the indirect nature of monetary transactions. Monies (or money substitutes) are not acquired to enjoy their subjective use-value in consumption, but with the intention of later exchange for more urgently desired commodities.[2] Since we can also understand how a similar desire motivates our counterparties, mutually consistent expectations emerge as foundational to the operation of monetary exchange: my willingness to exchange goods with A for money in the present rests upon an expectation that some future counterparty B will be willing to accept that money in a future exchange, which she will be willing to do in expectation that still others will do likewise, and so on. This pattern of expectations among economic actors is potentially stable if undisturbed, but also raises the question of how individuals throughout this network of exchanges reach such a pattern of expectations except by theoretical contrivance.

Carl Menger's *On the Origins of Money* (1892) explains how the expectations essential to money's role as a generally accepted medium of exchange develop as the cumulative result of the interactions among individuals attempting to navigate the marketplace. We begin by considering a pure barter economy whose only form of exchange is the bilateral exchange of commodities. Market activities in such an environment face severe impediments stemming from the need for transactions to be predicated upon a "double-coincidence of wants" between exchanging parties, which (absent intermediating institutions) is a significant restriction upon what kinds of trades can be made.[3] Desired exchanges that are not frustrated still require that a double-coincidence exist among some market participants, whose search for it rapidly increases in difficulty as the size of the market and the range of available goods expand.[4] Furthermore, market

---

[2] Where the monetary objects in use are themselves commodities that have nonmonetary uses, we should say more precisely that acquisition of those commodities *as money* (that is, beyond what would be otherwise acquired for consumption) is driven by indirect exchange.

[3] Menger (1892, p. 242) identifies the exchange of a single indivisible good for a number of items as a prime example, as the would-be buyer would have to ascertain the desired bundle, and then search for however many individual bilateral exchanges needed, a major chore in the best of circumstances and impossible in others (that is, where the needed goods are not simultaneously available).

[4] This description is idealized in several respects. It is evident when interpreting the *Diablo II* economy using this description that actors will simultaneously pursue a wide range of adaptations to mitigate search costs other than adopting a medium of exchange. In accounting for the underlying logic involved in the emergence of money, however, these can be disregarded as long as they do not reduce the costs of barter exchange to zero. (Indeed, when the Mengerian monetary-emergence process is approached from a general-equilibrium perspective, there is an important question of why money is needed at all, that is, what sort of deviations from the assumptions of perfect knowledge and frictionless exchange are essential to the use of money being efficient.)

participants are not generally looking for just any viable exchange, but are hoping for an exchange on the most favorable terms they believe they can get. This raises what are now familiar search-theoretic problems regarding what constitutes "favorable enough" terms to accept rather than continue the hunt.

Critically, the difficulty of finding alternative potential exchanges is highly dependent upon the sort of goods one is offering. Menger describes this property of a good as its salability, expressed in terms of the relationship between the period of time over which a good is intended to be sold and the extent of the discounting required to ensure a sale: relatively more salable goods require a lesser discount to liquidate on the spot, or, equivalently, require less time and effort to locate a buyer willing to pay "full price." The salability of goods within a given market, or across markets separated in space and/or time, depends both upon their intrinsic properties (extent of divisibility, possibility and cost of storage or transport, and so on) and the environmental and institutional circumstances in which they are offered (the stability and extent of demand, the overall level of economic integration, any potential cultural or legal regulation, and so on).[5]

From a pure barter economy involving goods with differential salability, Menger suggests, we will observe the emergence of a monetary commodity via the cumulative decisions made by self-interested market participants, without any of those choices having intended to create money. Individuals who enter the marketplace with goods of relatively low salability are, in comparison to vendors of more salable goods, less likely to find a desirable counterparty or any viable counterparty at all. (Obviously, there are commodities that are relatively unsalable because of the absence of demand for them, in which case even widespread adoption of a monetary unit is of little help.) However, the disadvantage imposed by the relatively low salability of one's goods remains even if we compare goods which over a "long enough" time period command the same total exchange value. Individual traders therefore have an incentive to hold the most salable assets possible, so as to maximize the number of potential exchange partners and more easily obtain the final commodities they desire.

By way of example, if we consider an individual "A" in possession of a valuable but relatively low salability good who is searching for a particular commodity "C," our expectation is that most of A's interactions will not result in successful exchange. None of the C producers A approaches are in need of what A has to

5 The third section discusses how properties of *Diablo II*'s game engine exert an influence upon salability (as well as price).

offer, and none of those who expressed interest in exchanging for A's product have been offering C in exchange. However, A may come to realize that not all of those would-be purchasers are alike: although none of them could satisfy the double-coincidence condition, some of them likely are offering commodities which, compared to A's product, are relatively more salable. It would be in A's interest to complete whichever of these exchanges will lead to acquiring the relatively most salable commodity "M." This improves A's situation, assuming that their expectations are correct regarding the relative salability of M, as it will now subsequently be easier to find a counterparty holding the desired end point C. The same logic would suggest a subsequent acquisition of some yet more salable commodity M' in exchange for M should the opportunity present itself, as that too would improve the chances of resolving the double-coincidence of wants.

Of course, it is possible that M and/or M' are not "generally" more salable commodities but are possessed of specific features that make them particularly likely to be desired in exchange by people possessing C;[6] when this same logic plays out across many individuals and commodities, however, it is likely to reveal some goods which, owing to a variety of factors, appear to have a generally high salability in a broad range of circumstances. Individuals who notice this, in turn, are likely to adjust their willingness to accept those goods in response, further enhancing their salability—something which, when subsequently noticed by later adopters, results in a similar upward revision, and so on. This cascade of increasing salability and corresponding increasing appeal of intermediary exchange creates a general expectation that individuals are willing to accept it as payment—or in other words, it allows one or more commodities to acquire the defining properties of a monetary good as a cumulative result of individual decision-making in the marketplace.

Menger's account of this *process* of monetary emergence provides a key insight into money's role in the economic system and identifies widespread salability (and thus, the factors which give rise to it) as the key property possessed by commodities which assume a monetary function. The social transition to money presents a case where not only is decentralized coordination among self-interested individuals possible given the appropriate institutional environment, but in

---

6 Examples of this sort of salability are ubiquitous in video games, most clearly in the various "premium" in-game currency units acquired predominantly or exclusively via direct purchase and which usually coexist with the in-world "money" and other "currency-like" gameplay resources.

which institutions themselves also originate as the unintended cumulative result of individual plans. The emergence of money has also taken on methodological significance and is sometimes seen as a prime example of a distinctive style of reasoning in the social sciences.[7] It is a topic of interest not only in monetary theory but also in its role in prompting the question Menger (1985 [1883], p. 146) identified as "perhaps the most noteworthy … problem of the social sciences: How can it be that institutions which serve the common welfare and are extremely significant for its development come into being without a common will directed toward establishing them?"

Since, as Menger identified, there is an underlying logic to the individual decision-making that results in the transition from direct barter to monetary exchange, contemporary examples of the process are rare—having already taken place nearly everywhere.[8] One of the great excitements (for political economists, at least) of the societies that arise in and around virtual worlds is the opportunity to study processes such as the emergence of money from a closer standpoint than is possible with more historically remote events: *Diablo II,* though undoubtedly ancient as an online game, is several thousand years closer to the present than the earliest known monetary systems. Furthermore, we have information regarding the institutional and economic environment available within *Diablo II* (and other similarly well-understood game engines) that are impossible to obtain for nonvirtual economies. Finally, as we will see, *Diablo II*'s artifactual nature allows its "initial conditions" to come far closer to those of the ideal-typical "pure barter economy" than would any historical society. Its environment is already characterized by many of the complementary institutions that constitute commercial society, including not only the full range of technological possibilities but also recognized and designated "market spaces" in which commerce is concentrated and a system of defined and enforced property rights, neglecting the adoption of a monetary unit. (In historical contexts where these institutions are not able to emerge full-grown prior to the rest of society, we would expect them to continually develop alongside monetary institutions.)

---

[7] This approach has a multitude of names, including the genetic-causal method, the compositive method, methodological individualism, and invisible-hand style explanations.

[8] One result of catastrophic hyperinflations is a similar process of cascading individual decisions that gradually erodes the monetary status of a medium of exchange. Even draconian currency restrictions, however, tend to result in the adoption of an alternative monetary unit rather than a return to barter exchange.

Diablo II as Economic Environment

Before we describe the environment of *Diablo II*, it may be useful to provide a few remarks on the crucially important question "Why bother?" If past experience is any guide, for one group of readers ("enthusiasts") most of the gameplay elements described in this section will be familiar, whether from *Diablo II* or other games, and recasting them in economic terms will be a valuable way to frame the rest of the discussion. At the same time, other readers may be generally unfamiliar with these sorts of game environments and find it useful to explore them before considering their economic implications. For these readers, the following description of *Diablo II* as a social scientific tool is essentially a "methods" section outlining a complicated experimental setup.[9] When the focus is on what the *Diablo II* experience offers to the development of monetary theory, this description focuses on certain elements of the game's environment and their impact on the resulting monetary institutions (Salter and Stein, 2015, 2016). They are selected because of their relevance to theoretical disagreements for which *Diablo II* provides a novel empirical data point. This approach helps to emphasize just how well the theoretical account relates the features of the game environment to its historical experience. The italicized toplines of each subsection identify the major elements of the game environment and their economic significance, which are then expanded upon in the subsequent discussions. Additional details of game mechanics or circumstances that are relevant to the economic circumstances surrounding particular cases are presented in the notes.[10]

---

[9] This setup includes conditions that would be unlikely to arise elsewhere, such as the experience of MMO *DC Universe Online*, which experienced an accidental hyperinflation—there having been no intention to disrupt the game's money supply at all. Instead, the rapid explosion in the supply of money resulted from a bug that allowed for mail duplication whose effects turned out not to be easily unwound.

[10] While much of this discussion is applicable to all published versions of *Diablo II*, it describes features that were only added in the game's expansion *Diablo II: Lord of Destruction*. This is the relevant environment for most online play and also for the economic interactions discussed here: characters within the expansion environment and those remaining in "classic" *Diablo II* did not interact (players with the expansion could convert a character from classic to expansion but never the reverse). Economically significant additions within the expansion include both runes and jewels as alternative uses for sockets, charms, and equipment additions, which rendered the previous "endgame" equipment obsolete. Particularly following the first major post-expansion patch release, the time between major adjustments by the developers also lengthens from months to several years.

Diablo II is populated by player-created characters whose effectiveness in gameplay is defined by nontransferable properties of class and build and by equipment selected for use. Equipment is transferable between characters, and the use-value of any given piece of equipment is heterogeneous between characters of different classes, builds, and existing equipment endowment.

Diablo II's primary gameplay features the player-character traversing the game world combating computer-controlled monsters, leveling up and obtaining better loot in order to fight more difficult monsters worth more experience and offering still better loot, a cycle that continues until a character reaches the "endgame" and the maximally difficult and rewarding monsters. The means available to any given character for dispatching the enemy differed based upon chosen class as well as by how the character was "built" via allocation of skill and attribute points rewarded to the character as they leveled up, and the statistics of equipped items. By the time characters reached the endgame, the dominant source of improvements in character efficiency was equipment upgrades rather than continued level progression. Equipped items were, with only a handful of restrictions, freely exchanged between characters—other characteristics could not be removed from the player's character or game account. For most of the lifetime of *Diablo II*, skill and attribute point allocations were irrevocable, and builds were often planned out prior to the character's creation to ensure the maximally effective allocation in conjunction with the character's intended equipment. Depending on one's class and even between different builds within the same class, an item could range in use-value from being practically mandatory to make the build function to no use whatsoever.

Characters had access to several technologies of equipment production, including as a direct reward for defeating computer-controlled monsters. The probabilistic rewards generated when loot-bearing containers are opened or monsters are slain represented the dominant but not exclusive source of character equipment: certain equipment was not found directly but produced through the correct combination of component items (which were dropped by monsters). Although of dwindling importance as characters approached the later portions of the game, equipment could be purchased from merchants in the game's various towns, and a few quests provided items as rewards, but these were only available to each character once on each of the three difficulty levels and were generated randomly. The level of output associated with any of these productive technologies were all ultimately associated with the efficiency with which the character (and the controlling player) could navigate the game environment quickly, minimize risk of death, and the speed at which they were able to defeat their intended targets: what made a character "powerful" within the context of the game environment and that character's level of output per unit time spent engaged in productive game actions were one and the same. (In contrast with many MMO environments where late-game production requires coordination among teams of specialized characters, nothing in *Diablo II*'s endgame was inaccessible for a lone online player.)

Along with the heterogeneity in the use-value of equipment, there was substantial variation in equipment properties themselves. Item generation was a probabilistic process which considered a series of weighted tables that defined the relative frequencies for the type of event in question, first determining whether any item would be generated at all and if so from what class of item. In addition to equipment, slain monsters could also drop consumable items, the gems and runes used in item modification and crafting, and piles of gold.[11] The precise type of item to be generated would be determined according to the relative frequencies defined among the options within a selected class, and finally when generating equipment would determine the level of rarity to be possessed by the object. It was then determined what, if any, additional properties beyond those of the "base item" any particular piece of equipment would possess.[12] When generated, items would fall to the ground in the game world, displaying their item type in color-coded text indicating rarity level. For experienced players, information of base item type and rarity usually was sufficient to quickly establish whether a given item was worth picking up to be identified—an assessment that needed to be swift given that objects once on the ground were freely available to whoever clicked on them first.

[11] As part of later additions to the range of endgame content, certain unique monsters also had a chance to drop a component required for access to the new endgame activity, which was adopted as another monetary commodity over time.

[12] Rarities ranged (in order of increasing quality and generally decreasing frequency) from broken or low-quality items worse than the default, to ordinary or "superior" items with only the base properties of the item or very slight bonuses, to common "magic" items with one or two additional bonus properties ("affixes," indicated by a pre- and/or suffix to the item's name), to "rare" items with more than two associated affixes, and finally "Set" and "Unique" items which possess predefined (although possibly variable) bonuses. Ordinary and superior items additionally had a chance to include one or more "sockets" for use with runes and gems, and items of any rarity could further be "ethereal" versions with improved properties but which could not be repaired (when reaching zero points of durability, they would be rendered permanently worthless).

Items of "magic" rarity or higher were generated in an "unidentified" state in which they could not be equipped and would not display their exact bonuses until the player took the additional in-game action of identification. Identified items included their full names when examined and (almost) complete information regarding their statistics to anyone viewing them (via mouse over) in an inventory or trade screen.[13] Most of the numerical properties possessed by any given piece of equipment or an associated affix were not precise set values but could fall within a range: possibly with a significant impact upon their prices. Information about these potential ranges, as well as similar data regarding the possibilities of generating different items, the weighting functions between rarities, and similar details, were generally accessible online either via a reference website provided by Blizzard Entertainment or from community-maintained sources. On account of the numerous margins available, the likelihood of finding an exact duplicate of a piece of equipment was vanishingly small for all but the least variable of Unique and Set items and ordinary items from common base item types. Finding equipment with appreciable exchange value in the player economy was infrequent, and for it to be an item with use-value for that character and build was correspondingly rarer still. To a first approximation, nearly everything dropped in the course of gameplay would be, from the player-economy standpoint, worthless.

The in-world medium of exchange was insufficiently salable to serve as the medium of exchange among players, given the limited role of purchase from the in-world merchants in player equipment acquisition. The online player economy was not the only economy in *Diablo II*: the world of Sanctuary (in which the *Diablo* franchise is set), or at least the entirety of the merchants and vendors with whom the player character can interact, employs some form of gold coinage as a universally accepted medium of exchange.[14] While in the player economy, gold appears never to have been a viable medium of exchange and, indeed, only on rare occasions do traders bother to assign it any value (in commodity terms) at all, it would be inaccurate to describe *Diablo II*'s currency as a failure. Considering

[13] Some information, associated with the item in the game's record keeping and related to the internals of item generation, was never displayed to the player within the game without modifications, none of which were by rule allowed while playing characters on the official servers. None of the information hidden from the player was relevant to an item's effect upon player statistics, but it did include information which was known to impact the expected results of some available item manipulations.

[14] How a single coinage came to circulate across not only the entirety of Sanctuary's continents but also both domains of the Afterlife is left unexplained.

gold's role in the game as a medium by which players interact with the game's merchants, it works perfectly well. Gold's uselessness for player-to-player exchange stems rather from a lack of demand on players' parts for more gold than can be acquired incidentally. This resulted partly from the ease of acquiring gold but predominantly because of the near-total irrelevance of purchasing items from merchants beyond the very early stages of character progression.[15]

The value of non-equipment items was derived from their role as inputs in the defined technologies of item manipulation available to players. Certain types of equipment could be generated with one or more available "sockets" into which players could place one of the items (gems, runes, and jewels), permanently consuming the placed object and "filling" one of the equipment's sockets in order to add additional benefits to equipment that varied according to the employed objects. Gems and runes both came in a limited number of homogenous subtypes,[16] while jewels were generated with affixes such as those found on magical equipment. Certain combinations of runes when placed into otherwise nonmagical equipment of the correct types resulted in the creation of "runeword" items that were comparable to those of Unique rarity, having fixed properties often unavailable from other sources—most builds' optimal endgame equipment was mostly comprised of Uniques and runewords. Along with their placement into sockets, gems, runes, and jewels served as consumable inputs for other available technologies for the creation or modification of equipment, the complete list of which was also available on the game's reference website.

Diablo II's game mechanics mutually reinforced the potential surplus available from exchange between characters, whose "tastes" in equipment were, due to the irreversibility of class and build (for most of the game's lifetime),

---

[15] Gold has other limitations, including having a fraction of one's held gold removed upon character death—however, for endgame characters (other than those in Hardcore mode, where character deaths are permanent), these losses are fairly trivial in comparison with the difficulty of recovering from the penalty to accumulated character experience that occurs upon death. The recurring costs that provide "sinks" for character gold are also outpaced by character income beyond the earliest stages of gameplay, outside of unusual cases.

[16] Gems were associated with both types, that is, ruby or diamond as well as ascending levels of quality up to "Perfect." Runes came in thirty-three types, each of which occupied a distinct rank in their internal ordering. Runes of increasing rank having a correspondingly higher threshold before they can be generated and a sharply decreasing relative frequency of generation even once that threshold was met.

effectively given and potentially heterogeneous. Since the primary productive technology's return in equipment and inputs to secondary equipment production techniques was stochastic, efforts to "produce" a desired object might be expected to yield, as a "byproduct" objects whose cumulative exchange value exceeds, maybe by orders of magnitude, that of the sought-after object. Along with the exchange-conducive features of these structures, which can be assessed in the abstract, the values associated with the tens of thousands of potentially variable parameters within the game (only a few of which are associated with individual effects of economic significance) "worked" in such a way as to make the abstract properties relevant within the game's online environment.

At the same time, the systems within the game relating to the process of realizing the gains from trade include design elements which present significant hindrances to search when compared with the exchange institutions of more recent online economies (including those of *Diablo III* while they lasted[17]).

Per-character storage was limited and costly, with the cost of storage of items and equipment being variable by type. Storage of inventory beyond that available to a single character involved additional costs, including the introduction of a risk of losses. Characters could only utilize a single piece of equipment corresponding to any given location (that is, a single pair of gloves, helmet, belt, and so on, each represented by a slot on the character's "paper-doll"), and any surplus equipment or other objects players wished to retain as property required the use of space either in the character's immediate inventory or their "stash" available only within the game's "towns" (safe zones serving as central hubs for interaction with vendors and other players in which no combat was possible). Each space was a rectangular grid divided into uniformly sized squares:[18] items and equipment ranged in size, at a minimum only a single square of the grid, with larger objects and equipment being of correspondingly greater dimensions. Characters could only take possession of objects (whether picking them up from the ground or via the trade interface) for which an open location of at least the required dimensions was available. The existence of "charms," a form of equipment which

[17] See the discussion in Chapter 6.

[18] Character inventories (and the temporary spaces used in the trade window) were 4 × 10, with the stash being 8 × 6; characters also acquired during the early portions of the game (but not immediately) an object with a 3 × 4 internal volume but occupying a 2 × 2 space, for a total of ninety-six "squares" of available space. ("Mule" characters were usually left in their initial state and thus could hold eighty-eight squares of items at maximum.)

provided bonuses, when held within the inventory brought this space into direct competition with player effectiveness. The one game resource that did not require inventory space was gold for which players have a separate, level-dependent capacity.

Characters possessed inviolable property rights over items within the spaces they "owned" in their inventories and stashes.[19] Outside of those areas, however, there were no property protections and some elements of significant risk: items on the ground were not only freely available to be picked up by other players but were also subject to the game's internal garbage disposal, which removed most "common" objects from the world once sufficient time had passed. Items, no matter their rarity, which remained on the ground when any given instance of the game was closed (usually immediately upon the disconnection of the last character from that game instance, but potentially a few minutes after that departure) were also permanently erased. Players wishing to hold additional goods beyond a single character's inventory capacity could create additional characters (and, if needed, additional accounts) purely for warehousing ("mules"). There were some costs associated with the creation of mule characters, particularly for players whose access either to their computer or the servers was limited, because of the requirement that characters spend a certain number of hours within game instances during their first few weeks following creation or risk deletion by the server. The practice of "muling" also had a definite ongoing cost, particularly for those without the ability to operate a second simultaneous connection to the servers because of the need for players to transfer objects between the characters they controlled. (The existence of a cross-character shared storage space, a "shared stash," was one of the most common modifications made for *Diablo II* and has subsequently become the norm in similar games.)

Moving items to and from one's mules was easiest with the help of a trusted confederate, both players joining a (password protected) game instance, with one remaining connected at all times while the other joined the game using various characters holding items to be shuffled between inventories. Handing the objects to be transferred via the trade interface to the assisting player was

[19] One substantial exception being counterfeits spawned by the various techniques of item duplication discovered over the game's lifetime (known collectively as "dupes"), which were at risk either of deletion in one of the intermittent efforts at curtailing server exploits undertaken by Blizzard or to randomly vanishing. Within the online community at large where the use of counterfeit equipment and other exploits was unproblematic, this risk was the primary basis upon which counterfeit items were discounted.

maximally secure against loss of the objects by means other than theft, but a more convenient alternative was throwing objects onto the ground as one character, leaving the game instance, and joining again using another character to pick items up.[20] The presence of the other player was required to ensure the game instance was not ended on the server (barring a general failure of the online servers) and, where communication was possible via means other than the game client, possibly able to recover items left in transit if the transferring player was interrupted midstream. (With two simultaneous connections, players could also perform this same process on their own, thereby eliminating any risk of defection by the counterparty but bearing all of the instability-related risks.) Transfer methods using public game instances involved greater risks of the item's being acquired by another party or lost.

The trade interface allowed for the simultaneous transfer of items between characters within the same game instance, with other forms of exchange opening up additional possibilities for opportunism. Although transfers between characters could never involve force, there was no in-game recourse for fraudulent activity. Characters within the same instance, while in town, could approach another player's character and request to trade, and when accepted both players would then interact via the trade interface. Items placed within one character's side of the trade window could be examined as if they were within the other character's inventory—so providing all the details regarding the properties of that item—but could not be manipulated in any way. Each player could also add gold to their side of an exchange, although this element of the interface was seldom used, and when both inventories had not changed in any way for a few seconds (to prevent more obvious potential efforts at deception as well as accidental transfers), players could indicate via a large checkmark button that they accepted the exchange. (Anytime the contents of either inventory changed, this was undone as another effort to forestall accidents and attempts at bad faith.) Once both players had done so, the game would automatically attempt to complete the transaction, adding the contents of each character's trade inventory to the inventory of the

[20] The prevalence of mule characters meant that often trades involved inventory held by a character other than the one for whom it was intended equipment, and allowing one's counterparty to complete this transfer directly following the completion of a sale was considered a courteous gesture in environments where sufficient trust was established regarding one's exchange partners.

counterparty or aborting the transaction if it exceeded either party's available inventory space.[21]

This kind of exchange was the sole means by which items could be directly moved from one character's inventory to another—removing directly coercive acts of theft or violence.[22] This also meant the absence of any means by which to enforce any transaction or contractual relationship other than simultaneous bilateral transfers in which only items (and gold) were to be exchanged.[23] Any departures from the immediate scope of the trade interface's automatic transfer meant the introduction of potential avenues for opportunistic behavior. Within the public trade games and their environment of near-total anonymity, only a slight possibility for repeat interactions,[24] and no external sanctions associated with dealing in bad faith, would-be scam artists were among the common irritations encountered while searching for potentially beneficial exchange partners—while players could never be robbed, they could certainly be fleeced.

Player efforts to facilitate successful coordination among potential exchange partners included norms and practices regarding in-game exchange activities and the creation of institutions external to the game environment intended to circumvent its inherent limitations. Exchange activities were oriented by the institutional rules of the trade interface only once a character accepted another's request to interact through it and only to the extent they were conducted within the limited range of outcomes allowed in that context. The remainder of the practices through

[21] Terms of trade that would require one party to offer more than forty inventory squares of objects in exchange for one item would thus involve an additional element of risk and therefore tend to be disfavored on the margin: the prevailing exchange ratio of conversion of the least valuable monetary commodity (Perfect Gems) to the commodity associated with items of intermediate value (the "Pul" rune) tended to remain at forty to one for most of any given Ladder season (at the beginning of which the economy was reset) before trending downward in the late-season economy.

[22] Transfers involving coercion were still possible between *players*, such as equipment theft resulting from a compromise of account login credentials.

[23] Excluding trades involving two highly desirable Unique charms, which could not be transferred using the trade interface, along with being atypical in several other respects—rather than being products of the usual item generation sources, one copy of each was rewarded upon defeat of certain endgame content, opening up the possibility of specialist production.

[24] The size of the player population relative to the maximum size of any single game instance making repeated chance encounters quite rare, even between players whose habits led to substantial overlap between their periods of active exchange seeking.

which exchanges are coordinated that are taken for granted when one thinks of a market—such as the one Menger imagines in his account of monetary emergence—have their origins within the online community rather than in the game's programming. Two tools were available for this purpose in the online environment. First, the interface included a messaging system consisting of unmoderated chat rooms, some of which were labeled as being for trading, and the ability to send and receive private messages and to designate certain accounts as friends who could be messaged as a group and about whom the server would send notifications regarding their status. Second, the manner in which game instances could be created and joined played a role: each game instance required a name not simultaneously held by another instance on the server.

For public games, unless fully occupied the name would be displayed (along with information about the presently connected characters, time active, any level restrictions if imposed, and an optional description of greater length than the name itself) among those potentially available. Players could also enter the name of the desired game instance directly (games created to require a password in order to connect were considered private and could only be accessed this way) and attempt to join. Certain names of game instances, notably "trade" and its nearby conjugations, came to signify instances intended to be for exchange interactions specifically. Players looking to join public trade games could therefore blindly request to join a game entitled "trade," creating one should it not exist, or attempting to join the hierarchy of secondary names if trade was full or set on too high a difficulty (as would be the case for most mules, were the difficulty set higher than the minimum). Since trades could only be conducted in town, and any character unable to access a higher difficulty level would be certain to have access to only the first (the location in which a new character begins the game), this was the focal location in which the distinctive ritual of public exchange interactions took place. Characters not presently in a trade interface bounced between characters with whom they had not yet interacted until one exited the previous trade and became available.

One player was then expected to display their items for inspection—traditionally whoever was slower to type the appropriate liturgical invocation "wug," shorthand for "what you got?" Once displayed, it was then expected that the initial party would either indicate items of potential interest or relatively quickly close the trade interface and move on to other characters and hopefully more desirable wares. This series of brief, brusque, and mostly futile interactions continued until a player had circulated between all the other characters in the game instance (up to seven) and then either disconnected and moved on to another game or waited and hoped for others to circulate.[25] Many players found public trade games an unpleasant experience, but the games had numerous shortcomings even for those less bothered. Using the trade interface was the least-bad method for informing potential partners about what was offered for trade. As a means of communication with other traders, it could display only those items held by the presently connected character and could be seen by only one other player at a time. Placing items into the trade interface by itself also communicated very little, providing no information to the other player regarding what would be desired in exchange for those items or the price expectations held by either player involved. Out of the pool of potential counterparties within a player's chosen region of online servers, public trade games were limited to only those players simultaneously engaged in the trade games, and of course standing in the starting town "wugging" to the limits of one's patience was time in which no production was taking place.

The potential gains from exchange therefore led players to commercial spaces outside the in-game client entirely. For some players, this meant eBay's gray market in virtual equipment,[26] but venues for coordinating exchanges entirely within the game environment's economy could be found on the numerous trade forums offered by message boards associated with *Diablo II* (including those on the official forums, d2jsp, and [of most importance for this work] diabloii.net). The use of these message boards allowed individuals to circumvent many of the limitations inherent when searching in game: posts expressing interest in a

---

[25] Trade game instances tended to go through a life cycle in which once created, there was usually a burst of activity as those actively scanning game names connected, then gradually filtered out again depending upon the overall activity of the trade pool at the time, quickly ossifying once more than two or three characters who did not contribute were connected. Along with the would-be confidence schemes mentioned before, free riders on the exchange activity included players begging for items or assistance of some form, and players looking mainly to show off some particularly rare or valuable object via the trade interface. (Because games above a certain duration would remain in existence for some time even after all players had disconnected, trade games during periods of relatively limited trading activity would also acquire a strange afterlife as individuals connected to them realized they were no longer active, and left.)

[26] eBay being, at least in the first few years of the millennium, among the venues of choice for the gray-market vendors.

particular exchange were advertised in a durable, public form even while players were not actively competing for limited visible chat space or circulating among trade games. Players' message board accounts also represented durable identities which could encompass multiple game accounts simultaneously, reducing some of the communications frictions encountered when swapping rapidly among characters on different accounts (as might occur for players connecting simultaneously on two computers, which promoted locating productive characters and mule characters on distinct accounts to allow for self-transfers). Message boards could also devise and enforce rules of conduct different from those associated with game accounts.

Diablo II's exchange institutions were very much a double-edged sword for the game's economic interactions. The existence and security of property rights enjoyed by characters in virtue of the game client's programming were more than enough to allow market processes to function, but interactions among strangers outside of the purview of the trade interface remained very low-trust wherever alternative institutional workarounds could not be devised. The trade interface's status as the only game element intended to support exchange activity meant the costs of coordination fell entirely on players, even once a commercial "hub" in game-name space and the patterns of interaction within the market had become settled institutions. All of those practices distinctive to the online environment a player would have to learn—often while being vigorously "flamed"—before having a chance to acquire the sort of day-to-day "market data" needed to make reasonable decisions. However, this also meant transactions were interactions between players directly, mediated at most by the ability to inspect and transfer the goods involved and, therefore, far less locked into a particular structure of commercial activity than is generally the case in virtual economies including greater automation of exchange institutions. Embedded in any implementation of an "auction house"-type exchange institution are a host of regulations upon exchanges concerning matters which in *Diablo II* were by default left to individual traders to determine and that could differ between trading forums. This of course has a significant bearing on why *Diablo II* is a particularly interesting environment from the standpoint of the Mengerian process of currency formation—and its focus upon the interactions among many traders within a decentralized market—compared either to the standardized "marketplace" of the *World of Warcraft* Auction House or the commodity markets of *EVE Online* or the (sadly now defunct) *City of Heroes*, where the game environment automatically enforces market clearing.[27] The monetary unit in which the auction house transacts also tends, for that very reason, to remain the medium of exchange in player-mediated transactions.[28]

In summary, *Diablo II*'s in-game currency was not something players were interested in obtaining through exchange—and, in light of this knowledge, it usually was not offered. The heterogeneous nature of characters and items that made exchanges potentially valuable also made the double-coincidence of wants needed to acquire a desired final item via barter that was much more costly to find. Players nevertheless found trading sufficiently worthwhile to generate and sustain specialized commercial institutions serving to facilitate coordination. The last such institution to consider is the system of monetary exchange adopted by players, evidence for the rudiments of which can be found quite early in the game's history. The player economy underwent several shifts of monetary unit in response to changes in the game's underlying parameters and gradually increased in sophistication over time.

The Monetary History of *Diablo II*

Diablo II's online experience can, from the perspective of its monetary institutions, be divided into three epochs corresponding to different versions of the game: the period prior to patch 1.09, beginning with the game's initial release in June 2000, and encompassing the economy of "classic" *Diablo II* and the release of the *Lord of Destruction* expansion the following year, concluding with the release of patch 1.09 in August 2001; the subsequent two-year period where patch 1.09 defined the online environment; and finally, the period beginning with the release of patch 1.10 in October 2003. These two versions included sweeping adjustments to the parameters of characters, monsters, and equipment and so represent points of discontinuity for the operation of the market processes within the online environment as well as being inflection points in the rate at

27 The design of the market-making institutions also represents another marginal increase to the complexity of the game design's "public policy" effects. The exchange interfaces in both *EVE Online* and *City of Heroes* generated persistent arbitrage opportunities: in the *EVE* case, this became extremely lucrative with sufficient capitalization and entirely disappeared when the interface element involved was "fixed" to remove it.

28 Of course, of the games whose economic systems I am sufficiently familiar with, the use of an auction house-type centralized market is usually only one of a host of differences in the economic interaction among players that also work to mitigate its abandonment in favor, initially, of barter exchange; with the exception of *Diablo III*, of course.

which such adjustments took place. The transitions from one of these game versions to the next were also associated with increases in the volume and quality of information available regarding players' exchange behavior. Even during the preliminary stages of this project a decade ago (see the early results in Salter and Stein, 2015, 2016), the economy in the early months after release was preserved mainly via descriptions written during the subsequent periods.

From these descriptions, it is evident that certain commodities acquired use in a monetary role even prior to the release of the game's expansion: the earliest version associated with the presence of a prevailing currency system is patch 1.05,[29] which spanned the sixth through ninth months following the game's launch. According to this account, the two items that formed the basis of the monetary system were a Perfect Gem (called the Perfect Skull) and a Unique ring (the "Stone of Jordan"), either of which could be converted to the other at a relatively stable exchange ratio. These commodities seem to have remained the focal currencies during the period of patch 1.06, the last update prior to the release of the expansion.[30] Both are items whose properties made them eminently salable commodities, as each cost only the minimal single inventory square to store, were homogenous and generally useful as equipment, and were in substantial nonmonetary demand, being the two inputs needed for the kind of item manipulation technology of most relevance in the pre-expansion environment. Due to unforeseen interactions between the implementation of the online server and the properties of certain item production technologies, it was also possible to acquire Stones of Jordan far more easily than had been intended.[31]

In this early instance, as in many others, the market data of the in-game economy reflected not only the game environment's economic variables but also

[29] https://web.archive.org/web/20030808095328/http://diabloii.net/columnists/a-items-origin.shtml.

[30] Reference to Perfect Skulls as foundational currency units was made in: https://web.archive.org/web/20030623160102/http://www.diabloii.net/columnists/a-bnet-trade2.shtml.

[31] Possessing the other two Unique rarity rings then in existence when starting a game instance meant that any Unique rarity ring generated would be a Stone of Jordan. Since merchants offering unidentified items ("gambling") were allowed to generate Unique rarity equipment, this presented a fairly certain potential source, the cost of which in in-game currency was circumvented following the discovery of means to determine whether an unidentified ring was of Unique rarity (information which was transmitted from the server to the game interface and could be intercepted *en route*).

influences coming from the wider society in which it is embedded. These were not always to deleterious effect: besides leading the exchange ratio between the two inputs to be lower than it would have been otherwise, it may have also made sufficient quantities available to allow for the circulation of monetary commodities against goods, rather than the more limited roles of supporting convertibility and serving as unit of account. The two sources invite contradictory inferences regarding whether the pre-expansion economy's monetary commodities were used as media of exchange, as one explicitly compares them to multiple denominations of dollar bills, while the other references the same economy's use of the Perfect Skull in the context of suggesting that one problem with 1.09-era public trades was the use of Stones of Jordan not merely as units of account but as a medium of exchange as well.

The Stone of Jordan continued to serve as a currency following the release of the game's expansion, while the Perfect Skull appears not to have remained a distinct monetary commodity.[32] While previous oversights allowing relatively easy acquisition had been removed, quantities sufficient to enable it to serve as a medium of exchange were made available via the continuous discovery of unintended techniques for item duplication. Taking advantage of these to "dupe" Stones of Jordan was of course tantamount to counterfeiting the in-game commodity standard, but the rate at which "duping" methods and other exploits were discovered and their increasing impact upon the game environment during patch 1.09 were closely related to the eBay gray markets of that period. Although undergoing increasingly severe inflation because of counterfeits able to avoid the anti-duplication measures, the Stone of Jordan seems to have remained in use as a monetary unit through the introduction of patch 1.10. (Were 1.09 to have remained the prevailing environment, the erosion of its monetary value and proliferation of other single-square, homogenous items would have led to the loss of its monetary function, much like the Perfect Skull.) The reactions among the online community as most formal and informal regulation of game exploits eroded make patch 1.09 a fascinating period, but except for the gradual obsolescence of legitimate production by bugged or exploit-produced equipment, the monetary institutions for in-game exchange between players remained fairly stable.

The introduction of patch 1.10 was intended as a major overhaul which made substantial changes to characters and equipment and adjusted the difficulty

[32] Most likely because the technology to which it was an input was no longer a relevant source of endgame equipment.

and rewards of the endgame, as well as addressing many of the long-standing issues plaguing the 1.09 online ecosystem. Comprehensive shifts in parameters meant corresponding shifts in the use value of items to builds, the relative efficacy of builds to each other, and so on, and exchange ratios shifted accordingly. Runes in particular increased in importance due to the introduction of high-power runewords, most requiring multiple runes from the rarest classes. The full range of new runewords and items, furthermore, was accessible only for characters created following the patch's release who opted to be "Ladder" characters comprising a distinct population from older characters, resetting the wealth of players in the Ladder environment to zero and creating a population devoid of lingering bugs and dupes, at least initially. (The Ladder environment has subsequently had additional periodic resets where its population was converted to non-Ladder and players again began afresh.) Since the introduction of patch 1.10, subsequent updates, including those whose additions were incorporated into the monetary system, have been marginal additions to the existing economic structure rather than overturning the system in the manner of the expansion or patch 1.10 itself.

The exchange institutions on the Ladder are even closer to the sort of economy envisioned by Menger, since here players could (and did) draw upon structures of in-game commercial coordination both internal to the game client and in other venues. A few months after the release of patch 1.10 also marks the earliest of the records available from the diabloii.net trade forum dedicated to the US East Realm, whose "archive" subforum had contained messages beginning with the recovery from a server error in January 2004 and running up until December 31, 2008.[33] These provide both a direct record of the exchange activity among forum members as well as a window into the prevailing exchange conditions within the commercial spaces of the Ladder itself.[34]

Due to selection effects, we would expect the individuals trading on message boards to be skewed toward players more invested in the game environment

[33] The collection of the archive subforum's contents took place initially in 2010 but was no longer accessible by 2013. As of the beginning of 2020, the "active" forum beginning January 1, 2009 (which has had little activity in recent years) is again publicly visible, but the archive subforum does not seem to have similarly reappeared; the author's record of the contents remains available upon request.

[34] The exchanges offered usually were one of three types: expression of one or both sides of a desired bilateral exchange, auctions, and inventory dumps listing everything a player had for sale.

than the population as a whole, although to what degree is uncertain given the absence of demographic information regarding players, characters, or the overall economy. The population on the diabloii.net forum was distinct from even those of the other major trading forums due to the forum's institutional commitment to "legitimate" play and the resulting supplemental regulations, most importantly the "Do Not Trade" list, comprised of any items notorious for being extensively duped. This did not completely divorce the forum's economic conditions from those of the Ladder population as a whole, since forum members were free to trade in-game (a ban on which would have been impossible to enforce in any event) and those who were not overt regarding their use of game exploits could remain traders in good standing absent other violations of the forum's rules. Thus, although the activity on the diabloii.net trade forum is a record of distinctively counter-cultural commercial interactions (which makes it fascinating in its own right as well as quite unlikely to emerge within an economy mediated via an "auction house"), there is plenty to indicate that the same monetary commodities and roughly the same exchange ratios prevailed in-game and on the forum. Traders make frequent reference to the state of current valuations in the economy as a whole or leave open the opportunity for negotiations by pleading ignorance regarding the present state of the market. Active traders on the forum sometimes undertook individual efforts to maintain up-to-date records of the prices one could expect common equipment to command—all of which appear to have eventually had the stock-ticker element abandoned.

Beginning from the earliest surviving records, the language in which players publicize the items they want suggests a widespread recognition of the underlying logic of differential salability driving the eventual emergence of money. Except in posts searching simply for a willing counterparty to a definite bilateral transaction, traders usually provided some indication of what they were interested in acquiring—their "In Search Of" (ISO) list, along with their "For Trade" (FT) list. To say an item can be found relatively frequently within trader's ISO lists basically implies that it possesses relatively high salability. ISO lists also commonly provided some indication of the relative importance assigned to each of the included goods, including ranking them or dividing the list into groups with greater or lesser priority. Where an explicit ranking is absent, inferences about the order can often be drawn from the formatting of the list. Among the goods listed as desirable but with a low priority, references are frequently made to various terms denoting a catch-all willingness to entertain offers made in terms of commonly saleable goods. In the early stages of the Ladder economy, the most frequent umbrella term for this category was "tradeables," while the comparable term in the non-Ladder economy was "currency." Gradually "currency" became the preferred term among traders within the Ladder economy as well. Traders often include runes alongside or within tradeables as a class of objects, although while tradeables decline over time, runes mainly increase in the amount of gradation expressed between rarity levels. One poster in the early portions of the records cuts directly to the core of the matter and concluded his ISO list with the entry "really anything of value that can be traded easily."[35]

Two components of the monetary system prevailing in patch 1.10 and subsequent versions seem to have stabilized quite early: first, the use of the Perfect Gem as the basic commodity monetary unit for items of limited value, connected to the monetary units used for more expensive items by exchange of Perfect Gems in bulk for individual runes of intermediate rarity; second, runes of intermediate rarity and up becoming the preferred monetary commodity of expensive transactions and wealthy traders. The price ratios among runes in the uppermost group appear to have been much less stable than the overall structure in which they were the highest-powered currency. Among the technologies introduced for Ladder characters by patch 1.10 were extensions of the capacity to combine runes of a given rarity to form the next highest rune: this introduced an arbitrage constraint on at least some exchange ratios.

The undesirability of constant exchange-rate fluctuations as can be found expressed early in 1.10 may be one reason behind the later emergence of a convention in which all of the runes past a certain rarity were grouped together as the interchangeable "high runes," although players would exclude certain runes (usually three in particular) of less use in the dominant runewords. Although the hierarchy of commodities within the monetary system therefore serves some of the functions of multiple denominations of a single currency unit, describing the monetary commodities and their hierarchical exchange ratios as being a single currency with different denominations is inaccurate (contra Salter and Stein 2016). Depending on what equipment players were attempting to acquire, there are frequent examples of traders deviating from the common exchange ratios, for instance by placing a premium on the type of Perfect Gem required for a certain transformation or by discounting currency units with no nonmonetary value to them against their normal exchange valuations.

[35] ThreadID #133323, originally posted on February 7, 2004.

The additional endgame content introduced in patch 1.11 involved the combination of a matched set of three items acquired from different locations to access boss encounters, each of which provided one of a second matched set of three items, which could be combined to access the concluding area and the principal reward. The variability in exchange value between versions for different classes serves as a useful proxy for the perception of their relative utility—as it happens, there was a significant gulf between the top two and the remainder mirrored across most other class-specific bonuses, which, while far from the ideal game balance, is at least another point that suggests consistency among the various exchange relationships within the player economy. The effect on the monetary system in particular was that both sets of items required for progression to the final area came to be adopted as other forms of currency, although with these too individual traders often varied their exchange ratios with respect to other monetary items or declined to accept them altogether. (The former of the two sets is also the first item adopted as a monetary unit whose storage cost exceeded a single inventory square, being 2 × 1 in size.)

As these additional monetary commodities entered into general use, several practices that began as occasional innovations for more easily completing transactions began to come into general practice. Traders provided lists of the exchange ratios among monetary commodities they considered equivalent, noting whatever exclusions or modifications they adopted or indicating that they adopted the common ratios. Similarly, a larger portion of traders inviting offers began to include what are effectively retail prices (but that were referred to, following eBay parlance, as BINs, or Buy-it-Nows), either in terms of a currency unit or a numerical currency value according to either their own or the "usual" exchange ratios. For trades negotiated in-game, this innovation would be redundant given the operation of the trade interface, but exchange conducted via the trade forums was considered sufficiently high-trust that most participants were willing, and many preferred, to complete transactions via "mule trade," in which one player transferred their side of the transaction to a mule located on an account created for this purpose, then sent their counterparty the login information. The counterparty would then replace the goods with payment, which could be retrieved later. This allowed for asynchronous communication and also asynchronous transactions.

Tracing these institutional changes reveals many individual threads or players who included retail prices, point systems, tables for conversion between commodities, and many other adjustments in the months and years prior to the point at which they became regular. Even after becoming fairly common in the exchanges of regular forum participants and being recommended as best practice for facilitating transactions, a large portion of the recorded activity was not uncommon in early 2004. In addition, while within the trade forum, under the watchful eye of the moderators and the sanction of the Do Not Trade list every effort was made to at least protect against illegitimate activities, they continued to be a routine part of most player interactions with the official servers and the gray markets. All of which is to say that there was still much messiness that remained part of the *Diablo II* economy even as player interactions were neatly bringing about a fairly sophisticated web of monetary commodities and exchange institutions.

Conclusion: What Changed in *D3*?

The evolution of exchange in *Diablo II* is even more interesting to consider given the reverse course followed by the digital economic system in its sequel *Diablo III,* which culminated in the near-complete removal of exchange as a game element and the decommissioning of its marketplaces.[36] As suggested in the section "*Diablo II* as Economic Environment," the game's mechanics ensured players would be in a position to benefit from trade, indeed, would be desperate to do so, given the heterogeneous use-value different builds associated with the same item, and suggested as well by the popularity of shared stash modifications for passing items between single-player characters. In contrast, *Diablo III*'s environment differed primarily in removing mechanics which, for all of their drawbacks, did increase the chances of finding a very good item *for someone else*. For example, irreversibility of character build meant this could occur for an item still intended for the character's class as well as other classes; builds for whom weapon damage was irrelevant disappeared, which reduced the desirability of exchange between the two populations; the importance of properties not associated by necessity with an item's level also meant items generated while not yet reaching the endgame were potentially endgame-relevant anyway, whereas in *Diablo III* they are certain to be obsolete. These changes and others are a step away from the factors in *Diablo II* that made exchange so appealing. They are defensible as improvements for other reasons, but on net, a substantial factor in the failure of the *Diablo III* auction house was a massive reduction in the extent to which the value of a character's production was contingent upon the ability to trade.

[36] See the discussion in Chapter 6.

In *Diablo III*, most items characters preferred to sell rather than use were either marginal downgrades or upgrades with sufficient exchange value to justify giving up the opportunity to take advantage of their marginally higher quality. The former case results in a market of hand-me-downs, while the indivisibility of equipment and transaction costs built in to the auction house make benefiting from cases of greater-than-optimal spread more costly, and possibly curtailed. To illustrate, consider "trifecta" gloves during the first few months after release, which because of the very limited heterogeneity among characters were strictly superior to gloves with any other combination of properties for every character of a class, regardless of build. The magnitude of this advantage was large enough that once characters had acquired a pair, the only potential upgrades to that character's gloves were the more moderate gains from using another pair with marginally better stat rolls. These demand conditions led to a price premium on higher values of the stats on "trifecta" gloves, one that became more pronounced the closer those stat rolls came to their maxima.

A player's choice whether to equip or sell a pair of these gloves that would be an upgrade for his character depends upon a comparison between the improvement provided by the gloves and the improvements to other equipment possible given their sale value. The built-in cut taken by the auction house lowers the realized sale value below the actual sale price and thus makes retaining the item relatively less costly. In addition, given the increasing marginal price effect of higher stat rolls, a pair of gloves with nine-tenths of the effectiveness of those found by the player could conceivably sell for half its price, so that the optimal decision from the player's standpoint would be to exchange the gloves his character found for a cheaper pair, pocketing the price differential between them. (Thinking about exchanges such as this makes more sense when the two items are distinguished by magnitude rather than type of effect.) In these situations, the indivisibility of items increases the costs of such "trading down," another marginal influence in favor of keeping and using items rather than selling them. (This also suppresses the entrance of "marginal" value items into the auction house, which makes it less likely for the gloves I want to ever be available.) Forgoing an institution you loathe when it does less for you than you anticipate is easier to do than for an intolerable but indispensable institution.

Diablo II's economic institutions and the hierarchical relationship among the commodities in its monetary system attest to the remarkable ability of individuals as economic actors to identify and exploit gains from trade—an ability we can also credit with the complete subversion of the game's official servers. The commodity standard and the many points where exchange ratios and programming quirks coincided, the counter-cultural ethic of playing without cheats, and the ever-present swindlers in public trade games all combined to make a wonderfully messy online community, but equally they provide an excellent case study of the natural logic of economic interaction in a barter economy, the same kind of economy that Menger realized could result in the emergence of money.

References

Menger, Carl. 1892. "On the Origin of Money." *The Economic Journal* 2 (6): 239–255.

———. 1985 [1883]. *Investigations into the Method of the Social Sciences with Special Reference to Economics*. New York: New York University Press.

Salter, Alexander W., and S. Stein. 2015. "Currency Emergence in the Absence of State Influence: The Case of Diablo II." *Cosmos + Taxis* 2 (2): 34–45.

———. 2016. "Endogenous Currency Formation in an Online Environment: The Case of Diablo II." *Review of Austrian Economics* 29 (1): 53–66.

Stein, S. 2015. "Cultural and Institutional Co-determination: The Case of Legitimacy in Exchange in *Diablo II*." In *Culture and Economic Action*, edited by Virgil Storr and Laura Grube. Cheltenham: Edward Elgar.

6

A Virtual Weimar

Hyperinflation in *Diablo III*

Peter C. Earle

As virtual fantasy worlds go, Blizzard Entertainment's *Diablo III* is particularly foreboding. In this multiplayer online game, witch doctors, demon hunters, and other character types duke it out in a war between angels and demons for control of a dark world called Sanctuary. The world is reminiscent of Judeo–Christian notions of hell, complete with fire and brimstone and the added elements of supernatural combat waged with magic and divine weaponry.

But between February and May 2013, various outposts in the world—Silver City and New Tristram, to name two—had more in common with Berlin in 1923 or Zimbabwe in 2007 than with Dante's *Inferno*. The culmination of a series of unanticipated circumstances—and, finally, a most unfortunate programming bug—produced a new and unforeseen dimension of hellishness within *Diablo III*: hyperinflation.

This chapter is outlined as follows: I begin with a literature review and exposition of the concepts of inflation and hyperinflation within the ambit of virtual economies—including a review of the means by which virtual monetary policy is conducted. I then briefly describe the method used to analyze the case of *Diablo III*. Finally, I offer a full account of the hyperinflationary saga.

Austrian Economics, Inflation, and Hyperinflation

In orthodox economics, the term "inflation" is used to mean a general rise in prices. In this chapter, though, we use the term in a different and more useful sense. The Austrian economist Ludwig von Mises (1924) described inflation as an increase in the supply of money in excess of the demand for money (that is, an increase not "offset" by an increase in the demand for money), resulting in the reduced purchasing power of money. Price increases are thus a direct result of this process, not its essence. From a practical perspective, as Henry Hazlitt (1964) wrote,

> [w]hen the supply of money increase[s], people have more money to offer for goods … Each individual dollar becomes less valuable because there are more dollars. Therefore more of them will be offered against, say, a pair of shoes or a hundred bushels of wheat than before. A "price" is an exchange ratio between a dollar and a unit of goods. When people have more dollars … [goods] rise in price, not because [they] are scarcer than before, but because dollars are more abundant.

Thus, inflation is not simply an increase in the supply of money within an economy; it is the increase in that portion, if any, not backed by a commensurate increase in specie: most commonly, market commodities like gold or silver (Menger, 1976). Today, in fact, most currencies are printed or created electronically by a central bank or currency board and are not backed by a commodity standard such as gold or silver. They are thus far more subject to politically inspired manipulation—the expansion of the money stock, in particular—and thus inflation. Mises (1953) noted that

> [t]hose applying these terms are not aware of the fact that purchasing power never remains unchanged and that consequently there is always either inflation or deflation. They ignore these necessarily perpetual fluctuations as far as they are only small and inconspicuous, and reserve the use of the terms to big changes in purchasing power. Since the question as to at what point a change in purchasing power begins to deserve being called big depends on personal relevance judgments, it becomes manifest that inflation and deflation are terms lacking the categorical precision required for praxeological, economic, and catallactic concepts. Their application is appropriate for history and politics ... The terms inflationism and deflationism, inflationist and deflationist, signify the political programs aiming at inflation and deflation in the sense of big cash-induced changes in purchasing power.

The term hyperinflation indicates monetary conditions characterized by high and accelerating rates of inflation. Several competing definitions of hyperinflation exist (as distinct from "merely" high inflation), with the strictest—

an increase of prices of 50 per cent in one month—defined by economist Phillip Cagan (1956) in his contribution to Milton Friedman's *Studies in the Quantity Theory of Money*.

In these circumstances, the prices of goods and services increase with mounting rapidity as the real value of the currency undergoing hyperinflation decreases, resulting in decreasing (and at some point, nonexistent) social propensities to save. Ultimately, the failure of prices to accurately reflect the scarcity of certain factors of production removes any ability to plan rational economic undertakings, and eventually both firms and individuals engage in a mounting "flight to real values": moving as quickly as possible from cash to goods in an effort to preserve purchasing power.

Hyperinflations have occurred throughout history. Outbreaks during the Crisis of the Third Century in Rome and during the Tang Dynasty in China are occasionally cited as early instances, but whether they constitute hyperinflation or "merely" severe inflationary episodes is contentious. Another ancient episode, cited by Spalding (1917), harkens back to thirteenth-century Persia:

> During the year 1294, Persia was going through bad times: the King, Kai-Khatu, had squandered the country's funds at such a rate that the national exchequer was practically empty, and all efforts to raise money at Baghdad and Shiraz were fruitless. At last, some brilliant member of the king's court seems to have brought to the notice of his sovereign and the Treasury officials a species of paper money … A scheme for its issue was forthwith drawn up, submitted to Kai-Khatu, approved by that august gentleman, and promptly put into circulation in Persia … All gold and silver money was called in and notes given in exchange, and circulating offices … were set up throughout the country … They were issued at Tabriz, in the month of Zilkadeh, 693 (Sept–Oct 1294), and merchants and shopkeepers were forced to accept them. In three days, Tabriz was a wilderness, and trade there at a standstill … Naturally the paper money immediately became a depreciated medium of exchange … and a horse worth 15 dinars was sold for 150. All caravan traffic ceased.

Hyperinflation is the economist's equivalent of an astrophysicist's quasar cluster or a marine biologist's dolphin "stampede": a rare exhibition of a unique set of circumstances which arise infrequently and are closely studied when they materialize. Such events are exotic enough that they become legendary: for instance, many individuals who know little about monetary policy are aware of the case of Zimbabwe from 2007 to 2009 or are familiar with the defining instance of monetary collapse in the post-WWI Weimar Republic. Studies of Germany between 1920 and 1923 are especially common and include works by economists such as L. Albert Hahn (1924), Ludwig von Mises (1924, 1978), Constantino Bresciani-Turroni (2007 [1931]), and Frank Graham (1932), among others. Studies of other hyperinflationary episodes include but are not limited to China during the 1940s (Campbell and Tullock, 1954), pre-revolutionary France (White, 1959), Hungary between 1945 and 1946 (Bomberger and Makinen, 1983), Greece between 1943 and 1946 (Makinen, 1986), Bolivia between 1984 and 1985 (Bernholz, 1988), and Taiwan from 1945 to 1952 (Makinen and Woodward, 1989). There are also several comparative surveys by Sargent (1982), Capie (1991), Calder (2009), and Saboin (2018).

Virtual Economics

Virtual economics is a small but growing field, with early work done by Castronova (2002) and Lehdonvirta (2005). Studies of virtual currencies have included Denapolis West (2005) and Lederman (2007). The virtual currency of the predecessor to *Diablo III*, *Diablo II* (released in 2000) was studied as well in Salter and Stein (2016). Game developers implement and control virtual money, which is essentially a type of unregulated digital money, for use by members participating in their game or virtual community. While it is generally forbidden by games' terms of service for "closed virtual currencies" (virtual currencies which are bound to use exclusively within a specific game or community) to have any connection with the real economy, a gray market often forms for individuals to exchange virtual currencies for real-world assets. When forbidden, the market for exchanging real-world assets for virtual currencies constitutes a de facto black market.

Digital Hyperinflations

Because the virtual currencies created and used within virtual economies are digitally created and not commodity-backed—therefore, not particularly dissimilar from current real-world currencies—those like *Diablo III*'s "gold" are fundamentally fiat currencies. Possibly the earliest identification of an outbreak of virtual inflation, formerly identified by the portmanteau "MUDflation," occurred on April 6, 1993, in which a poster explained that

> [s]omebody in the post mentioned something about MUDs [multi-user dungeons] having an inflation problem. The response I have for this is: YES!!! The reason is intuitively obvious even to the most casual observer – when a mobile recreates itself whole from nothingness, it also creates more coinage. So the amount of money in the economy goes up and up and up … Anybody got any other ideas on how to deal with MUDflation? :-)

MUDs tended to be largely text-based and therefore rather simple games with consequently simple economies. With the arrival of the first MMORPGs came more sophisticated game economies, more frequent outbreaks of digital inflation, and ultimately the first digital hyperinflations. (It is critical to note that because of a paucity of data, the difference between a "merely" high inflation and hyperinflation in a virtual context is purely subjective. Having said that, accounts of prices rising on a daily basis are suggestive of extreme inflationary conditions.)

Two particular cases document previous episodes of particular relevance to this chapter; both were similarly caused by "duping" bugs: programming errors wherein an ordinarily quotidian in-game action causes currencies or goods to be multiplied, sending supply shocks rippling through the virtual economy. The first, described in 2001 in an article titled "Pimps and Dragons," unfolded in *Ultima Online* as follows:

> The [in-game] kingdom … has a single unit of currency, a gold piece that looks a little like a biscuit. A network of servers is supposed to keep track of all the gold, just like it keeps track of everything else on the island, but in late 1997 bands of counterfeiters found a bug that allowed them to reproduce gold pieces more or less at will. The fantastic wealth they produced for themselves was, of course, entirely imaginary, and yet it led, in textbook fashion, to hyperinflation. At the worst point in the crisis, Britannia's monetary system virtually collapsed, and players all over the kingdom were reduced to bartering. (Kolbert, 2001)

In the popular *EverQuest* as well, on December 16, 2003, a blogger reported as follows:

> Thanks to several independent observers for forwarding information about a money hemorrhage in EverQuest. Apparently a little bug appeared on an NPC [Nonplayer character] that allowed the conversion of any amount of cash into 10 times its value, almost instantly. The first sign of a problem: plummeting prices of [game] platinum pieces in terms of dollars … [w]hat

> does a money dupe really do? Well, it raises the prices of all the goods in the economy.

Nintendo's *Animal Crossing: New Leaf* also saw a massive inflation due to a duping error in 2013.

Armamentarium of the Virtual "Central Bank"

Within the fairly straightforward gaming framework in *Diablo III*, the virtual currency—called "gold"—is employed for purchasing weapons and repairing battle damage. Over time, virtual gold can be used to purchase ever-more resources for confronting ever-more dangerous foes. In virtual economies, the primary instruments used to control the money supply are "faucets" and "sinks." Faucets are ways through which currency is injected into the game. This generally involves players receiving currency from the game system itself as opposed to other players. In such situations, the received currency is created anew. Sinks are ways through which currency is removed from the game. This typically involves players paying currency into the game system itself as opposed to other players. In such situations, the paid currency is destroyed. Examples of faucets and sinks in *Diablo III* include:

Faucets

Drops: When a player defeats a foe, he or she often receives a reward of virtual gold or a good saleable for virtual gold.

Rewards: The game involves the player undertaking "Acts," and within each act are a number of "quests." For completing these, players are typically awarded virtual gold.

Buyers: Players can sell items to "in-game" (computerized, nonhuman) buyers, receiving virtual gold.

Sinks

Repairs: Over time, a player's equipment will become damaged in combat and suffer wear-and-tear, requiring periodic restoration from an in-game craftsman in exchange for virtual gold.

Forging: Players pay virtual gold to an in-game blacksmith for weapons.

Rakes: Using the gold auction house costs players both a listing fee and a transaction fee, removing virtual gold from the economy.

Consumables: Players can purchase potions, scrolls, and other items from vendors for virtual gold.

Methods

Accounts of the implementation of monetary policy and their effects are generally categorized into two categories: empirical and narrative. As summarized by Angelopoulou (2007),

> [t]he empirical literature starts from the principle that systematic monetary policy is endogenous and therefore the only way to identify the effects of monetary policy is to isolate exogenous monetary policy shocks and estimate their impact on a number of endogenous variables … An alternative way to explore the effects of monetary policy is to use official records (monetary policy minutes, press releases, reports) to identify distinct shifts in monetary policy and understand the intentions of the monetary authorities.

Nelson (1989) and Sumner (1997), for example, utilized the business press to analyze expectations during the Great Depression. Hinchman and Hinchman (1997) explain that

> [n]arratives in the [social] sciences should be defined provisionally as discourses with a clear sequential order that connect events in a meaningful way for a definite audience and thus offer insights about the world and/or people's experiences of it.

At its core, a narrative account is characterized by illustrating an event via a chronological ordering of meaningful events relevant to a specific thesis or audience. In the case of *Diablo III*, because the firm operating the game is privately owned, there are no publicly available minutes or official notes regarding internal decisions or lack thereof. This account, therefore, employs the narrative approach: to construct this rendering, I employ communications from players on the official Blizzard company message board as well as press releases, company announcements, and a variety of other sources.

Early Concerns

Diablo III was first released in May 2012, and there seem to have been early concerns among players that gold sinks within the game were insufficient. As early as June 2012, one site noted,

> [M]ost of us (probably including Blizzard) assumed that the Blacksmith would be widely used — he was, after all, the only major gold sink in

> the game … but dropped items alone selling in the [auction house] have been enough to satiate the appetite [of players] and crafting is … a waste of [gold] when one could easily buy an optimal item from the [auction house] rather than pumping 50 to 170K of gold into [a Blacksmith-crafted weapon]. (Gamerluck, 2012)

The establishment by Blizzard of a real money auction house ("RMAH") alongside a virtual gold auction house in the game provided players with an incentive to both farm the game for real-world profits and to pursue arbitrage opportunities. The RMAH was also created, at least in part, to disincentivize players from patronizing third-party markets outside the game. Nevertheless, bots—automated game participants whose sole purpose is to farm the game world for items to sell—quickly emerged.

Several weeks after the game's debut, an anonymous blogger claimed there were at least 1,000 bots active 24/7 in the *Diablo III* game world, allegedly "harvesting" (producing) 4 million virtual gold per hour. Although skepticism about anonymous sources is often justified, it does seem that most of the gold generated by the ruthlessly productive, rapidly adapting bots found its way to third-party vendors through a black market which undercut the prices in the sanctioned in-game auction houses.

The combined effect of heavy bot activity and insufficient sinks immediately influenced the gold markets, and inflationary pressures soon became apparent. One exasperated player complained in August 2012:

> I purchased most of my gear for around 5 mil [gold] early on. I've been farming for awhile [and] have saved around 30 million gold [but now] I can't upgrade the gear I have ... Where is all this money coming from? Why is everything so expensive? (Blizzard, 2013)

With gold prices falling, prices began spiking in certain goods. Another player noted with curiosity:

> [Y]esterday Fiery Brimstone was 150K, now almost 300K. Each time I hit refresh it seems to be going up a bit[.] (Blizzard, 2013)

As in real-world economies, the price effects of monetary inflation arose unevenly throughout the *Diablo III* game world: prices did not change at the same time or to the same extent.

Gold Floors versus Black Markets

The RMAH had minimum and maximum dollar amounts hard-coded (fixed) by developers for in-game gold transactions: $0.25 minimum, $250 maximum. Market participants were also limited to dealing in increments of a certain size, called a "stack." The stack was initially set to 100 K gold. But as gold prices fell owing to rapidly building supply, the stack size was changed in August 2012 to 1 million. This practice, known as redenomination, is a fairly standard (if cosmetic) method of addressing inflation, but was viewed by some players as tacit devaluation.

Historically, this is a classic means of dealing with runaway inflation. For example, it was used, to no avail, in Zimbabwe:

> Zimbabwe will slash 10 zeros from its currency from August 1, central bank Governor Gideon Gono said on Wednesday in another attempt to bring relief to consumers ravaged by hyperinflation … Gono in mid-2006 removed three zeros from the local dollar to make life easier for shoppers forced to carry huge piles of cash to make even the simplest purchases, but the move was followed by sharp price rises … "This (re-denomination) is just to overcome the absurd difficulty of having to deal with all those zeros but it does not address the root cause of the problem," John Robertson, an economic consultant, said. (Banya, 2008)

It was also applied during the (ongoing) hyperinflationary crisis in Venezuela.

> President Nicolas Maduro late Wednesday announced a two-week delay to a planned currency redenomination to Aug. 20, when Venezuela will lop five zeroes off the refurbished bolivar and also link it to the country's Petro cryptocurrency. By "anchoring" the Sovereign Bolivar, as the new currency will be called, the Petro will help stabilize the economy, Maduro said in a speech on state television … Maduro's initial redenomination plan called for slashing three zeroes from the Strong Bolivar notes to be replaced with the Sovereign Bolivar. This new delay comes after Maduro postponed a planned June rollout until Aug. 4. (Orozco and Zerpa, 2018)

Whether in real or virtual worlds, the impact of redenomination upon the rate of inflation is cosmetic. One player, addressing the *Diablo III* developers and managers via message boards, lamented the increasing inability to conduct profitable trading in view of the pending redenomination.

> If you're changing the [price] of gold from 0.25 per 100,000 to 0.25 per 1,000,000 I would like to cancel my gold auctions before you do that. You're completely shifting the market in less than a day, and those of us that have auctions listed that will be affected by this change cannot cancel them until after the patch hits, which is potentially too late. (Blizzard, 2013)

To be clear, at the time at which the redenomination was introduced, gold was still trading above the floor rate. But despite limiting the minimum price, price floors (and caps) do not change the prevailing supply or demand. Thus, inefficiencies are created by the authority setting the floor (or cap) and subsidized by market participants. And by preventing markets from clearing, price floors give black markets a target to undercut, and this is what began to occur in *Diablo III*. An added effect of transactions being undertaken outside of the game is that the 15 per cent fee levied upon transactions in the auction house—another gold sink intended to fight inflation—was neutralized.

Another player predicted,

> [T]his [change] will likely have 2 effects … [it] could kill the private 3rd party market for gold and hopefully discourage botting … [but] because the real money price of gold is decreasing [in the real money auction house] … [g]old will become cheaper as botters flood the market in an attempt to unload their massive surplus of gold before it becomes absolutely worthless … This decision will further destabilize the economy [as in the gold auction house] prices shoot from 100,000 gold to 1,000,000 gold … [or] 10,000,000 gold to 100,000,000 gold … The same would happen if the [Federal Reserve] decided to suddenly release a flood of currency into the U.S. Economy. (Blizzard, 2013)

By early 2013, the gold price had fallen to the exchange floor set by the game managers—$0.25 per million—and players began to show signs of concern. One asked,

> [Are] there any plans of lowering the floor of gold[?] … It has been at 0.25 for about 2 weeks now … should I sell my gold now before it gets lowered? (Blizzard, 2013)

With the gold price dropping precipitously and the added possibility of sudden or random intervention in the game's markets by Blizzard developers, some players were undoubtedly distracted from playing in favor of attempting to strategically protect their eroding virtual savings.

A Delirium of Stacks

Economically, the tipping point in the transformation from inflation to hyperinflation is characterized by a profound drop in the outstanding demand for money: when holders of money expect the supply of money to increase—particularly without any sense of timing, bounds, or other guidance—monetary demand in the present drops in favor of surrendering money for vendibles. As Rothbard (2011) commented on inflation,

> [T]he ultimate runaway stage [is] the collapse of the currency. The public takes panicky flight from the money into real values, into any commodity whatever. The public's psychology is not simply to buy now rather than later but to buy anything immediately. The public's demand for cash balances hurtles toward zero.

The focus of holders of currency, therefore, devolves into an effort to capture known, present purchasing power against the high likelihood of its decline in value in the near future. Saving—in any event, delaying consumption—is chastened; and if a cycle of declining purchasing power and rapidly rising prices ensues, ultimately, the propensity to hold money declines precipitously and may fundamentally disappear.

In July 2012, in the early stages of the inflation which would become hyperinflationary nine months later, one player warned that

> Blizzard just announced that the drop rates for [certain] items are going to be doubled … if you haven't already, you should consider converting your current gear to cash … since real $ [are] the best hedge against gold devaluation[.] (Blizzard, 2013)

If historical cases of hyperinflation—real, and now virtual—have one thing in common, it is the instinct among its victims to blame the symptoms rather than the disease. The Austrian economist Hans Sennholz (1979) noted that during the German hyperinflation, "intrigue and artifice" were believed to be at work. Similarly, a handful of *Diablo III* players, frustrated about the decimation of their purchasing power, expressed increasing suspicion of manipulation and conspiracy theories.

> [W]hy [are] certain items priced [s]o astronomically high? Many of them are not even that good yet cost 100's of millions of gold … I have about

> 45,000,000 gold saved up [and] check every few days to see if I can get any upgrades that are worth the gold, but … everything is vastly overpriced … clearly controlled by the gold sellers. (Blizzard, 2013)

And, predictably, any number of baleful remedies were proposed: these included daily taxation, virtual gold levies, and—incredibly enough—increasing the amount of virtual gold in the economy.

While the RMAH prices for virtual gold rallied occasionally, the prevailing direction of black-market prices for virtual gold was inexorably lower as third-party sellers undercut the in-game gold floor. In February 2013, patch 1.0.7 was rolled out, introducing a range of new gold sinks intended to sop up ever-increasing virtual gold; they included new weapons and items not eligible for sale on the RMAH. In early March 2013, with gold prices continuing to decline, a player made the following diagnosis:

> [A]dditional gold sinks [are] unfortunately comparable to spitting on a fire ... [they] do nothing to limit the core issue which is that players are earning gold faster than they [want] to spend it. Repairing is not a … good gold sink as it works best [for] players who are [dying]. … Crafting is the same, works well on players who can get the items to craft with … but leaves players with limited gold supply out of the picture … The amount of gold that drops … needs to be nerfed, and not softly. (Blizzard, 2013)

The effort appears to have been futile, as virtual gold supply continued to grow.

By Cagan's (1956) definition, the *Diablo III* economy appears to have entered hyperinflation between February and March of 2013, when the black-market price of gold fell from $0.20 per million to $0.05 per million—a decline of over 75 per cent in a few weeks. At around that time, a player commented that he was

> watching the markets collapse and gold become worthless … So you feel rich that you have a billion or two in gold[?] … [W]ell guess what, you aren't … there is nothing you can invest in to hold value. The only thing worth anything has become $$$. (Blizzard, 2013)

With a sardonic irony that markets sometimes display, real-world currencies had assumed the role of commodity gold, and virtual gold had gone the way of all flesh and fiat currencies.

This, however, was still only the penultimate stage. On May 7–8, 2013, Blizzard rolled out patch 1.0.8, which contained the seeds of the last surge of gold superabundance. (A software patch specifically targeting a bug is often called a "hotfix.") One change was the altering of the gold stack size from 1 million to 10 million per $0.25: a simultaneous redenomination and 90 per cent devaluation (sitting, as the price was, at the RMAH floor) of virtual gold, targeting black-market rates of roughly 4 cents per 10 million. In addition, a bug within the patch allowed users to cancel transactions in the auction house before completion, essentially allowing them to double their gold on demand.

In just a few hours, the already gold-swamped economy saw trillions more created: a mammoth deluge of, by then, worthless virtual gold chasing finite goods, driving prices upward in leaps and bounds. It was, at last, the hyperbolic blow-off characteristic of real-world hyperinflationary episodes. Some of the price increases (in *Diablo III* gold) are shown below:

Figure 6.1 (Assorted) Prices during *Diablo III*'s hyperinflationary episode (January–May 2013)

	2013 avg price	1-6 May avg price	7-8 May price	15 May price
radiant star amethyst	17.4M	41.2M	85.8M	26.1M
radiant square ruby	187K	260K	337K	375K
flawless square topaz	491	5,170	8,700	8,600
star emerald	764K	1.1M	106M	797K
tome of jewelcrafting	694	3,400	3,100	1,350

Source: http://www.diablo3farming.com/.

When hyperinflation occurs in the real world, individuals often shift to barter as the availability and variety of necessities dwindle; a common manifestation of that phenomenon takes the form of swapping food for skilled labor. However, when hyperinflation exists in the virtual world, people will disappear from chat channels, the locations where trade took place. They turn away because the real-world hierarchy of needs—shelter, sustenance, and so on—do not exist in the virtual world.

Aftermath

Blizzard quickly closed the in-game auction houses and audited transactions which took place during the blowout, banning players who took advantage of the bug. Which is to say, players who demonstrated a pattern of capitalizing upon the "dupe" error by entering and canceling transactions repeatedly were banned, and the proceeds of their trades donated to charity. The gold stack size was also moved back from 10 M to 1 M.

In May 2012, the price of virtual gold was approximately $30 per 100,000 or $0.0003 per gold (Gamerluck, 2012). In the days surrounding the final, atmospheric spike of hyperinflation, roughly May 7–8, 2013—and bearing in mind that these prices may be erroneous, stale, or merely indications of interest—one site showed *Diablo III* gold being offered by four major third-party sellers at an average price of $1.14 per 20 million, or $0.000000057 per gold: one ten-thousandth its market price one year earlier (MMOBux, n.d.).

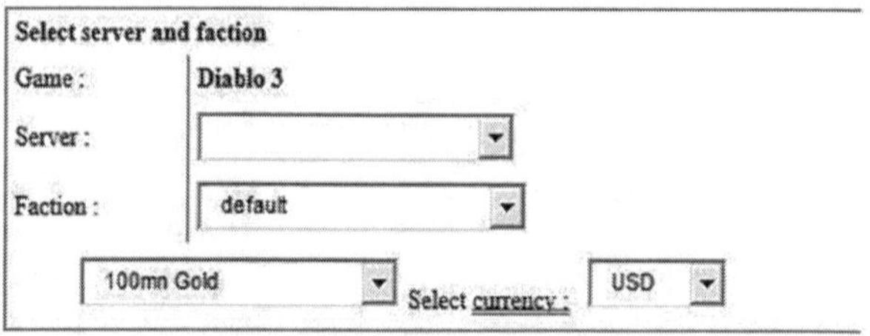

Trusted Sellers:

Amount	Price	Quick link	Shop profile	Shop rating
20mn Gold**	$ 0.78	Buy Now	EpicToon	★★★½☆
20mn Gold**	$ 0.80	Buy Now	InGameDelivery	★★★★½
20mn Gold**	$ 0.99	Buy Now	Koala Credits	★★★★½
20mn Gold*	$ 1.99	Buy Now	Avatarbank	★★★★½

Source: mmobux, http://www.mmobux.com/compare/d3/diablo-3-gold.

In the RMAH, virtual gold was simultaneously priced at $0.39 per million.

Several weeks after the hyperinflation was in retreat, an infographic published by Blizzard on May 25, 2013, announced that the size of the *Diablo III* money stock stood at 648,510,803,462,686 (nearly two-thirds of one quadrillion) gold pieces (Blizzard, 2013). Without any data regarding the starting amounts of gold in the economy, it remains an exercise for the reader to determine whether this amount was more likely in line with intentional game design or a product of unfettered game money creation.

Conclusion

In-game economies are private and players are voluntary members, so there is no explicit mandate to developers to ensure rigid control over inflation as one often sees (however rarely pursued) in real-world economies. That said, knowing that gaming experiences can be upended by economic missteps, there is a clear business interest for gaming firms in keeping virtual currencies and their greater economies as a whole stable.

Frequently, hyperinflationary episodes have ended by substituting a currency outside the political and central banking control of a nation for the sovereign currency. In the early 1990s, during Serbia's hyperinflation,

> [t]he authorities could not print enough cash to keep up. On Jan 6th, 1994, the dinar officially collapsed. The government declared the German mark legal tender … [which] end[ed] the hyperinflation. (Hanke, 1999)

Two obvious solutions for managers of virtual economies include more vigilant bot restrictions and close—indeed, real-time—monitoring of faucet output, sink absorption, prices, and user behaviors. More critically, though, whether structured as auctions or exchanges, markets must be allowed to operate freely, without caps, floors, or other artificialities. Unrestricted (real) cash auctions would, for the most part, preempt and obviate black markets.

One also surmises, considering the level of planning that goes into designing and maintaining virtual gaming environments, that some measure of statistical monitoring and/or econometric modeling must have been applied to the *Diablo III* game world. The Austrian school has long warned of the arrogance and naïveté intrinsic to applying rigid, quantitative measures to the deductive study of human actions. Indeed, if a small, straightforward economy generating detailed, timely economic data for its managers can careen so completely aslant in a matter of months, should anyone be surprised when the performance of central banks consistently breeds results which are either ineffective or destabilizing and, in any event, wholly responsible for generating unintended consequences?

This analysis is by no means intended to equate the actions of game development firms with the policies of governments or central banks nor to malign their indisputably talented managers, designers, and programmers.

There is no doubt a fear among game designers that a fixed amount of in-game currency would reward the first, most active players, who would then save ("hoard") their winnings and leave decidedly fewer opportunities for later or less active players; online gaming is a business, after all. But this is essentially the theoretical underpinning of the Keynesian concept of a "liquidity trap." This is countered by economists who note that in the real world, there is always some level of consumption. Considering that individuals need to eat, shelter, and clothe themselves, even in the most desperate times expenditures may be pared back severely, but never completely disappear, and certainly not en masse.

How best to accomplish regular, periodic player consumption is beyond the scope of this article, but a mild, persistent deflation in a virtual world—not unlike what the United States experienced throughout most of the nineteenth century—would benefit newer players and encourage longer-term players to remain active.

While their actions may ultimately generate similar outcomes, central planners seek and wield power whereas the actions of commercial gaming interests are undertaken to compete with other online entertainment providers by delicately balancing opportunities for newer players with the need to continually challenge experienced players. Sargent (1982) offers a fitting coda:

> In discussing [hyperinflation] with various people, I have encountered the view that the events described here are so extreme and bizarre that they do not bear on the subject of inflation in the contemporary United States. On the contrary, it is precisely because the events were so extreme that they are relevant. The … incidents we have studied are akin to laboratory experiments in which the elemental forces that cause and can be used to stop inflation are easiest to spot. I believe that these incidents are full of lessons about our own … if only we interpret them correctly.

Decision-makers at online gaming firms can and should be forgiven for failing to anticipate the perilous and unpredictable torsions of rapidly expanding money supplies; nevertheless, the events of the spring of 2013 provide a stark reminder of the power and inescapability of the laws of economics—even within the virtual realm.

References

Angelopoulou, Eleni. 2007. "The Narrative Approach for the Identification of Monetary Policy Shocks in a Small Open Economy." Working papers 55, Bank of Greece. SSRN.

Banya, Nelson. 2008. "Zimbabwe to Re-Denominate Dollar by Lopping Off Zeros." *Reuters*. Accessed on July 25, 2019. https://www.reuters.com/article/

us-zimbabwe-currency/zimbabwe-to-re-denominate-dollar-by-lopping-off-zeros-idUSHUN11302620080731.

Bernholz, Peter. 1988. "Hyperinflation and Currency Reform in Bolivia: Studied from a General Perspective." *Journal of Institutional and Theoretical Economics* 144 (5): 747–771.

Blizzard. n.d. "Blizzard Forums." Accessed on May 13, 2013/July 25, 2019. https://us.battle.net/forums/en/.

Bomberger, William A., and Gail E. Makinen. 1983. "The Hungarian Hyperinflation and Stabilization of 1945–1946." *Journal of Political Economy* 91 (5): 801–824.

Bresciani-Turroni, Constantino. 2007 [1931]. *The Economics of Inflation: A Study of Currency Depreciation in Post-War Germany*. Translated by Millicent E. Sayers. Auburn: Ludwig von Mises Institute.

Cagan, Phillip. 1956. "The Monetary Dynamics of Hyperinflation." In *Studies in the Quantity Theory of Money*, edited by Milton Friedman. Chicago: University of Chicago Press, pp. 25–117.

Calder, Tara M. 2009. "Hyperinflation in Zimbabwe: Money Demand, Seigniorage and Aid Shocks." Institute for International Integration Studies (IIIS) discussion paper no. 293. SSRN.

Campbell, Colin D., and Gordon Tullock. 1954. "Hyperinflation in China, 1937–49." *Journal of Political Economy* 62 (3): 237–245.

Capie, Forrest. 1991. *Major Inflations in History*. Cheltenham: Edward Elgar.

Castronova, Edward. 2002. "On Virtual Economies." CESifo Working Paper Series No. 752. SSRN.

———. 2003. "New Bout of Inflation in EverQuest (blog post)." December 16, 2003. https://terranova.blogs.com/terra_nova/2003/12/new_bout_of_inf.html.

Denapolis West, Kristina B. 2005. "Real Concerns in Virtual Property." Available at SSRN 1154234. https://papers.ssrn.com/sol3/papers.cfm?abstract_id=1154234.

Diablo III. n.d. "Diablo III: 1 Year Infographic." Accessed on July 25, 2019. https://us.diablo3.com/en/game/anniversary-infographic/.

Elliott, Jane. 2005. "Narratives and New Developments in Social Sciences." In *Using Narrative in Social Research: Qualitative and Quantitative Approach*. London: Sage Publications Ltd, pp. 1–16.

Gamerluck. June 13, 2012. "Diablo 3 Gold Price Analysis in Black Market!" Accessed on July 25, 2019. https://www.gamerluck.com/Diablo-3-Gold-Price-analysis-in-black-Market--news-200-html.Diab

Graham, Frank. 1932. "Exchange, Prices and Production in Hyper-Inflation: Germany, 1920–23." *Journal of the Royal Statistical Society* 95 (1): 119–122.

Hahn, L. Albert. 1924. "Zur Frage des sogenannten 'Vertrauens in die Wahrung'." Archiv fur Sozialwissenschaft und Sozialpolitik 52 (2): 289–316.

Hanke, Steve. 1999. "Dinar Inflation." Mises Institute. Accessed on July 25, 2019. https://mises.org/library/dinar-inflation.

Hazlitt, Henry. 1964. *What You Should Know about Inflation*. Princeton: D. Van Nostrand Company, Inc.

Hinchman, Lewis P., and Sandra K. Hinchman. 1997. "Introduction." In *Memory, Identity, Community: The Idea of Narrative in the Human Sciences*. New York: State University of New York, pp. xii–xxxii.

Irwin, Jon. 2013. "Is Animal Crossing the Dark Future of Our Virtual Economy?" *Kill Screen*. Accessed on July 24, 2019. https://killscreen.com/articles/auguries-virtual-economy/.

Kolbert, Elizabeth. 2001. "Pimps and Dragons." *New Yorker*, May 21, 2001. Accessed on July 24, 2019. https://www.newyorker.com/magazine/2001/05/28/pimps-and-dragons.

Laidler, David E., and George W. Stadler. 1998. "Monetary Explanations of the Weimar Republic's Hyperinflation: Some Neglected Contributions in Contemporary German Literature." *Journal of Money, Credit, and Banking* 30 (4): 816–831.

Lederman, Leandra. 2007. "'Stranger than Fiction': Taxing Virtual Worlds." *New York University Law Review* 82 (March). SSRN.

Lehdonvirta, Vili. 2005. "Virtual Economics: Applying Economics to the Study of Game Worlds." In Proceedings of the 2005 Conference on Future Play (Future Play 2005). Lansing, MI.

Makinen, Gail E. 1986. "The Greek Hyperinflation and Stabilization of 1943–1946." *The Journal of Economic History* 43 (3): 795–805.

Makinen, Gail E., and G. Thomas Woodward. 1989. "The Taiwanese Hyperinflation and Stabilization of 1945–1952." *Journal of Money, Credit, and Banking* 21 (1): 90–105.

Menger, Carl. 1976. *Principles of Economics*. Translated by James Dingwall and Bert F. Hoselitz. Institute for Humane Societies, New York: New York University.

Mises, Ludwig von. 1953. *The Theory of Money and Credit*. Translated by J. E. Batson. New Haven: Yale University Press.

———. 1978. *On the Manipulation of Money and Credit*. Translated by Percy L. Greaves, Jr. Dobbs Ferry: Free Market Books.

MMOBux. n.d. "MMO Currency Research, News, and Reviews." Accessed on May 13, 2013. https://www.mmobux.com/compare/d3/diablo-3-gold

Nelson, Daniel B. 1989. "Was the Deflation of 1929-1930 Anticipated? The Monetary Regime as Viewed by the Business Press." HGB Alexander Foundation.

Orozco, Jose, and Fabiola Zerpa. 2018. "Venezuela Delays New Currency Rollout, Slashes More Zeroes." *Bloomberg*, July 25, 2018. https://www.bloombergquint.com/markets/venezuela-delays-new-currency-rollout-slashes-more-zeros.

Romer, Christina D., and David H. Romer. 2012. "Friedman and Schwartz's Monetary Explanation of the Great Depression: Old Challenges and New Evidence." Berkeley: University of California.

Rothbard, Murray N. 2011. "Money, Banking, and Calculation." In *Economic Controversies*. Auburn: Ludwig von Mises Institute, pp. 683–892.

Saboin, Jose. 2018. "The Modern Hyperinflation Cycle: Some New Empirical Regularities." IMF working paper no. 18/266. SSRN.

Salter, Alexander W., and Solomon Stein. 2016. "Endogenous Currency Formation in an Online Environment: The Case of Diablo II." *The Review of Austrian Economics* 29 (1): 53–66.

Sargent, Thomas J. 1982. "The Ends of Four Big Inflations." In *Inflation: Causes and Effects*, edited by Robert E. Hall. Chicago: University of Chicago Press, pp. 41–98.

Sennholz, Hans F. 1979. "The Age of Inflation." Belmont: Western Islands.

Spalding, William F. 1917. *Eastern Exchange Currency and Finance*. London: Sir Isaac Pitman and Sons.

Sumner, Scott. 1997. "News, Financial Markets, and the Collapse of the Gold Standard: 1931–1932." *Research in Economic History* no. 17: 39–84.

Tach, Dave. 2013. "Inflating Animal Crossing's Economy, One Bug at a Time." *Polygon*. Accessed on July 24, 2019. https://www.polygon.com/2013/7/27/4561246/animal-crossing-new-leaf-inflation.

White, Andrew. 1959. *Fiat Money Inflation in France*. New York: The Foundation for Economic Education, Inc.

7

The Facilitate or Acquire Decision

The Tipping Points for Strategies toward User-Generated Content in Massively Multiplayer Online Game Platforms*

Robert Conan Ryan

Introduction

This chapter turns the reader away from the discussion of video game monetary economics to a broader issue: video game business strategy for MMO game companies. Instead of asking how video game economies work, here we look at how video game companies manipulate both their internal capabilities and their external industrial environment to increase their competitive performance. At the end of the day, a video game company is usually a for-profit firm like any other, looking to increase its financial performance through business strategy (Gidhagen, Ridell, and Sörhammar, 2011).

Scholars have not closely examined the best competitive strategies that platform-based firms use to cope with competitive pressures from user-generated content (Bogers and West, 2012). Sometimes user-generated content increases revenues by increasing overall platform usage, but other times it can decrease revenues by cannibalizing the core product offerings. This chapter uses transaction costs theory and the literature on the informal economy (Godfrey, 2011; Chen, 2005) to analyze MMO firm strategy. Three MMO mini-case studies on *Rage of Bahamut*, *Minecraft*, and *Dota 2* address why MMOs face a "facilitate or acquire" decision for management of user-generated content.

* The author would like to thank Dr Barry Mitnick and Dr Ravi Madhavan at the University of Pittsburgh for ongoing mentorship and co-authorship; Dr Matthew McCaffrey for excellent editing and vision for the book; and his father, John Ryan, for support and editing on this chapter.

Gray markets[1] are a fascinating, and yet under-theorized, phenomenon (McGahan, 2012). Often confused with black markets, gray markets are places where humans conduct "socially legitimate" economic transactions but with little regard to existing formal (legal) business institutions (Webb et al., 2009; Chen, 2012; Maloney, 2004). Black markets deal directly in goods and services deemed socially irredeemable, whereas gray market actors' productive and exchange activities contribute positively to welfare. Each *gray firm*, no matter whether an individual, an *ad hoc* group project, or an organization, chooses grayness to achieve some goal while also avoiding costly institutional obligations and legal formalities required of *white firms*.

Gray firms may thrive if the costs of institutional formalization exceed the benefits. Gray transaction types are diverse, including conducting "handshake" informal agreements, impromptu bartering, using peer production in "common" spaces (Benkler, 2002), the used product aftermarket, and *parallel markets*—a business model that cheaply resells legal goods through informal trade networks to bypass official marketing channels, arbitraging local price differences (Lindauer, 1989). The most common gray firm in the world is probably an "under the table" service worker in the household-to-household economy, such as teenagers who do small amounts of yard work and childcare (Chen, 2005).

However, gray high-tech interactions are also common, especially in advanced economies (Castells and Portes, 1989). Open-source software contributors, hardware hackers at makerspaces, Silicon Valley subcontractors who use immigrant or globally outsourced staffing, and PayPal-based international trading are varied examples of knowledge-intensive environments for informal innovation and exchange. Still, gray technology firms tend to be tiny and nonthreatening (Williams, 2006), since retaining their earnings and scaling up requires investment in formal management, contracts, and taxes.

Problem Statement

Scholars need to resolve a theoretical controversy (Pasquale, 2016): when should high-tech firms formalize and acquire the activities of gray firms (forged from

[1] Note that this color-selection scheme is based on past literature. The use of the word "market" here is extremely broad and does not refer to only price-driven auctions; indeed, gray markets and gray firms are a diverse heterodoxy of socioeconomic behavior. Formal markets and firms have *legally standard* rules and accounting, whereas gray entities use only *ad hoc* rules. These gray entities have fuzzy business models that can be interpreted in flexible ways and straddle the gap between markets and firms (Powell, 1990; Benkler, 2002).

user-generated content), and when should they instead facilitate the expansion of partner gray market in the form of a public and "free" commons? Current theories are unclear about the basic strategies white firms can use to cope with adjacent gray activities. We especially need a clear strategic framework for managing lucrative digital platforms, which are major attractors for modern gray entrepreneurship.

On the "acquire" side of the argument, internet-based companies such as Task Rabbit, Etzy, Fiverr, and Mechanical Turk have proven it is possible to monetize, formalize, and curate "gig economy" transactions, that is, ex-gray firm activities. These firms rely on a business model of collecting fees for curating "two-sided" matching platforms (Mitnick and Ryan, 2015; Pasquale, 2016; Tiwana, 2014). Still, they must leave some profitable "breadcrumb" opportunities to attract innovative gig workers, or else greatly reduce overall market entrepreneurship and chase talent into other industries (Burtch, Carnahan, and Greenwood, 2018). Platforms acquire and integrate the most lucrative transaction types.

On the "facilitate" side of the argument are scholars of open-source innovation, the digitized economy, and futurism. These scholars argue that gray markets need not always be viewed from a competitive perspective (Chen, 2005; Chandna and Salimath, 2018; von Hippel, 2016; Benkler, 2002; Awunyo-Vitor, Dadson, and Abankwah, 2012). Gray markets fill in the gaps where businesses and governments are under-responsive, especially in very dynamic industrial environments (Siqueira, Webb, and Bruton, 2016; Malerba et al., 2007). Facilitating them can create perpetual knowledge spillovers.

Take social media, for instance. Many informal groups meet through Facebook to fill a gap that neither government organizations nor business organizations fill in the physical world. Facebook can learn valuable information from informal activities such as crowdsourcing and Big Data analysis (Doan, Ramakrishnan, and Halevy, 2011). Facebook often facilitates the gray market rather than directly attacking it, because it commercializes the resulting "Big Data" patterns that the informal "crowd" cannot fully exploit, rather than the gray activities themselves. Strategy scholars such as David Teece (1986) long ago explained that firms benefit from *complementary* activity in their vicinity—aka complementarities between one firm's internal capabilities and the external capabilities of other firms. Complementarities include marketing *word-of-mouth* (Chen and Xie, 2008), the *spillover effects* of localized learning (Audretsch and

Feldman, 2004; Martin, 2002; Hayek, 1945), and *network externalities* from holding a powerful central network position (Katz and Shapiro, 1985).[2]

Thesis: The White–Gray Strategic Matrix

To resolve the apparent paradoxical tension, we must distinguish level of complementarity and rivalry on *two different axes* (low/high) rather than viewing them on a single axis. Any given market segment can be sorted into one of four categories, each of which implies one dominant white firm strategy. Herein is presented a new two-dimensional framework—the *White–Gray Strategic Matrix.* This four-quadrant matrix sorts gray markets in terms of levels of knowledge spillovers for complementary effect and levels of organizational complexity that produce rivalry pressures. The four basic strategic alternatives for white firms are: *ignore, litigate, facilitate,* or *acquire* the gray firms. Because these strategies are abruptly different, correctly assessing the "tipping point" between gray market transaction types is critical to the success of white firms.

This essay proceeds in three parts:

Part One develops a simple, yet powerful 2 × 2 framework for the degree of complementarity and rivalry between white and gray firms. The White–Gray Strategic Matrix rests on two key low/high dimensions: *knowledge spillovers* (a major cause of complementarity) and *transaction complexity* (a major cause of rivalry). The four response strategies—ignore, litigate, facilitate, and acquire—align with each of these four quadrants.

Part Two of this essay examines the tipping point between facilitation and acquisition strategies for the White–Gray Strategic Matrix. Three illustrative mini-cases of MMOs isolate the winning and losing strategies. In this industry, the focal white firms are the designers and hosts of MMOs—that is, the platform "hosts" for short. Hosts face the challenge of balancing game designs that capture revenues (white) with designs that permit informal user-innovators to innovate, exchange, and optionally monetize (gray). The case analysis provided here

---

[2] Note that this is not quite the same analysis as deciding how open to make a platform. Boudreau (2010), for example, found that firms in the handheld computing devices industry which widely granted platform access to software developers fared well, but firms who surrendered control over the platform governance had negligible results. This question of platform governance versus openness is important to digital platform strategists but does not touch upon the level of informality or the strategic attitude toward gray markets.

suggests that MMORPG developers should acquire the financial exchange and production of in-game items that confer a competitive advantage on players (that is, positional goods) and control sale of alternative game versions.

Part Three argues for a research program centered on broadening the investigation of this framework and toward a multifactor model of complementarity and complexity. Due to space constraints and to maintain the readability for a broad social science audience, the analysis here is intentionally shallow and will need much further empirical support from strategic management and economic research.

PART ONE: The White–Gray Strategic Matrix

This part builds the White–Gray Strategic Matrix through eight sections: (*a*) a review of gray markets, (*b*) investing in the gray economy, or investing in formalization? (*c*) defining the relationship between white and gray markets, (*d*) separating black from gray markets, (*e*) gray markets around high-tech platforms, (*f*) gray complementarities, (*g*) gray rivalry, and (*h*) the White–Gray Strategic Matrix.

1. A Review of Gray Markets

To begin to frame the problem of white firm response to gray firms, we must first understand how the broader economics literature has characterized the informal economy, and why recent scholars are challenging this view, especially as it pertains to online and platform-based business models.

According to classic theory, the informal economy is a legally noncompliant, inefficient, and ineffective rival of the formal economy. Scholars of economic development have sought to find ways to develop informal sectors to increase economies of scale, innovation, tax revenues, and even labor rights (Williams and Nadin, 2012a, 2012b; Thai and Turkina, 2014; Lindauer, 1989). If the classic view of the informal economy were logically sufficient, economic development would eliminate gray markets and advanced economies would see a per capita decrease in informal activity. White firms would steadily reduce their dependence on informal labor and monetize and commoditize all transactions.

Global gray market statistics

The evidence suggests a more complex story (Mukherjee, 2016; Chen, 2012). As national GDP levels rise, the per capita gray activity grows in absolute per capita terms, with only a slow decline as a percentage of GDP (Schneider and Buehn, 2017). The current estimate for middle-income countries is that the gray economy adds about 40 per cent to formal GDP. The Organisation for Economic Co-operation and Development (OECD) average of advanced economies is closer to 17 per cent, yet gray activity never declines in absolute terms. For example, according to the International Monetary Fund (IMF) (2019), Germany is 16th overall in nominal GDP per capita at $48,264; therefore, its additional gray market is estimated at 17 per cent: $8,205. In contrast, Ecuador is a middle-income country ranked 100th overall in GDP per capita at $11,718. The estimated Ecuadoran gray-market size is roughly $4700—barely over half of the German informal economy, per capita. However, scholars have noted that the internet gray economy is very hard to estimate as it demonetizes many transactions that are still economically important (Gaspareniene and Remeikiene, 2016). The GDP percentage declines may be a grand illusion, obscured by the notorious difficulty in measuring informal transactions. Some scholars, using proxy measures of gray activity, suggest we should double our estimates (Schneider and Buehn, 2017).

Upstream production and downstream aftermarkets

An important point of clarification must be made about what counts as a gray market. Many business authors use that terminology to narrowly refer to gray wholesaling and retailing of white manufactured goods, such as gray sales of brand-name fashion items (see a full discussion in Antia, Bergen, and Dutta, 2004). Viral marketing is another digital aftermarket dominated by gray firms. But what the literature often ignores is that much of gray market activity is not exchange, but micro-production upstream of a firm. As the reader assuredly knows, much of the in-game content for MMOs now comes from nonemployee users of games; but most of the classic scholars of gray economics have overlooked user-generated content and focused on social media, exchange platforms such as eBay, and purposeful internet labor markets such as Amazon's Mechanical Turk.

Gray transactions as peer-to-peer networks

Castells and Portes (1989) and Benkler (2002) published two of the most influential works on the topic of peer-led organizations and their dominance in the informal economy. Both made convincing arguments that advanced economies incorporate digital technology that increases decentralized and demonetized labor—that is, tiny, informal, flexible, and quick-evolving economic relations in a networked economy. Much of this labor deals in outsourced microtransactions, labeled the "gig economy" (Friedman, 2014), but also heavily overlaps with the concepts of lead-user innovation (von Hippel, 2016) and hacking (Levy, 1984). The sociologist Powell (1990) explains all informal economic activity as "networked" economic exchange—a third major alternative to the market/firm dichotomy of organizational forms in Oliver Williamson's work on transaction costs theory (1973).[3] Digital platforming made informal organization dramatically easier, faster, and global. High-tech firms recognized they can either facilitate gray innovations and activities as an external complement to their core activities or incubate and acquire (formalize) the best activities.

Lax enforcement

Most gray firms are knowingly exempted from the enforcement of prevailing rules for large-scale business activity, either because the enforcement costs exceed the benefits or because the gray-firm activities are deemed qualitatively different enough to be nonthreatening to formal contacting. If gray firms directly encroach on mainstream value chains, they threaten the legitimacy of mainstream institutions and the success of law-abiding large firms (De Filippi, 2014).

Informal economics and economic development

Some scholars of economic development argue that gray markets are merely underdeveloped white markets (Williams and Nadin, 2012a, 2012b; Siqueira, Webb, and Bruton, 2016). From this perspective, all informal economic activity can and will eventually be replaced with formalized innovations. Governments would not let gray entities achieve large scale, and business rivals will use formal property rights to eliminate profit from the gray market—if there are any ideas worth the effort. Private sector entrepreneurs persistently search for clever business models for formalization, thereby capturing profits and making it difficult to

[3] Some authors, such as Michel Bauwens (Bauwens, 2006; Kostakis and Bauwens, 2014), have gone so far as to suggest that networked transactions will become the dominant form in the post-capitalist economy. Bauwens refers to this future as a "commons-based society." He argues that the commons used to be a huge part of the recognized feudalist economy. In other words, what we call the informal economy is really the civic commons but was politically disenfranchised during the first industrial revolution. Capitalist institutions disincentivize peer-to-peer exchange and incentivize capital accumulation and centralization. Libertarian leftists, such as Bauwens (2006) and Carson (2010), claim the internet and the "homebrew" digital revolution created new socio-technical conditions that re-empower the commons and increase "copyleft" practices.

earn high wages from any gray activity (Chen, 2005). From the perspective of *transaction costs*, a white firm can outperform the gray market through hierarchical organization (Chen, 2005; Williamson, Wachter, and Harris, 1975).

2. Investing in the Gray Economy, or Investing in Formalization?

Transaction costs and property rights

Every little routine step of behavior taken on digital platforms is a special case of the broad theoretical notion of a *transaction*. The classic argument for why firms such as MMO game companies choose to formalize their business model is that investors believe that the intellectual and physical property rights managed by the MMO firm can be monetized, scaled, and appropriated at profit. J. R. Commons, one of the pioneers of transaction cost economics, pointed out that a price-based transaction is one based around the exchange of ownership rights, but some transactions bypass that step and ignore property rights (Commons, 1934; Kaufman, 2003). Commons argues a price is paid for legally enforceable ownership claim, not really for the object itself. Thus, firms who are unconcerned with ownership rights and are not motivated by perpetual revenue growth would also be unconcerned with formal transaction accounting and would manage nonmonetized exchanges or legally unenforceable property rights. Many users generate content without any concerns for owing it or monetizing it (von Hippel and von Krogh, 2003; Baldwin and von Hippel, 2011). The creators of user-generated content cannot enforce their exchange rules or property rights to the full extent of the law—thus, they are not fully committed to playing within the formal *field of transactions* in business society.

Gray finance

Consider, also, that politics can drive some radical investors to develop gray markets as a form of institutional rebellion—cryptocurrencies (Richter, Kraus, and Bouncken, 2015; De Filippi, 2014; Levine, 2019). The inventor of Bitcoin, Satoshi Nakamoto, made political statements about radical liberalization of financial activity. Many early investors wanted to use it as a global solution to facilitating black market (that is, Silk Road) and gray market (that is, Craigslist) trading. Economists estimate that the demand for cryptocurrency increases in larger gray markets (Polasik et al., 2015).

An example of a massive gray industry is marijuana cultivation in the United States. Due to gaps between state and federal regulations, much of the industry is informal. Cash-based marijuana transactions are still mostly quasi-legal at the time of this publication, and federal laws still prevent marijuana companies from using mainstream banking, interstate trade, and other typical business institutions and infrastructures. To cope with quasi-legality, cannabis firms try gray cryptocurrencies and other services, but they are aware they are investing in a gray market competing somewhat with federally recognized medicines, with an uncertain timeline to formalization.

3. Separating Black from Gray Markets

Although it is not central to our investigation, a quick word about black markets is appropriate. Gray activities are routinely misrepresented as less-threatening versions of *black markets*. However, the gray/black distinction is easy to make. For black markets, societies have made formal rulings to declare either the business *process* (that is, fraudulent accounting or child labor) or the business *products* (that is, the illegal drug trade or counterfeit goods) to be a negative sum game for society; consequently, societies actively enforce stiff sanctions against such content and processes (Webb et al., 2009; Lindauer, 1989).

Furthermore, it is obvious that most black markets "crowd out" white market activity. With a misallocation of capital and labor toward high negative externalities, harmful contraband lowers the overall production possibility frontier. Gray markets, however, do not usually crowd out demand for legitimate products and services (Mukherjee, 2016), they merely compete with the institutions that enforce contracts—such as courts, patents, and regulatory bodies (Chen, 2005, 2007).

4. Gray Markets around High-Tech Platforms

Virtual worlds, social media, gig economy platforms, and online game platforms are becoming the dominant arenas for gray markets in advanced economies (Tiwana, 2014). Such industries sustain not only lively gray markets that offer little chance of economic rents on patents but also large economic spillovers from neighbors' highly imitable knowledge (Teece, 1998). A growing percentage of business activity takes place in digital platforms or markets under the supervision of a formal firm. Large platforms such as Instagram, YouTube, and Amazon not only provide direct opportunities to advertise and to sell products but also provide opportunities for other indirect business activity. There are social influencers on Facebook's many platforms who monetize their influence in creative ways, and Facebook must choose to either look the other way or discourage such activity.

User-generated content is often hard to monetize. Informal commercial success on these platforms follows a steep power law: most gray firms in the peer economy make negligible revenues, with a tiny elite making exponentially large earnings (Kenney and Zysman, 2016; Brynjolfsson, Hu, and Smith, 2006; Jarvenpaa and Lang, 2011).

Free innovation and the wisdom of crowds

Gray knowledge markets are large "forums" of information that range from everyday consumer groups to specialized technical wikis. Because these spaces have no property rules or restrictions, they are accessed by anyone. Even though individual content creators have little chance of a big hit, the Big Data platforms can reliably turn a profit on their extreme economies of scale. Digital media firms produce and harvest the "wisdom of crowds" and steer markets with informal influencers (Surowiecki, 2005). von Hippel (2016) refers to large pools of publicly sharable knowledge as communities of *free innovation*.[4] High-tech firms tend to exploit free innovations by filing for legal protection of derivative, yet patentable, works (Osterloh and Rota, 2007). High-tech firms have used *open innovation* strategies where they rely on external sources for innovation. This strategy, in part, copes with the digital age—open innovation reduces risks in a fast-moving, turbulent, yet easily imitated and re-distributed, technologies (Enkel, Gassmann, and Chesbrough, 2009).

5. Gray Complementarities

In low-tech markets, knowledge spillovers are quite minimal because the economic activities are so simple that they provide little opportunity for recombination. High-tech markets are rich with knowledge that can be recombined and used in myriad ways. There is no doubt that knowledge-intensive markets create large knowledge spillover opportunities (Täuscher and Laudien, 2018; Kenney and Zysman, 2016; Teece, 2018; for a taxonomy of platform business models, see Lang, Shang, and Vragov, 2015). The dominant firms control the market by installing a large user base, creating a platform that provides a panoply of complementary goods to the primary technology (López and Roberts, 2002; Schilling, 2003; Langlois, 1990, 1992). In some cases, such as online video

4 See also the related concept of corporate communities of creation (Sawhney and Prandelli, 2000). Instead of being pools of gray activity, communities of creation are cross-organizational networks of peer production that support the technical employees of many firms in high-tech industries.

games, there is also a core software "product" around which the platform activity revolves (Haefliger et al., 2011).

White platforming removes the possibility of an infinite gray regress. The infinite nesting of gray firms within a purely informal value chain—that is, a chain beginning with all gray inputs and ending with only gray outputs—would result in a purely gray economy. In the case of white platforms, all gray activities must therefore be complementary to some white activity at some point in the value chain.

The question for digital platform hosts becomes how many transactions on that chain are better suited as white or gray. For example, eBay permits a fair amount of gray activity, whereas Amazon aims for somewhat higher formalization but still relies heavily on consumer feedback on products.

Rivalry between white and gray firms

In classic transaction cost theory, rivalry is caused by offering a competitive alternative for transactions (Williamson, 1973). For example, Amazon and Walmart both offer consumers access to goods at the best possible prices and the most convenient delivery options. They each have complex business processes for managing transactions but use somewhat different process capabilities for achieving results (Pitelis and Teece, 2009). These two firms are rivals because they provide two alternative systems for retail transactions embedded within the transactive ecosystems managed by two different firms. Both firms have restrictions on which goods it will offer and tend to discourage informal production they cannot police with property rights. A dedicated gray market, such as Craigslist, makes it possible to either get the same goods through different means or to get competing goods not allowed on these two retail platforms. From this point of view, firm rivalry between platform-based firms is driven by the existence of alternative business processes for the same goods.[5]

For another example, consider cryptocurrency firms such as Ripple that are built around formal business processes. However, Ripple began as an informal firm due to their complete sidestepping of traditional financial practices with cryptocurrency. Whereas Ripple Labs is a private firm that is speculated to be

[5] Although Amazon and Walmart do offer exclusive products on their platforms, they are not fundamentally threatened by diverse sourcing of products, variety of content, or informal steps to their global supply chain. They are only fundamentally threatened by better ways to get the same thing or undercutting gray channels.

going public soon (Caplinger, 2018), Etherium is an example of a cryptocurrency firm that stayed large, crowd-based, and effectively informal. These two firms support market processes that both provide havens for many gray legal segments. Major platforms often find that these transactions are a scalable threat and better formalized than left open. In an attempt to prevent revenue loss to such outsiders, Facebook is launching its own legally embedded cryptocurrency, Libra (Paul, 2019). Facebook believes it can create more value by administering its own affiliated cryptocurrency transactions. Facebook chose to acquire similar capabilities rather than facilitate existing cryptocurrency and blockchain-based activities.

6. The White–Gray Strategic Matrix

This section explains how each one of the four quadrants of the matrix leads to a dominant strategy.

The purpose is to begin the foundation for a framework to analyze the strategic organizational design of gray markets. By combining the effects of knowledge spillovers and firm complexity, we can begin the foundations of a framework. Emphasis is placed on the facilitate/acquire decision tipping point in high-tech markets—one of the most difficult and yet common decisions for digital platforms to make. See the originally devised Table 7.1 below.

Table 7.1 The White–Gray Strategic Matrix

	High spillover field (High complementarities)	**Low spillover field (Low complementarities)**
Low complexity firm (Low value chain rivalry)	Informal high tech, not complex Competitive move: facilitate	Informal low tech, not complex Competitive move: ignore
High complexity firm (High value chain rivalry)	Informal high tech, complex Competitive move: acquire	Informal low tech, complex Competitive move: litigate

Source: Author (Robert Conan Ryan).

Strategy one: facilitating the gray knowledge commons

According to the White–Gray Strategic Matrix, high-tech white firms should facilitate in environments with high complementarities and low rivalry. The facilitate strategy involves maximizing participation levels, drawing a diverse pool of tiny gray firms, but deterring them from growing to a formal scale. The industries that best fit this strategy are based on knowledge spillovers from user-generated information rather than gray business process innovations. The facilitating firm hopes to increase the variety of offerings with user-generated content but sees no path forward for the routine formalization of user contributions. This strategy works best when the white firm already possesses dominant process innovations for managing user content and sees no threat to its core business or revenues from rival process innovations. In other words, those gray processes that do exist—such as rival websites that share and disseminate downloadable free content—offer no value-added. Acquisition of such rivals would not add value to the focal firm's capabilities.

Strategy two: creating proving grounds and acquiring

Some industries create opportunities for repeated process innovations that are so good that they create a scalable, and rival, gray supply chain. Evidence indicates that the larger and more complex the platform, the more they benefit from a strategy of ongoing internalization of new software process innovations (Fichman and Kemerer, 1997). A high-tech white firm should plan to repeatedly acquire capabilities from the gray knowledge pool if the targeted gray innovations are process innovations. The acquire strategy involves converting microscale gray activities into more complete and scalable innovations through formal business processes. It should not be used when the gray market content is more valuable and voluminous than any emerging business processes. Successful white firms might also use business models that directly interact with informal yet sophisticated labor; however, they run a great risk of losing revenues to such firms as they develop loyal consumers. This essay coined the concept of "a proving grounds" as an intentional incubation of gray businesses toward formal status.

For a clear illustration, let us consider Innocentive, a B2B platform host that matches research and development (R&D) projects with consultants. Due to the complexity and diversity of relationships that form around open innovation activities, many small groups of businesses find each other and decide to repeatedly work together. Such subgroups are gray firms that spontaneously emerge from an entanglement of project teams. As the bargaining power of these subgroups becomes large and routine, they may decide to bypass Innocentive entirely, cutting into their core business of brokering B2B deals. Thus, it is in the best interest of Innocentive to acquire such research subnetworks that pose a threat to their core activities.

Strategy three: ignoring informal markets

This third strategy arises when the business cannot find highly complementary gray markets, but also have not felt any pressure from scalable gray businesses. These situations occur in highly commoditized industries with very little product or process innovation. Under such circumstances, the gray market is composed of nonthreatening, petty trades that have low profitability. The focal white firm will ignore adjacent gray transactions. For example, ticket scalpers are still common because preventing resale can lower total attendance to events. Scalpers quickly buy tickets for popular events and then resell them for a higher price once all the tickets are sold out. However, the reselling margins are now typically small enough that the cost of attacking this tiny-scale aftermarket is often greater than the effort is worth.

Strategy four: litigating informal bureaucracies

The fourth strategy is a defensive approach, whereby white firms use the legal system to increase pressure on gray firms. In such markets, there are scant opportunities to innovate products but very strong scale economies for organized processes. For example, medical marijuana sellers find that moving one level up the distribution chain creates large savings; so, individual consumers have a strong incentive to cooperatively buy in large batches, resell the remainder, and repeatedly expand on their gray market sales. When gray firms can easily become larger and more sophisticated, anyone might rapidly change roles from petty trader to a coordinator of an alternative supply chain or market. Classic litigation strategies target parallel resellers who do not receive permission from goods manufacturers or firms whose gray activity is sliding into black-market territory.

The ignore or litigate decision

For an example of the ignore or litigate decision, consider daycare. Established daycare operations can avoid wasting resources by simply *ignoring* the perpetual gray market for casual babysitting transactions; yet, most daycares should sink costs into *litigating* sophisticated home "popup" daycare operations that undercut licensed professional work (Smith, 2016). A transactional analysis could spot the tipping point where a firm decides to litigate, such as litigating pop daycare transactions that are sliding into the black-market category, as some unlicensed behaviors are dangerous for children. However, since the "ignore or litigate" side of the matrix applies mostly to these lower-tech environments, this essay focuses only on analyzing the "facilitate or acquire" decision. [6]

The facilitate or acquire decision

Strategy tipping points for high-tech market segments center around *facilitation* or *acquisition*. Rather than argue that some markets strictly favor one or the other, the White–Gray Strategic Matrix is built around difference in business models. In software industries, the user must engage in some sort of process to complete a transaction—such as interact with ecommerce shopping carts, navigate menus or gaming controls to interact with other players in a game, chat on forums, or agree to peer-to-peer trades. Each business model is designed to monetize some transaction types, give some transactions away for free, and ignore other possible transaction types. The most important issue for high-tech gray markets, therefore, is which transaction types are best suited for each strategy. In other words, given that a transaction type is a useful part of a business model, should the white firm facilitate the transaction outside of the boundaries of the firm or acquire that transaction?

Part Two: The Tipping Point from Facilitate to Acquire in the MMO Industry

This part has four brief sections: (*a*) three mini-cases in the MMO industry, (*b*) ignoring complementarities in *Rage of Bahamut*, (*c*) *Minecraft* and the gray economy, and (*d*) *Dota 2* and the shift to acquire.

Three Mini-Cases in the MMO Industry

To better understand the decisions an MMO firm makes to manage the gray market, we now turn to three mini-case studies. Before stampeding into a broad, multi-industry analysis of the White–Gray Strategic Matrix, the critical task here is to conceptually justify the strategic "tipping point" between facilitation

---

[6] This framework has a kinship to the classic Miles and Snow Prospector-Analyzer-Defender-Reactor framework. In the Miles and Snow framework, the Prospector and Analyzer strategies are dominant because they involve embracing continuous change. The Defender and Reactor strategies are often losers, as they involve resisting change. Similarly, the White–Gray Synergy framework focuses on the dominant Facilitate and Acquire strategies. See Parnell (2016) and Fiss (2011) for recent attempts to reinvigorate the Miles and Snow Typology.

and acquisition with the case analysis of business transactions that exemplify these strategies. In internet-based and high-tech segments, most firms have struggled to manage their relationships with gray markets, either overshooting or undershooting these two strategic stances. Here, we shall look at one firm, Mobage, a platform that failed to strategize appropriately and mismanaged an initially popular game, *Rage of Bahamut* (developed by Cygames); Microsoft, who struck on a clever facilitation strategy for their popular game *Minecraft*; and Valve, a prospecting game platform that struck on a repeatable acquisition strategy, first deployed for their in-house developed game, *Dota 2*.

Only recently have business scholars and economists appreciated the scale of the industry and the importance of MMO platform strategy. Some readers may be shocked to hear that the top ten grossing MMOs have greater lifetime revenues than the top ten Hollywood blockbusters of all time. In the first year of sales, top ten grossing Hollywood films typically fall between $400 million and $2 billion, but that number rapidly declines thereafter (De Vany, 2003). But the top MMOs earn that much annually *for many years in a row*! This is largely because people spend only a few hours on each movie, but MMO gamers spend hundreds or even thousands of hours a year on a game. At a deeper level, this time commitment is driven by the user-generated content that keeps the game fresh, the communities exciting, and the lead users coming back instead of moving on. Scholars have studied the user communities (Burger-Helmchen and Cohendet, 2011) but barely from a business strategy perspective.

The MMO industry is an ideal place to examine how the White–Gray Synergy framework works. MMOs are highly dependent on user-generated content and attract users who like to contribute to the game content. They must discourage gray markets that are at highest risk of devolving into a cesspool of black-market activity; yet, if the game host is too jealous and greedy about revenues, it will scare off highly influential lead users and "whales" (big spenders) and lose business to more gray-friendly MMOs. Gray firms are affiliated with players who are competing, and their interests entangled in competition. Some MMOs have a very casual "sandbox" format, with only playful competition, whereas other games are high-stakes competitions where very large sums of money are spent during combat to "pay to win."

Three rival transaction types

These mini-cases draw attention to three types of rivalrous transaction types: *financial exchanges* where players seek items for in-game competitive advantages, the *productive exchanges* that produce items for player advantage, and, *alternative versions* of the game. See Table 7.2 for a breakdown of the three tipping points for MMO facilitate or acquire strategy. A case shall be made here that most of the rival gray activity centers around the production of positional goods (Schneider, 2007). A positional good is a good that ranks consumers based on their relative consumption, either in terms of quality or quantity. Items that confer competitive advantage to a player are positional goods, because paying directly leads to a player's competitive rank in many MMOs.

Table 7.2 Three Facilitate or Acquire Tipping Points in MMOs

	Exchange transactions	**Productive transactions**	**Alternative game versions**
Facilitate **(Low value chain rivalry)**	No positional goods trading Create a support infrastructure that facilitates free content trading and downloading, which do not result in competitive player advantages	No positional goods making Sell low-priced content modding tools to facilitate user-generated content that does not result in competitive player advantages	No alternative versions Do not facilitate content that results in new game versions
Acquire (High value chain rivalry)	Positional goods trading Monetize and acquire user-generated code that facilitates financial exchanges for competitive player advantages	Positional goods making Monetize and acquire user-generated code that leads to competitive player advantages	Alternative versions Monetize and acquire user-generated code that leads to new game versions

Financial exchanges outside of the control of the platform, such as monetized exchange community for valuable in-game items leading to competitive advantage, take revenues away from in-game exchanges. A platform can make most of its money by selling players "pay to win" options on its marketplace. Second, gray firms that directly produce in-game resources for other players' use, or for their own use, might take away revenue from official game exchanges, but even worse, it will cause the entire game mechanic to become dependent on a shadow economy. Third, gray firms might produce alternative versions of the game itself, leading to a rival game variant that draws players away from the core game. Examples of competitive advantages within a game include stronger attacking, defense, or restoration of exhaustible competitive resources. Top players are often the hackers (lead users) who create popular game "mods": derivative innovations to a software developers' main product. Simple mods might result in game content and complex mods create rival game versions.

A classic example is the game *Half-Life 2*—a game whose various user versions ended up being more popular than the original. Gary's Mod is perhaps the most famous of these. One of the first mods to be intentionally sold as an add-on tool for a commercial product (Champion, 2013), Gary's Mod has been sold well over a million times on the Valve platform, which also distributes the *Half-Life 2* game.

Case One: Ignoring Complementarities in Rage of Bahamut

The first mini-case is the game *Rage of Bahamut*—abbreviated here as "Rage." The author of this chapter was an active player of this game as a participant observer and played at the highest level of competition. In preparation for this mini-case, the author interviewed several highly ranked players to derive a consensus story. Jim Perkins and Duncis Distmannis were two of these top players who have also been highly ranked in multiple other MMOs. They provided their perspective on why *Rage of Bahamut* fundamentally failed.

Created by a small Japanese game developer, Cygames, *Rage* was one of the top grossing smartphone apps of 2013 and a leading MMO until its sudden demise in 2015. It is now known as an odd "flash in the pan" that quickly collapsed into obscurity because of the developers' business strategy. Cygames blamed a shift in the marketplace but fans blamed mismanagement (Dennison, 2017). The developers produced high-level artwork and servers that rarely crashed. However, they also initially ignored the gray market. In a desperate move to correct their error, they made it worse by attempting to litigate to protect revenues. Despite high initial demand for *Rage*, this ill-conceived strategy directly led to a rapid demise. At its peak, *Rage* hosted around two million active accounts worldwide and several million inactive accounts—however, once they went on a widespread campaign to kick top performers off the platform, they lost their user base. What they had failed to appreciate was that their ignoring of the gray market led top players to consider it necessary. "Litigating" the top players by seizing their expensive assets and canceling accounts caused a panic and inflationary sell-off.

Game mechanics

Rage was a clan-based game, where up to forty player accounts joined a single clan to battle other clans online (Wikipedia, 2020). The core game mechanism was built around digital trading cards. Each player could own nearly unlimited amounts of items but could only use five cards at a time—that is, either a five-card attack deck or a defense deck. Rather than detailed live combat action, interpersonal battles are resolved with one winner who has the highest total score. For example, player A could attack player B and generate 10,000 points of damage. If Player B's defense is 10,000 or greater, the defense wins. There is also a random element that makes each card sometimes trigger bonus damage. Clans battle other clans by staging "Holy Wars." During each Holy War event, clans are paired up randomly with rival clans for hour-long battles, usually over the course of three days (72 hours = 72 battles). Hundreds, or even thousands, of individual battles between rival pairs of players take place within an hour time window. At the end of the time window, the team that scores the most damage against the other is the winner. Between Holy War events, players invest time gathering resources to improve their decks.

Overpricing and the gray market

The most important item in *Rage of Bahamut* is Holy Powder (HP) because you need to spend one use of powder per attack during a Holy War. If you have 100 HP, you can attack 100 times for your clan and possibly score up to 100 victories. Thus, players would spend almost all their time collecting cards or trading their rare cards with other players to get more HP. The game offers a very minimal "quest" system that gives free cards and HP, but most good cards are acquired as prizes for high clan ranking in Holy Wars or by gambling on a randomized card pack that costs real dollars. The primary way to acquire HP or cards, though, was paying US dollars for it through the official game marketplace.

Rage has a "pay to win" dynamic: you either pay with money or with effort. *Rage* marketplace initially priced HP at one dollar per unit; moreover, good cards are not available for guaranteed purchase, only through a low percentage chance in a "loot box." Considering that battles take less than 10 seconds and that players can easily spend $100 on a loot box before drawing a very powerful card at random, these obscenely high prices chased nearly all serious players to the gray markets to find discounts. A player could spend more than $100 per hour to win a game.

Within months after debuting, the gray market prices steadily declined from $1.00 per unit of HP. Clever entrepreneurs used various means to arbitrage casual sales of HP and cards, and resellers of these game assets used various misinformation tactics to create "artificially scarce" digital goods. Some players created "farming" systems. What they did was open many anonymous accounts, complete the early quests to get free cards and HP, and then resell those items. Since the first few hours of play give you over 35 HP and a few hundred cards, this was worth over $35 in the early months of the game. Players from poor countries saw this as part-time job and would farm these assets by hand. Later on, even more sophisticated hackers created bots that would automatically farm these assets and trade them. Some major hackers would sell bot accounts for $10 each or amass massive resources for themselves. By the end of the first year, nearly all top players used some sort of farming strategy.

Eventually, gray market entrepreneurs routinized many other clever transactions, including Holy War banking and insurance, Holy War tax systems, PayPal-based HP exchange markets, and meta-clans that pooled and rotated player assets across multiple clans through Facebook or other platforms. By the end of the second year, after an explosion of increasingly complex gray market activity, Cygames had peaked in financial performance and the platform host, Mobage, began a campaign to attack players who used the gray market. By spying directly on player accounts, they identified a number of "whales" who had flagrantly discussed their gray dealings through the official Mobage forums. Once the purging began and the asset seizures started, there was a huge sell-off of assets. The gray market crashed to the point where HP were worth less than a penny each. Interest in the official game markets dwindled to near nothing.

Resolution

What followed was a mass exodus of top players to other MMOs where the gray markets were still thriving. Mobage and Cygames fundamentally failed in their platform design. The open trading rules for peer-to-peer exchanges, combined with poor planning of their overall business model and forums, made it possible for users to construct elaborate gray firms who facilitated and insured alternative development strategies. Top players conspired to form massive markets of informal business services whose revenues collectively exceeded Cygames's profits. While Cygames initially ignored these gray markets, their bigger mistake was not realizing that *their entire combat system depended on the gray market.* Instead of acquiring rival services to formalize these markets, they simply litigated. Cygames chose to repeatedly ban high-ranking players they suspected were hackers or had built their decks entirely through the gray market. Since nearly all high-ranking players used the gray market, Cygames was essentially trying to ban nearly all of its highly active users for breaking the end-user license agreement. Other developers have learned from this mistake and provided "quickstart" services for new players, such as "time advancing" items sold on their internal marketplace, integrated aftermarket services with fees per transaction, and deterrence of meta-clan production schemes.

Minecraft: The Facilitate Strategy

Minecraft is a MMO game that is predominantly based on user-generated content but with very low competitive pressure (that is, low player interest in positional goods). It is a giant sandbox world that feels a lot like the Lego universe of brick-building. *Minecraft* gameplay involves live action with player-controlled avatars, computer-generated monsters, and a "crafting" system where players build items from combinations of raw materials. We shall not describe this case in nearly such detail as the last one, as most people are now familiar with it. *Minecraft* is one of the most successful children-targeted games of all time, reaping billions of dollars for Microsoft (Wikipedia, 2020). Early on, the company struggled with its Intellectual Property (IP) strategy but eventually settled into a process for separating formal from informal content (Schlinsog, 2013). Their policy is to protect user rights for creating and sharing user-generated content; however, their end-use license agreement also prevents users from sharing and editing officially licensed *Minecraft* code. They do not focus on providing the user a path to commercialization of code; instead, they only encourage gray firms to provide truly free content within game. Out-of-game merchandise in the physical world is licensed.

For example, websites such as *minecraftmods.com* persist in offering independent free mods to the core game but the website cannot charge for these add-on services, and the items do not lead to competitive advantage in *Minecraft* game competitions. Firms that use the facilitation strategy will construct a business model that maximizes relationships with innovative gray spaces upstream, downstream, or both. The knowledge commons provide complementary knowledge to *Minecraft*'s core strategy: an installed base for the core game, which sells for around $20–$50x, depending on the edition and on the hardware (that is, Xbox or PC). Many successful white firms are moving toward the *Minecraft* platform strategy to facilitate (Brunt, King, and King, 2020).

Dota 2 and the Shift from Facilitate to Acquire

The third mini-case is Valve, a company that provides thousands of games for downloadable purchase and a variety of community and support services for these games through its successful online gaming platform, Steam. Steam provides remarkably well-planned modding communities for popular MMO titles. The flagship MMO on the Steam platform is *Dota 2*, one of the top ten grossing MMO games worldwide from 2014 to 2019 and a pioneer of MMO business strategy (Tan, 2017). *Dota 2* partially credits its surprising longevity, millions of monthly players, and financial success to Valve's strategy in cocreating and managing user-generated game content. In 2016, *Dota 2* was the first major game on Steam to fully commit to an acquire strategy, as we shall discuss here.

Dota 2 benefitted from transitioning from a popular strategy of facilitation of forums and light user artwork to a more involved form of commercial user modding that split revenues with formerly gray firms (Musabirov et al., 2017). Valve debuted this approach by offering users a "Custom Game Pass" for the first time in 2016 (Thursten, 2016). This custom pass requires users to pay a flat fee for access to some combination of user-generated content and official modifications in one package. The original price of access was one dollar per month, but to reduce the nuisance factor, users now pay for annual passes. Instead of merely supporting minor user artwork, the Custom Game Pass offered a comprehensive game modification so significant that the user-based version plays like a fully rival version of *Dota 2*—in this case, like a "dungeon crawler MMO" instead of an "open world MMO." Instead of merely offering user-generated clothing or weaponry, the game mechanics and maps for the Custom Game Pass are notably different. The new game mechanic was so popular that other Valve gamers requested "Season Passes" for their preferred games, such as Cities: Skylines and Surviving Mars—which are not even in the MMO category, instead involving city building as a primarily solitary gaming activity.

Part Three: Conclusion, Limitations, and Future Directions for Research

Conclusion and Limitations: The Matrix

This paper developed a two-level framework, the first level being the White–Gray Strategic Matrix. What is unknown is how far and wide this White–Gray Strategic Matrix applies beyond user-generated content in video games. There is reason to believe that it could apply to the role of the government and any firm that deals with informal activity whatsoever. In the future, the model needs to be measured either as sets of necessary conditions, such as using Qualitative Comparative Analysis (QCA) analysis or as multifactor analysis models. This is because no true business model need be so one-dimensional. There are several different activities such as governance, trade, production, customer service, and so forth, each of which could be treated independently or in a strong strategic unison. Thus, future work can explore the measures and constructs—a more granular business model analysis.

Conclusion and Limitations: The Tipping Points

This paper presented an analysis of the "tipping points" between facilitate or acquire strategies in MMOs, as caused by transaction types within a specific industry. Future work should examine if strong strategic analogues exist in related industries. The transaction types were analyzed by *ex post* qualitative analysis of three mini-cases. It is recommended that future studies also consider *ex ante* theorizing as to why platforms seem to be purveyors of positional goods, despite being dependent on gray markets and commons. It is expected that some markets may have a tipping point determined by other factors than those used in this paper. However, it is likely that all firms in cultural goods industries that sell positional goods affect the relative rank order of users (Schneider, 2007) such as fashion, higher education, sporting goods, and luxury goods.

Applying the Framework to Government Activities

Some government policymakers look down on gray markets as a nuisance and assume formalization is always a net welfare gain (Schneider, 2012). But what about the persistent gray markets thriving in advanced economies—could they not be opportunities for government facilitation as gray social services and cultural goods production? Advanced economies are knowledge-driven and so the gray market for knowledge-type innovations persists even after institutions are well developed. Some scholars have argued for a "partner state" that supports an independent peer-production sector with its own legal system (Kostakis and Bauwens, 2014) and market segments.[7] The partner state can provide income

[7] A partner state is one that facilitates the commons-based society, based on direct democracy, sharing economics, and peer-production projects (Bradley and Pargman, 2017). Peer projects require significant labor from both creators that produce content and curators that manage organizational processes (Benkler, 2002; Kostakis and Bauwens, 2014). Thus, gray entities are neither a proper market nor firm but are a primordial form of human organizing that can evolve into a variety of business models depending on how the "partner state" decides to structure the rules (Heffan, 1997).

and other incentives for its citizens who contribute to digital commons, and thus can greatly impact the quantity and quality of gray activity.

In lieu of a partner state, the informal economy is relegated to a support role for formalized business, but a partner state could fully legitimate "the commons" as an alternative sector of power.

Studies of Business Models and Formalization Processes

A deeper and broader version of this framework may also help to explain the process by which new business models are legitimized (Lee and Hung, 2014; Webb et al., 2009). Consider the "sharing economy" pioneers, such as file sharing, ride sharing, cryptocurrency, and blockchain firms (Kassan and Orsi, 2012; Iansiti and Lakhani, 2017). Their business opportunities presented potential alternatives to the classic institutions of transportation and of money. While benefitting from legal haziness in the fledgling years of the industry, a few emerging entrepreneurs disrupted the customer bases of software retailers, taxi services, and even of traditional finance with app-based finance. It remains to be seen what the strategic tipping points are for those industries. Gray business models can vary greatly in dimensions such as explicitness of copyleft convictions, monetization, profit motive, permanence, and structural complexity.

The Perpetual Grayness of Entrepreneurship

An extension of this model could better explain the point when entrepreneurs decide to go formal, the value of new hybrid organizational forms, and how to spot emerging opportunities. Recent evidence indicates that informal fields of socioeconomic activity are often proving grounds for young digital entrepreneurs (Chen, 2012; von Hippel, 2007; Webb et al., 2009; Browder, Aldrich, and Bradley, 2017). Entrepreneurs find radical commercial opportunities in gray knowledge commons such as hobby forums, open-source technology, hackathons, and university clubs. Start-ups often sell their first products on a handshake basis without documentation. Technology entrepreneurs explore emerging categories of products or business models, testing strategies with lawless markets. Thus, a big chunk of high-tech firms is always passing through this primordial stage of development. Venture pioneers from Bill Gates at Microsoft, Steve Jobs at Apple, and Bre Pettis of Makerbot are CEOs who famously built their core offering on the community of open-source prototypes. It remains to be seen how many MMO industry user offshoots become heavyweight entrepreneurs.

References

Antia, Kersi D., Mark Bergen, and Shantanu Dutta. 2004. "Competing with Gray Markets." *MIT Sloan Management Review* 46 (1): 63.

Audretsch, D. B., and M. P. Feldman. 2004. "Knowledge Spillovers and the Geography of Innovation." In *Handbook of Regional and Urban Economics*, vol. 4, edited by J. V. Henderson and J. F. Thisse. North Holland: Elsevier, pp. 2713–2739.

Awunyo-Vitor, Dadson, and Vincent Abankwah. 2012. "Substitutes or Complements?: Formal and Informal Credit Demand by Maize Farmers in Ashanti and Brong Ahafo Regions of Ghana." *International Journal of Agriculture and Forestry* 2 (3): 105–112.

Baldwin, C., and E. von Hippel. 2011. "Modeling a Paradigm Shift: From Producer Innovation to User and Pen Collaborative Innovation." *Organization Science* 22 (6): 1399–1417.

Bauwens, M. 2006. "The Political Economy of Peer Production." *Post-autistic Economics Review* no. 37: 33–44.

Benkler, Y. 2002. "Coase's Penguin, or, Linux and 'The Nature of the Firm'." *Yale Law Journal* 112 (3): 369–446.

Bogers, M., and J. West. 2012. "Managing Distributed Innovation: Strategic Utilization of Open and User Innovation." *Creativity and Innovation Management* 21 (1): 61–75.

Boudreau, K. 2010. "Open Platform Strategies and Innovation: Granting Access vs. Devolving Control." *Management Science* 56 (10): 1849–1872.

Bradley, K., and D. Pargman. 2017. "The Sharing Economy as the Commons of the 21st Century." *Cambridge Journal of Regions, Economy and Society* 10 (2): 231–247.

Browder, R. E., H. E. Aldrich, and S. W. Bradley. 2017. "Entrepreneurship Research, Makers, and the Maker Movement." *Academy of Management Proceedings* 2017 (1): 14361–14367.

Brunt, C. S., A. S. King, and J. T. King. 2020. "The Influence of User-Generated Content on Video Game Demand." *Journal of Cultural Economics* 44 (1): 1–22.

Brynjolfsson, E., Y. J. Hu, and M. D. Smith. 2006. "From Niches to Riches: Anatomy of the Long Tail." *Sloan Management Review* 47 (4): 67–71.

Burger-Helmchen, T., and P. Cohendet. 2011. "User Communities and Social Software in the Video Game Industry." *Long Range Planning* 44 (5–6): 317–343.

Burtch, G., S. Carnahan, and B. N. Greenwood. 2018. "Can You Gig It? An Empirical Examination of the Gig Economy and Entrepreneurial Activity." *Management Science* 64 (12): 5497–5520.

Caplinger, Dan. 2018. "Is a Ripple IPO Coming in 2018?" *The Motley Fool*, January 24, 2018. Accessed on January 5, 2020. https://www.fool.com/investing/2018/01/14/is-a-ripple-ipo-coming-in-2018.aspx.

Carson, K. A. 2010. "The Homebrew Industrial Revolution: A Low-Overhead Manifesto." Booksurge. Creative Commons Attributions-Share Alike 3.0 License.

Castells, M., and A. Portes. 1989. "Introduction." In *The Informal Economy*, edited by A. Portes, M. Castells, and L. Benton. Baltimore, MD: John Hopkins University Press, pp. 11–33.

Champion, E. 2013. *Game Mods: Design, Theory, and Criticism.* Lulu.com.

Chandna, V., and M. S. Salimath. 2018. "Peer-to-Peer Selling in Online Platforms: A Salient Business Model for Virtual Entrepreneurship." *Journal of Business Research* 84: 162–174.

Chen, M. A. 2005. "Rethinking the Informal Economy: Linkages with the Formal Economy and the Formal Regulatory Environment." WIDER research paper no. 2005/10, April 2005.

———. 2012. "The Informal Economy: Definitions, Theories and Policies." WIEGO working paper no. 1, August 2012.

Chen, Y., and J. Xie. 2008. "Online Consumer Review: Word-of-Mouth as a New Element of Marketing Communication Mix." *Management Science* 54 (3): 477–491.

Commons, J. R. 1934. *Institutional Economics: Its Place in Political Economy.* New York: MacMillan.

De Filippi, P. 2014. "Bitcoin: A Regulatory Nightmare to a Libertarian Dream." *Internet Policy Review* 3 (2): 1–12.

De Vany, A. 2003. *Hollywood Economics: How Extreme Uncertainty Shapes the Film Industry.* London and New York: Routledge.

Dennison, Kara. 2017. "Cygames Pulls the Plug on IOS Support for Rage of Bahamut." *Crunchyroll*, January 29, 2017. Accessed on January 29, 2020. https://www.crunchyroll.com/anime-news/2017/01/29/cygames-pulls-the-plug-on-ios-support-for-rage-of-bahamut.

Doan, A., R. Ramakrishnan, and A. Y. Halevy. 2011. "Crowdsourcing Systems on the World-Wide Web." *Communications of the ACM* 54 (4): 86–96.

Enkel, E., O. Gassmann, and H. Chesbrough. 2009. "Open R&D and Open Innovation: Exploring the Phenomenon." *R&D Management* 39 (4): 311–316.

Fichman, R. G., and C. F. Kemerer. 1997. "The Assimilation of Software Process Innovations: An Organizational Learning Perspective." *Management Science* 43 (10): 1345–1363.

Fiss, P. C. 2011. "Building Better Causal Theories: A Fuzzy Set Approach to Typologies in Organization Research." *Academy of Management Journal* 54 (2): 393–420.

Friedman, G. 2014. "Workers without Employers: Shadow Corporations and the Rise of the Gig Economy." *Review of Keynesian Economics* 2 (2): 171–188.

Gaspareniene, L., and R. Remeikiene. 2016. "Shadow Economy Estimation Methods: Digital Shadow Economy Assessment Aspect." 9th International Scientific Conference "Business and Management 2016." Vol. 34. May 12–13, 2016. Vilnius, LITHUANIA.

Gidhagen, M., O. Ridell, and D. Sörhammar. 2011. "The Orchestrating Firm: Value Creation in the Video Game Industry." *Managing Service Quality: An International Journal* 21 (4): 392–409.

Godfrey, P. C. 2011. "Toward a Theory of the Informal Economy." *The Academy of Management Annals* 5 (1): 231–277.

Haefliger, S., E. Monteiro, D. Foray, and G. von Krogh. 2011. "Social Software and Strategy." *Long Range Planning* 44 (5–6): 297–316.

Hayek, F. A. 1945. "The Use of Knowledge in Society." *The American Economic Review* 35 (4): 519–530.

Heffan, I. V. 1997. "Copyleft: Licensing Collaborative Works in the Digital Age." *Stanford Law Review* 49 (6): 1487–1521.

Iansiti, M., and K. R. Lakhani. 2017. "The Truth about Blockchain." *Harvard Business Review* 95 (1): 118–127.

IMF. 2019. *World Economic Outlook 2019*. International Monetary Fund website. Accessed on December 1, 2019. https://www.imf.org/external/error.htm?URL=http://www.imf.org/en/Publications/WEO/weo-database.

Jarvenpaa, S. L., and K. R. Lang. 2011. "Boundary Management in Online Communities: Case Studies of the Nine Inch Nails and ccMixter Music Remix Sites." *Long Range Planning* 44 (5–6): 440–457.

Kassan, Jenny, and Janelle Orsi. 2012. "The Legal Landscape of the Sharing Economy." *Journal of Environmental Law & Litigation* 27 (1): 1–17.

Katz, M. L., and C. Shapiro. 1985. "Network Externalities, Competition, and Compatibility." *American Economic Review* 75 (3): 424–440.

Kaufman, B. E. 2003. "The Organization of Economic Activity: Insights from the Institutional Theory of John R. Commons." *Journal of Economic Behavior & Organization* 52 (1): 71–96.

Kenney, M., and J. Zysman. 2016. "The Rise of the Platform Economy." *Issues in Science and Technology* 32 (3): 61–69.

Kostakis, V., and M. Bauwens. 2014. *Network Society and Future Scenarios for a Collaborative Economy*. London: Springer.

Lang, K., R. Shang, and R. Vragov. 2015. "Consumer Co-Creation of Digital Culture Products: Business Threat or New Opportunity?" *Journal of the Association for Information Systems* 16 (9): 766–798.

Langlois, R. N. 1990. "Creating External Capabilities: Innovation and Vertical Disintegration in the Microcomputer Industry." *Business and Economic History* 19: 93–102.

———. 1992. "External Economies and Economic Progress: The Case of the Microcomputer Industry." *Business History Review* 66 (1): 1–50.

Lee, C. K., and S. C. Hung. 2014. "Institutional Entrepreneurship in the Informal Economy: China's Shan-Zhai Mobile Phones." *Strategic Entrepreneurship Journal* 8 (1): 16–36.

Levine, L. 2019. "Digital Trust and Cooperation with an Integrative Digital Social Contract." *Journal of Business Ethics* 160 (2): 1–15.

Levy, Steven. 1984. *Hackers: Heroes of the Computer Revolution*. Garden City, NY: Anchor Press/Doubleday.

Lindauer, D. L. 1989. "Parallel, Fragmented, or Black? Defining Market Structure in Developing Economies." *World Development* 17 (12): 1871–1880.

López, L. E., and E. B. Roberts. 2002. "First-Mover Advantages in Regimes of Weak Appropriability: The Case of Financial Services Innovations." *Journal of Business Research* 55 (12): 997–1005.

Malerba, F., R. Nelson, L. Orsenigo, and S. Winter. 2007. "Demand, Innovation, and the Dynamics of Market Structure: The Role of Experimental Users and Diverse Preferences." *Journal of Evolutionary Economics* 17 (4): 371–399.

Maloney, W. F. 2004. "Informality Revisited." *World Development* 32 (7): 1159–1178.

Mangram, M. E. 2012. "The Globalization of Tesla Motors: A Strategic Marketing Plan Analysis." *Journal of Strategic Marketing* 20 (4): 289–312.

Martin, S. 2002. "Spillovers, Appropriability, and R&D." *Journal of Economics* 75: 1–32.

McGahan, A. M. 2012. "Challenges of the Informal Economy for the Field of Management." *Academy of Management Perspectives* 26 (3): 12–21.

Mitnick, Barry M., and Robert C. Ryan. 2015. "On Making Meanings: Curators, Social Assembly, and Mashups." *Strategic Organization* 13 (2): 141–152.

Mukherjee, D. 2016. "Informal Economy in Emerging Economies: Not a Substitute but a Complement!" *International Journal of Business and Economic Development* 4 (3): 16–27.

Musabirov, I., D. Bulygin, P. Okopny, and A. Sirotkin. 2017. "Deconstructing Cosmetic Virtual Goods Experiences in Dota 2." Proceedings of the 2017 CHI Conference on Human Factors in Computing Systems.

Osterloh, M., and S. Rota. 2007. "Open Source Software Development—Just Another Case of Collective Invention?" *Research Policy* 36 (2): 157–171.

Parnell, J. A. 2016. "A Business Strategy Typology for the New Economy: Reconceptualization and Synthesis." *Journal of Behavioral and Applied Management* 3 (3): 207–232.

Pasquale, F. 2016. "Two Narratives of Platform Capitalism." *Yale L. & Pol'y Rev* 35 (309): 309–319.

Paul, Kari. 2019. "What Is Libra? All You Need to Know about Facebook's New Cryptocurrency." *The Guardian* Online, January 18, 2019. Accessed on January 5, 2020. https://www.theguardian.com/technology/2019/jun/18/what-is-libra-facebook-new-cryptocurrency.

Pitelis, C. N., and D. J. Teece. 2009. "The (New) Nature and Essence of the Firm." *European Management Review* 6 (1): 5–15.

Polasik, M., A. I. Piotrowska, T. P. Wisniewski, R. Kotkowski, and G. Lightfoot. 2015. "Price Fluctuations and the Use of Bitcoin: An Empirical Inquiry." *International Journal of Electronic Commerce* 20 (1): 9–49.

Powell, Walter W. 1990. "The Transformation of Organizational Forms: How Useful Is Organization Theory in Accounting for Social Change?" In *Beyond the Marketplace: Rethinking Economy and Society*, edited by Roger Friedland and A. F. Robertson. New York: Aldine de Gruyter, pp. 301–329.

Richter, C., S. Kraus, and R. B. Bouncken. 2015. "Virtual Currencies Like Bitcoin as a Paradigm Shift in the Field of Transactions." *International Business & Economics Research Journal (Iber)* 14 (4): 575–586.

Sawhney, Mohanbir, and Emanuela Prandelli. 2000. "Communities of Creation: Managing Distributed Innovation in Turbulent Markets." *California Management Review* 42 (4): 24–54.

Schilling, M. A. 2003. "Technological Leapfrogging: Lessons from the US Video Game Console Industry." *California Management Review* 45 (3): 6–32.

Schlinsog, Melinda J. 2013. "Endermen, Creepers, and Copyright: The Bogeymen of User-Generated Content in Minecraft." *Tulane Journal of Technology & Intellectual Property* 16: 185–206.

Schneider, F. 2012. "The Shadow Economy and Shadow Economy Labor Force: What Do We (Not) Know?" IZA Discussion Paper Series #6423. Institute for the Study of Labour, Bonn.

Schneider, F., and A. Buehn. 2017. "Estimating a Shadow Economy: Results, Methods, Problems, and Open Questions." *Open Economics* 1 (1): 1–29.

Schneider, M. 2007. "The Nature, History and Significance of the Concept of Positional Goods." *History of Economics Review* 45 (1): 60–81.

Siqueira, A. C. O., J. W. Webb, and G. D. Bruton. 2016. "Informal Entrepreneurship and Industry Conditions." *Entrepreneurship Theory and Practice* 40 (1): 177–200.

Smith, W. L. 2016. "Untold Number of Illegal Day Care Centers Are Popping up in Apartment Buildings and Homes throughout the Five Boroughs. How Are Parents to Know If They're Safe?" *NY Daily News* Online, Febuary 11, 2016. Accessed on January 1, 2020. http://interactive.nydailynews.com/2016/02/illegal-day-care-centers-popping-up-throughout-NYC/.

Surowiecki, J. 2005. *The Wisdom of Crowds.* New York: Anchor Press.

Tan, D. N. 2017. "Owning the World's Biggest ESport: Intellectual Property and DOTA." *Harv. JL & Tech* 31 (2): 965–989.

Täuscher, Karl, and Sven M. Laudien. 2018. "Understanding Platform Business Models: A Mixed Methods Study of Marketplaces." *European Management Journal* 36 (3): 319–329.

Teece, D. J. 1986. "Profiting from Technological Innovation: Implications for Integration, Collaboration, Licensing and Public Policy." *Research Policy* 15 (6): 285–305.

———. 1998. "Capturing Value from Knowledge Assets: The New Economy, Markets for Know-How, and Intangible Assets." *California Management Review* 40 (3): 55–79.

———. 2018. "Profiting from Innovation in the Digital Economy: Enabling Technologies, Standards, and Licensing Models in the Wireless World." *Research Policy* 47 (8): 1367–1387.

Thai, M. T. T., and E. Turkina. 2014. "Macro-Level Determinants of Formal Entrepreneurship versus Informal Entrepreneurship." *Journal of Business Venturing* 29 (4): 490–510.

Thursten, C. 2016. "Valve to Add Custom Game Pass to Dota 2." *Pc Gamer*, March 15, 2016. Accessed on January 29, 2020. https://www.pcgamer.com/valve-custom-game-pass-interview/.

Tiwana, A. 2014. *Platform Ecosystems: Aligning Architecture, Governance, and Strategy.* Burlington, MA: Morgan Kaufmann.

von Hippel, E. 2007. "Horizontal Innovation Networks—by and for Users." *Industrial and Corporate Change* 16 (2): 293–315.

———. 2016. *Free Innovation.* Cambridge, MA: MIT Press.

von Hippel, E., and G. von Krogh. 2003. "Open Source Software and the 'Private-Collective' Innovation Model: Issues for Organization Science." *Organization Science* 14 (2): 209–223.

Wikipedia. 2020. "Rage of Bahamut." Accessed on June 11, 2020. https://en.wikipedia.org/wiki/Rage_of_Bahamut_(TV_series).

Webb, J. W., L. Tihanyi, R. D. Ireland, and D. G. Sirmon. 2009. "You Say Illegal, I Say Legitimate: Entrepreneurship in the Informal Economy." *Academy of Management Review* 34 (3): 492–510.

Williams, C. 2006. *The Hidden Enterprise Culture: Entrepreneurship in the Underground Economy*. Cheltenham: Edward Elgar.

Williams, C. C., and S. Nadin. 2012a. "Tackling the Hidden Enterprise Culture: Government Policies to Support the Formalization of Informal Entrepreneurship." *Entrepreneurship & Regional Development* 24 (9–10): 895–915.

———. 2012b. "Tackling Entrepreneurship in the Informal Economy: Evaluating the Policy Options." *Journal of Entrepreneurship and Public Policy* 1 (2): 111–124.

Williamson, O. E. 1973. "Markets and Hierarchies: Some Elementary Considerations." *American Economic Review* 63 (2): 316–325.

Williamson, O. E., M. L. Wachter, and J. E. Harris. 1975. "Understanding the Employment Relation: The Analysis of Idiosyncratic Exchange." *The Bell Journal of Economics* 6 (1): 250–278.

8

Mod the World

How Entrepreneurs Learn from Video Game "Modding" Communities

William Gordon Miller

> But mods can do a lot more than just modernize a game. Mods can transform an old title into something entirely new and far better.
>
> —Rafi Letzter, *Business Insider*[1]

Gaming provides both a great source of entertainment as well as a welcome mental release for the end of busy days. However, for certain players, it represents something more as well—a chance to create. For them, opportunities to inject their own visions into the worlds they explore offer exciting new ways to stoke their passions and give back to the gaming community. These innovators, known colloquially as "modders," not only correct the inherently frustrating mistakes made by developers but also bring fresh new content to the games we know and love. After all, what would the Bethesda worlds of *Fallout* and *Elder Scrolls* be like today without the dynamic hand of the modder? Would multiplayer online battle arenas (MOBAs) actually exist? How about the incredible new technical marvels displayed in the massive open worlds of Rockstar franchises *Grand Theft Auto* and *Red Dead Redemption*? Not to mention the incredible prevalence of the MMORPG.

The list goes on and on, but truly, gamers owe much to the industrious and creative minds of modders. For those unfamiliar with this practice though, what exactly do I mean by "modders" and "modding"? Poor (2014, p. 1250), in his qualitative and quantitative overview of this phenomenon, offers an excellent definition:

---

1 See Letzter (2015).

> Modding, from *modifying*, is the act of a changing a game, usually through computer programming, with software tools that are not part of the game. This can mean fixing bugs, modifying content to improve it, or adding content. But modding is not an activity taken on by those at game companies—developers release patches and downloadable content, not mods. Modding is instead done by players and fans of the game … Modding is more than adjusting the preferences or game settings, it is making changes that cannot be made through the game as it is.

What might we say about these individuals in a grander sense? More precisely, do they matter beyond the confines of the games they modify? This chapter aims to partially answer this question, and (SPOILER ALERT) the answer is a resounding YES! How so? In terms of entrepreneurial learning (and ultimately judgment; see Foss and Klein, 2012), the modding community as a whole provides a rich source of untapped innovative potential upon which certain game developers (that is, the firms of the video game industry) draw to overcome creative roadblocks. By tapping into this pool of informal, but uniquely creative, individual talent, these developers harvest novel ideas that respond to real consumer demand, allowing even the most niche tastes of gamers to be satisfied and/or commercialized. Furthermore, this phenomenon highlights the role that informal communities more broadly might play in bringing about unprecedented levels of value creation.

Though arguably their relevance extends to multiple domains outside of this narrow confine as well, I argue that their role in facilitating the entrepreneurial development of video games showcases perhaps one of their most salient features. To support my argument, I specify three categories in which the modding community, broadly defined, has contributed (and continues to contribute) to the growth of games from major developers:

1. **Traditional modding**, exemplified by Valve's *Dota 2* and Bethesda's *Elder Scrolls* and *Fallout* franchises.
2. **Quasi-modding**, portrayed by games such as Mojang's *Minecraft,* Sony's *Little Big Planet* franchise, and Ubisoft's new Story Creator Mode in *Assassin's Creed Odyssey*.
3. **Multiuser dungeons (MUDs)**, notable for their influence on the development of *EverQuest* and MMORPGs more broadly.

In doing so, I root this analysis in the well-established construct of absorptive capacity (Cohen and Levinthal, 1990).

In addition to the firm-level ramifications, I propose that this discussion of modding and informal communities makes three primary contributions to our understanding of its economic impacts at the industrial and societal levels of organization. First, from a methodological individualist perspective (Boettke, 2012), the micro-foundations of how firms engage in an entrepreneurial action highlight the emergent nature of economic activity that ultimately informs our understanding of higher-level phenomena. To that end, I primarily rely on Foss and Klein's (2012) judgment-based approach, which emphasizes intuitive reasoning in a context of structural uncertainty. By explicating how entrepreneurs make these judgments, this discussion provides some clarity into one way that firms collectively influence emergent economic processes and overall individual well-being—namely, learning through user experimentation and modification. Notably, this ties in well to the discussion in Chapter 9 concerning Valve's economic organization, as this company makes extensive use of these individualized processes.

Second, understanding this aspect of the micro-learning processes within the video game industry also informs our understanding of similar activity in other industries and spheres of economic life. Looking to several diverse strands of literature such as those dealing with user innovation and entrepreneurship, alternative entrepreneurial environments, and the emerging sharing economy made possible by smart technology, a number of parallels between video game modding communities and overall market activity become readily apparent. For example, the case of Apache security software's use of innovation toolkits (Franke and von Hippel, 2003) highlights the ways in which modding processes take place in other industries, and the maker movement (Browder, Aldrich, and Bradley, 2019) showcases the potential for environments of modular production and informal enthusiast interactions to define the next generation of entrepreneurship. Essentially, modding forms a key element of all economic activity as consumers and producers alike rely on new and dynamic means of exchanging tacit information. This chapter primarily adds to this point by providing extensive detail about a particularly salient form of modding and detailing how firms can benefit from these learning processes. This in turn emphasizes certain connections between market activity in all domains, regardless of the particular good or service being offered. In addition, it builds on the discussion in Chapter 7 concerning gray markets, as modding offers yet another way in which firms can gauge consumer demand.

Overview of Modding

To begin, it is important to note that video game "modding" consists of two fundamentally different types, *partial conversion* mods and *total conversion* mods. Arakji and Lang (2007, p. 199) describe these forms as varying in regard to the "extent of alteration of the game elements." Partial conversion mods constitute relatively minor additions or tweaks to a game such as adding new content (for example, new music, artwork, character models, objects, and so on) or modifying existing content to fit some particular purpose. However, the key characteristic of this type of mod dictates that the "base" game remains fundamentally the same (that is, the root mechanics do not change; changes simply result in new or modified content). On the other hand, total conversion mods represent a fundamental change in the overall nature of the game, with products that constitute entirely new derivative experiences. They typically enable new functionalities, with holistic changes in both content and mechanics.

The first major historical example of traditional modding (though MUDs, discussed later, predate this form) comes from *Castle Wolfenstein*, an early 1980s' game for the Apple II computer. The mod, entitled *Castle Smurfenstein*, replaced all in-game Nazi enemies with Smurfs. The popularity of modding grew from there. In 1993, with the release of *Doom* (from id Software), the game developers decided to include a WAD (which stands for "Where's All the Data?") file separate from the main game engine that allowed players to develop their own content and levels for the game. This proved to be hugely popular and launched the widespread appeal of modding in game communities (Dyer, 2016).

Since the 1990s, the practice of including modding capabilities in large commercial games has become quite common, at least for PC games. Console modding would come later and with some limitations—the first major example being *Unreal Tournament 3* in 2007 and, more recently, *Fallout 4* in 2015 (Grayson, 2015). However, for the most part, modding remains largely a phenomenon for PC gaming, though this could change in the near future as console platforms strive to compete for increased market share through the introduction of new features. Regardless, mods in the PC gaming arena have proven quite illuminating regarding the practice's overall potential and ramifications for the industry as well as society.

Before moving on, a couple of examples of notable games using mods may help the reader to understand what they look like in practice. One example includes a particularly prolific modding community in *Elder Scrolls V: Skyrim*, released in 2011 from Bethesda Softworks. While most Bethesda games include modding capabilities of some sort, this specific game developed quite a reputation for them, partly because the base game was so well received. Some notable mods in this game allow users to update the in-game world map with additional texture and details (making it easier to navigate and interpret), incorporate an enhanced user interface (to sort through menus more efficiently), reorder the events of the game (to suit individual playstyles), remove wait times for vendors (to speed up the buying and selling of loot), alter the heads-up display (to show or remove desired on-screen information), and much more (Livingston et al., 2019).

Yet another example, this one illustrating the potential of total conversion mods, comes from *XCOM: Enemy Unknown*, released by Firaxis Games and Feral Interactive in 2012, and its expansion pack *XCOM: Enemy Within* (released in 2013). This turn-based strategy game, in its official form, already contains a massive amount of content providing players with numerous options for highly customizable gameplay. As such, the major mod, entitled *Long War*, is all the more impressive. Introducing hundreds of changes, it extends the campaign, makes the game more difficult, and adds a large amount of content (for example, soldier classes, voice packs, equipment, new mechanics, and so on). Notably, the developers were so impressed with the success of the mod that they brought in its creators to work on launch-day mods for the official sequel, *XCOM 2*, released in 2016 (PC Gamer, 2017). For reference, other popular games incorporating extensive modding capabilities include *Grand Theft Auto 5*, *Minecraft*, the *Just Cause* franchise, and the *Civilization* franchise.

To manage and access all these mods, users (provided they own the game they intend to modify) simply need a platform or user interface to interact with its respective library of user-created content. Such platforms include Nexus Mods, Mod DB, the Steam Workshop, Curse Mods, and the Bethesda Creation Club. Granted, it is possible to mod a game without the use of one of these interfaces, but it requires sufficient technical knowledge on the part of the player to ensure that the mod runs as expected and avoids technical hiccups. Thankfully, the aforementioned platforms enable a simplified means of searching and installing mods for essentially any game (Casper, 2017; Dey, Massengill, and Mockus, 2016).

Theoretical Foundation

Absorptive Capacity and Networks

A primary topic of interest to scholars studying the potential gains from organizational learning revolves around the notion of absorptive capacity (ACAP).

Dating back to Cohen and Levinthal (1990), this concept essentially deals with the returns to innovation resulting from a firm's capability to assimilate, integrate, and synthesize a diverse base of knowledge that will enable further learning to occur. In short, it provides a foundation upon which new information acquired from external networks can be readily put into useful practice. Notably, Todorova and Durisin (2007) offer a reconceptualization of this important construct, emphasizing Cohen and Levinthal's (1990) discussion of the recognition of value. Their revised model, as seen in Figure 8.1, thus offers a potentially fuller understanding of the construct.[2]

Figure 8.1 A Model of Absorptive Capacity

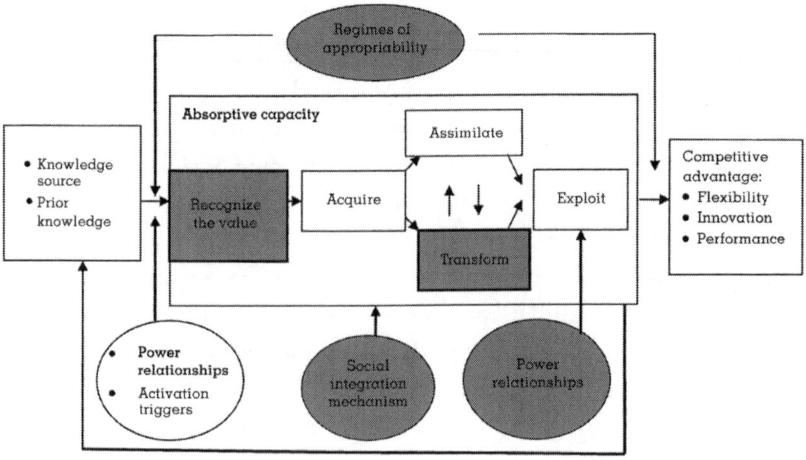

Source: Todorova and Durisin (2007, p. 776).

Given the complexity of the above model (Figure 8.1), a few simplifying notes are warranted in relation to the current discussion. Essentially, the relevant takeaways are as follows. First, in order to effectively make use of a new idea, a firm must possess related knowledge that allows it to integrate the idea into its internal activities. Upon recognizing a new idea's value, a firm's ACAP thus consists of an ability to acquire, assimilate, transform, and exploit the new information. This ultimately results in a competitive advantage relative to other firms in the industry and increases the firm's knowledge base. Finally, various contextual factors influence this process at each stage as seen (for example, intellectual property rights, social norms, relationships with key input providers, and so on).

[2] For yet another conceptualization, see Zahra and George (2002).

Consequently, the commercialization of new innovations fundamentally depends on the firm's ability to properly absorb and leverage a new idea, but this also impacts the firm's ability to effectively absorb new knowledge in the future (that is, organizations are path-dependent). Therefore, a more diverse set of ideas (as exemplified by modding communities) fundamentally provides a more diverse ACAP.

In addition, a diverse literature on the nature and organization of formal versus informal knowledge networks (Allen, James, and Gamlen, 2007; Anklam, 2005; Cross and Parker, 2004) further emphasizes the importance of this distinction (though these works mostly deal with the internal R&D structures within firms). A notable exception is Kreiner and Schultz (1993) who describe the Danish biotech community in which informal collaborations or relationships are formed across organizations, thereby facilitating a great degree of strategic innovation, despite being hampered to some degree by managerial fiat. Yet another includes Aken and Weggeman (2000, p. 140) who explore what they term the "Daphne-dilemma," or the trade-offs between managing such informal networks for efficiency purposes and allowing creativity to flourish in these circles. They, however, broadly define informal networks in terms of social relationships developed within an industry (or across formal industries).

This chapter extends this notion by suggesting that informal enthusiast communities, which are formally unconnected to the firm or industry, often help spur such innovation by developing new ideas and acting as proxies for organizational exploration. Importantly, individuals in these communities do not necessarily have official connections to the industry they may be serving and, often, their "services" are unintentional. As discussed further in the fourth section, gaming enthusiasts who participate in modding exemplify this function in their ability to experiment with novel, creative ideas upon which entrepreneurs and firms later draw.

Entrepreneurial Judgment

Turning to the economic ramifications of this learning process, a newer approach to entrepreneurial action integrates the traditional theory of the firm with more recent theories emerging from the field of entrepreneurship. Termed the judgment-based approach or JBA (Foss and Klein, 2012, 2015), this framework essentially states that the locus of entrepreneurship is the resource owner who bears the full weight of uncertainty (or the "unknown unknowns," to borrow an infamous line from Donald Rumsfeld). Within this environment, resource owners engage in subjective judgmental decision-making to allocate their scarce resources toward the ends they believe to be most worthwhile or productive. In turn, the market evaluates the quality of their decisions (or judgment) by assigning either a profit or a loss, hence generating feedback that can be incorporated into future decisions (see Figure 8.2). Importantly, since no market for judgment exists (that is, you cannot buy or sell it[3]), entrepreneurs organize into firms (conceived here as a bundle of human and capital resources) in order to make final decisions.[4]

Figure 8.2 Entrepreneurial Judgment

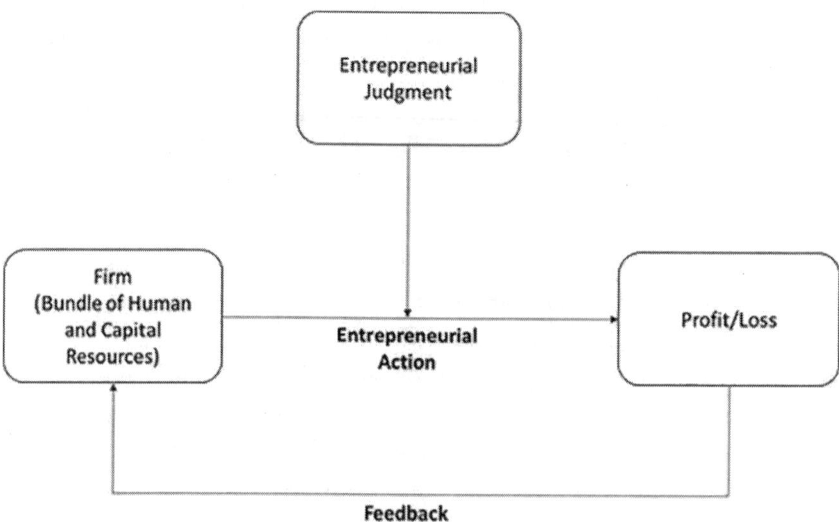

Source: Author's own figure.

For the purposes of this chapter, I focus on how learning from informal external environments impacts the returns to this judgmental decision-making, primarily in terms of knowledge flows. Thus, by integrating the diverse literatures

---

[3] One potential criticism of this claim lies in the observation that entrepreneurs might frequently hire consultants to help them make decisions. However, one must remember that in deciding whether to take or not to take a consultant's advice, an entrepreneur inherently makes a judgment regarding the quality of that advice. Since the entrepreneur holds the final say in such decisions and experiences the residual profits or losses associated with those decisions, judgment ultimately lacks the ability to be traded like other goods.

[4] Various refinements and extensions of this framework include a focus on how entrepreneurs deal with different types of uncertainty (Packard, Clark, and Klein, 2017) and the contextual and institutional factors at play (Foss, Klein, and Bjørnskov, 2019).

on absorptive capacity, networks, and entrepreneurial judgment, I show how firms theoretically improve the outcomes of their decision-making through learning from the wisdom of the crowd. As such, this leads to the improved economic performance of the firm, marginally facilitating entrepreneurial progress in the economy (Holcombe, 2006).

Thus, in highly dynamic industries, I suggest that informal networks (as defined by crowdsourced knowledge) will be more valuable than formal networks for three primary reasons. First, they unleash creative potential as they draw upon agents that, by definition, possess a more varied outside perspective and who, consequently, generate a greater diversity of ideas. Second, since these agents are typically sourced from the consumers a particular firm serves, their ideas collectively reflect the underlying demand for products and services that a given supplier must provide. Third, through engaging with these crowdsourcing communities, firms can identify talent that may later be brought formally into the firm, thus increasing future ACAP through the acquisition of valuable human capital. At the end of this process, moreover, the quality of the firm's entrepreneurial judgment moderates (either positively or negatively, dependent upon the revealed abilities of the entrepreneur) the final outcome on innovation performance. Along with the extant literature, this basic logic forms the foundation for the following five propositions:

Proposition 8.1: *In highly dynamic industries, the wisdom of the crowd will positively contribute to future ACAP, particularly in the form of idea diversity.*

Proposition 8.2: *ACAP impacts innovation performance through two primary channels. The first reduces innovation performance by increasing organizational rigidities. The second raises innovation performance through better firm capitalization of technical knowledge/resources.*

Proposition 8.3: *Learning through the wisdom of the crowd mitigates the firm rigidity effect by introducing greater idea diversity.*

Proposition 8.4: *Entrepreneurial judgment either increases or reduces the effect of absorptive capacity on innovation performance depending on its underlying quality.*

Proposition 8.5: *Innovation performance feeds back into absorptive capacity leading to an iterative process.*

Figure 8.3 presents my complete model for highly dynamic industries. Summarizing the five propositions above, it illustrates a series of simple relationships highlighting the contrasting impacts of ACAP on innovation performance through organizational rigidities and increased technical capabilities. In addition, it provides my intuition regarding the impacts of informal (represented by the "wisdom of the crowd" construct) as opposed to formal external networks on this overall process, specifically for highly dynamic industries. Lastly, it incorporates the iterative effects of entrepreneurial judgment and innovation performance on a firm's overall absorptive capacity.

Figure 8.3 Crowdsourcing Knowledge in Highly Dynamic Industries

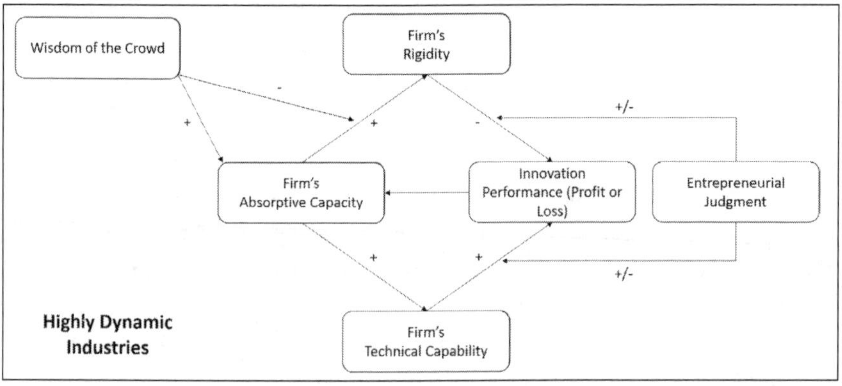

Source: Author's own figure.

Moving into the next section, I now consider this model in terms of three separate conceptualizations of the modding phenomenon—traditional modding, quasi-modding, and MUDDING. While not intended to be an exhaustive account of how crowdsourced networks facilitate learning, this discussion does provide for an illustrative account of how learning takes place among seemingly disorganized end users and how this learning injects fresh, novel ideas into already dynamic, but perhaps routinized, firms.[5]

Three Types of Modding

This section provides an overview of the three aforementioned styles of modding proposed for this analysis as embodied in several notable games. For each style, I

[5] Notably, an extensive parallel literature exploring this phenomenon of user innovation exists in the field of innovation (for example, Baldwin, Hienerth, and von Hippel, 2006; Bogers, Afuah, and Bastian, 2010; Bogers and West, 2012; Franke and Shah, 2003; von Hippel, 2006; Lakhani and von Hippel, 2004; Lüthje, 2004; Shah, 2006; Shah and Tripsas, 2007; Tietz et al., 2005; von Hippel, 1976, 2005). The current chapter seeks to root such work in a more solid theoretical foundation as well as provide some new insights for economics and the gaming industry.

present mini-case studies examining how they respectively take shape in the real world, and I emphasize links to their mainstream adoption by major development projects. As such, this approach enables a closer look into how established or emerging firms in the video game industry learn from the wisdom of the crowd and commercialize novel ideas through the application of user innovation (see note 8).

Traditional Modding

The impact of this first type of modding (and arguably the most salient) is captured by a particularly notable genre, the multiplayer online battle arena (MOBA), which evolved out of a simple mod for Blizzard Entertainment's highly successful real-time strategy (RTS) game, *Warcraft 3*. Pulling from various online accounts and quasi-ethnographic experiences, the following case study demonstrates how a gaming community spontaneously emerged (Miller, 2018) to create a new genre and, more importantly, how Valve, a major game developer, capitalized upon this collective learning process to take the genre mainstream. By internalizing and acting upon the "wisdom of the crowd," the studio went on to generate enormous value for the industry through its creation of one of the top MOBA games to date, *Defense of the Ancients 2* (aka *Dota 2*). Evidenced by *Dota 2*'s current monthly peak-player base (approximately 700,000 to 1 million; see SteamCharts, 2019a), $238 million in revenue (as of 2015; see Walker, 2016), and major tournament prize pools totaling over $100 million (as of June 2017; see Stubbs, 2017), Valve's profitable foray into leading a major-studio adaptation of the popular MOBA genre provides keen insight into the value of learning from the crowd.

As Dean (2014) illustrates, the origin of *Dota 2* (and MOBAs more generally) actually dates back to a heavily modified map entitled "Aeon of Strife" from Blizzard Entertainment's highly popular *Starcraft*, released in 1998. Though not much to look at by today's standards, this map featured a revolutionary concept in which players controlled a single powerful hero unit as opposed to an entire army. In contrast to the original concept of *Starcraft*, in which players engaged in real-time strategic decision-making regarding base construction and individual unit command, this seminal MOBA sub-game tasked players with defending three lanes of traffic in which automated waves of AI soldiers attack the opposing side's main base. In each lane stood a series of towers which players defended (attacked) in order to reach the other team's base. The end goal was to successfully reach the opposing base and destroy it (Stasiukaitis, 2017).

This simple concept later laid the foundation for the popularization of the genre with a mod called "Defense of the Ancients" (or DOTA), created for Blizzard Entertainment's subsequent RTS, *Warcraft 3*, released in 2003. Created by a modder known as Eul, this sub-game refined the earlier concept to include support for ten players and further develop the RPG elements (for example, skill trees, experience levels, weapon and armor shops, and so on) to encourage player progression. Over the next five years, countless iterations and refinements of the model were developed by a large community of over 1.5 million users, including notable (within the genre) leaders such as Steve "Guinsoo" Freak, Steve "Pendragon" Mescon, and Abdul "IceFrog" Ismail. In 2009, two independent titles based on the DOTA model were released, one of which became a major commercial success. Since then, numerous titles have emerged within the MOBA genre (over thirty), though not all have been particularly successful.

Dota 2, officially released on July 9, 2013, to glowing reviews, stands in stark contrast. After a two-year public beta phase in which players tested the game and its developer, Valve Software, conducted server stress-tests, *Dota 2* formally entered the market to much applause. Since then, the overall player base has grown to 11.19 million as of January 2019, higher than in some recent years but lower than the all-time high of 13.02 million in June 2016 (Statista, 2019). In addition, the franchise has been incorporated into the growing popularity of eSports with the introduction of The International (TI) tournament in 2011, which has since become an annual event. Since 2015, this tournament boasts the largest prize pool of all such competitions, growing annually to more recently top $24 million in a single year (Prescott, 2017). Thus, *Dota 2*, initially borne out of a niche idea, truly epitomizes the value of the "wisdom of the crowd." Furthermore, it provides a great example of the potential of traditional modding for entrepreneurial learning.

Quasi-Modding

A second type of modding takes the form of "quasi-modding," or the ability of players to create and contribute to a game through developer-designed systems. Though variants of this approach existed prior to the more recent era of gaming[6] (that is, 2005 onward beginning with the seventh generation of console gaming), this type of modding really went mainstream with the release of games such as Sony's *Little Big Planet Franchise* in 2008 and Mojang's *Minecraft* in 2011. Here,

[6] A notable example includes earlier entries into the popular franchise *RPG Maker* from ASCII and Enterbrain.

I discuss the quasi-modding inherent in these games as well as in an ongoing development with Ubisoft's new "Story Creator Mode" in *Assassin's Creed Odyssey*.

Three key features distinguish this form from the previously discussed traditional form of modding. First, quasi-modding does not require its participants to possess any sort of coding proficiency. Instead, developers preload a wide range of creative tools into a user-friendly interface and, as such, even laypersons can design and build to their heart's content. For example, the game *Minecraft* largely consists of using a predesigned graphical user interface (GUI) to explore a practically endless[7] three-dimensional (3D) world and build structures (as well as other oddities such as functional computers and console emulators). Of course, this also creates a much more limited window of potential innovation (dependent upon the range of freedom the developer allows) but, as with traditional modding, the result originates entirely in the users' minds and imaginations. As such, quasi-modding remains emergent, though it might be considered a sort of bounded emergence. Notably, *Minecraft* enables the use of traditional modding as well, so in one sense, it might be considered an exemplar of both traditional and quasi-modding.

A second way in which quasi-modding differs relates to the conceptual divide between game and development. Whereas with traditional modding, the process involves actions taken outside of the game itself (that is, usually within some programming software), quasi-modding typically occurs in-game and, many times, comprises a part of the game. For example, a core feature of the *Little Big Planet* experience revolves around its player-creation tools. Players, using in-game unlockable content as well as imported content, can develop original artwork, characters, and even entire levels and stories. The newer entries even enable players to come up with novel gameplay mechanics. All of this new material can be shared to the cloud enabling other players to see and interact with each other's creations. Notably, this approach to gameplay resonates strongly with the gaming community as partially evidenced by the *Little Big Planet* community's creation of over 10 million levels.[8]

A final, but related, distinction of quasi-modding deals with the endogeneity of the modding process itself. Since the modding environment consists of an

7 The game world in *Minecraft* is procedurally generated *ad infinitum*, so the only real limitation on its size rests in the user computer's processing and memory capacity.

8 Exact statistics on this franchise are relatively hard to come by. The level creation number comes from the website https://lbp.me/home/. Other loose numbers from various online sources peg the total sales to be in the multi-millions, but an exact number is difficult to verify. Given its overall robustness, longevity, and sustained player base, however, the franchise can presumably be considered a successful endeavor.

internal part of the game (as opposed to the exogenous, external environment of traditional modding), developers possess a direct feedback mechanism and, thus, beyond simply pulling novel ideas from the community concerning potential new content, they can actually refine and improve the overall modding experience. This expands the overall potential of quasi-modding over time and, as such, causes it to gradually emulate many of the characteristics of traditional modding. For example, consider Ubisoft's new "Story Creator Mode" in *Assassin's Creed Odyssey*, an immersive open-world adventure game. This new feature enables players, via a web-based application, to create full questlines in game using much of the same programming language and software that went into the base game's original development, albeit with a user-friendly interface.

MUDs

A third type of modding, referred to colloquially as MUDs,[9] dates back to the mid-1970s. These text-based applications enable users to build out worlds, explore those worlds, and socialize with other users in the process. In Richard Bartle's (2003, p. 4) *Designing Virtual Worlds*, the cocreator of the first MUD defines "virtual worlds" (his more encompassing term for MUDs)[10] as possessing the following four characteristics:

1. Characters represent *individual* players "in" the world and consists of a single entity, regardless of any other units the player may or may not control.
2. These worlds exist in *real* time.
3. Players *share* these worlds (key distinction).
4. These worlds are *persistent.*

Furthermore, since these game worlds developed on-screen as simple lines of code and text, the real enjoyment and immersion for players came not from

---

9 The acronym MUD typically refers to "multi-user dungeon," but other variations include "multi-user dimension," "multi-user domain," and "multi-user dialogue," among others. Given the wide range of applications, the exact terminology largely depends on context, though generally, they all consist of some sort of text-based adventure (adventure being used in the broadest sense).

10 Bartle's (2003) definition notably includes more modern MMORPGs, which I distinguish from earlier MUDs. This gets to one of his points about the difficulty of terminology in describing various genres. It largely depends on the context being discussed. Nevertheless, his definition, for my purposes, provides a solid delineation from non-MUDs and holds with the addition of one more characteristic—these worlds are entirely represented by text (that is, no graphical display).

seeing the action but rather imagining it in their minds. Consequently, despite a lack of visual and auditory feedback, the potential capacity for world-building arguably maintained much wider boundaries than most gamers know today. Notably, fans of this genre largely wax nostalgic about these "glory days" of RPG gaming and adventuring (Olivetti, 2011).

The first widespread adventure game using this format, though not technically a MUD itself, emerged with Will Crowther's *Colossal Cave Adventure* (more commonly referred to as just *Adventure* or *ADVENT*) in 1975, and it set the stage for the development of the MUD genre just a few years later. Comparable in feel and tone to the popular nondigital role-playing game *Dungeons and Dragons*, *Adventure* allowed users to live out a similar experience only with the computer programmer serving as the dungeon master (that is, the game's facilitator and director), thus enabling individual engagement with this style of gameplay. However, this benefit also constituted its major limitation—it only facilitated one player at a time![11]

Not until the 1978 release of *MUD* (eventually called *MUD1* to distinguish it from sequels and the genre name), however, by Roy Trubshaw, a student at England's Essex University, did the world receive a truly multiplayer text-based game. Later serving as the basis for the genre's name, the title of this game originated in part as a tribute to another single-player adventure game's many variants called DUNGEN (see Tim Anderson and Bruce Daniel's *Zork*). What *MUD* gave players consisted of a novel concept in which they might work together to solve various puzzles and drive the creation of a new socialized universe. After Trubshaw's hand off of the *MUD* project to Richard Bartle, another Essex student, a new trend kicked off in which aspiring developers created whole new worlds, ones that could be shared and developed by a growing community of MUDDERs (Bartle, n.d.). Importantly, these self-contained worlds came about for different purposes but, ultimately, most became adopted by the role-playing community (Olivetti, 2011). The limit of their potential rests in the extent of their players' imaginations.

The nature of MUDDING then lends itself neatly to the analysis of entrepreneurial learning in this context for three reasons. First, given the theoretically limitless bounds of human imagination, the creativity of MUDDERs provides a rich source of new ideas for both content- and mechanic-driven

[11] Other adventure games included *Zork*, *Planetfall*, *The Hobbit*, and *The Hitchhiker's Guide to the Galaxy* (Olivetti, 2011).

consumer innovations. Second, unlike the other forms of modding, the focal games tend to not be well recognized outside of their niche communities, but they ultimately provided the inspiration for well-known graphic-based titles such as *EverQuest*, which popularized the modern-day MMORPG. Third, though this form of modding largely fell out of style in the 1990s, many MUDDING communities still exist, thus enabling a direct comparison of its influence in the past and the present. Though the current chapter does not delve into present-day MUDDING, its existence does provide an opportunity for an extension of this analysis.

Discussion

What does this all mean for the individual learning processes of game developers? Thinking back to the theoretical model presented in the last section, I argue that each of the forms of modding discussed earlier satisfy my core propositions, albeit in somewhat different ways. In this subsection, I elaborate further on the applicability of the earlier case studies to this model.

Regarding Proposition 8.1, the gameplay development and acquisition of the legal rights for *Dota 2* expanded Valve's portfolio, both in terms of formal intellectual property and fundamental experience. While significant legal challenges delayed this process to some extent, eventually the company won and secured the rights. This enabled particular branding strategies such as the declaration that "*Dota*" had become its own word, and it allowed Valve to capitalize upon previous genre name-recognition. Furthermore, the onboarding of IceFrog to help create *Dota 2* enabled the developer to benefit from the unique community-based insights that made the root game so successful in the first place and, by relying on the lessons learned by earlier modders, they externalized the costs of experimenting with this new genre to the community. Quite plausibly, factors such as these enhanced the overall future ACAP that Valve brought into the mainstream marketing of the *Dota* brand and subsequent development of *Dota 2*.

For quasi-modding, this process takes place in a different fashion. Since the platform for innovation is provided directly by the developers, they possess a direct pool of knowledge from which to draw. In addition, given the relative simplicity of the process compared to more traditional modding, this potentially makes the pool much larger. To some extent, this formalizes the network, but provided free entry and exit onto the platform, the individuals generating useful knowledge and ideas essentially still come from the larger population and, consequently, likely remain immune to any standardized thinking within the industry itself. For example, consider *Minecraft*. The worlds and structures that the players develop, the ways in which they interact, and the workarounds they use to solve in-game problems ultimately guide the developers in further improving the overall experience. In *Little Big Planet*, much of the same can be said, but particularly notable with this game is that Sony actually brought on two of its most productive and dedicated fans from the earlier games to work on the franchise's third entry (Solomon, 2014). Time will tell if we see similar occurrences with *Assassin's Creed Odyssey's* new "Story Creator Mode," but if history tells us anything, this form of modding seems to be quite lucrative for developers interested in the innovative potential of their player bases.

In terms of MUDs, learning from the crowd might be thought of as not only beneficial but also practically necessary. Given that these programs largely existed in the void of early gaming history, developers relied upon one another to try out their creations and build upon them. With the large proliferation of varying MUD types (for example, MOOs, MUCKs, MUSHes, TinyMUDs, DikuMUDs, LPMUDs, and so on) and especially with the ease of sharing that the internet eventually brought, aspiring developers sought to provide their own spins on familiar ideas and create wholly unique experiences. In the case of DikuMUDs, this eventually led to the creation of the breakout graphical hit *EverQuest*, the first widely popular MMORPG.[12] It essentially consisted of providing graphics for the ever-popular DikuMUD. In fact, as Bartle (2003, p. 25) explains:

> If there ever was a case of being in the right place at the right time, *EverQuest* (EQ) is it. It was basically a DikuMUD with a graphical client bolted on—the similarities are so close that under legal threat its server programmers were forced to sign sworn statements to the effect that they didn't use any actual *DikuMUD* code in *Everquest*.

Whatever the specific similarities to *DikuMUD* though, no doubt that its developer, Sony Online Entertainment, drew significant inspiration from the class of MUDs preceding *EverQuest*. This game would go on to itself garner huge success and provide inspiration for future MMORPGs such as *Star Wars Galaxies*, *Dark Age of Camelot*, *Final Fantasy 11*, and arguably every game in this

[12] Other notable graphical experiences predated this game (for example, *Meridian 59*, *Ultima Online*, and so on), but none achieved the seemingly overnight success that *EverQuest* enjoyed (Bartle, 2003).

genre succeeding it. However, the lessons and ideas coming from this game owe their origins to the highly informal niche communities found in the world of MUDDING.

Moving on to Proposition 8.2, while I lack robust data on the internal rigidities that individual game companies face, I offer some speculation in terms of the broad situation with which game developers generally must deal. In developing and releasing a new game, firms in the gaming industry face immense costs, both in terms of money and time. For AAA games (that is, blockbuster games), modern-day estimates for financial budgets range from $20 to $200+ million, though a great deal of imprecision exists due to developer secrecy (Superannuation, 2014). In addition, major games today can take as long as ten to fifteen years to complete (Frank, 2016). Given this, major developers tend to shy away from intensely radical experiments, suggesting an inherent rigidity among such firms (that is, they favor the tried-and-true models of the past, perhaps with slight alterations). Consequently, though I cannot definitively pinpoint a "rigidity magnitude" for the studios in my sample, I can confidently state that certain rigidities inherent to the industry also must be dealt with by these firms as well. Given this, it stands to reason that any method of reducing these rigidities will increase the level of desired innovation by such developers. Further studies should help to verify this claim, but nevertheless, I hold that it is a highly plausible one to make.

Building on this assumption provides some intuition for Proposition 8.3 that the "wisdom of the crowd" can help mitigate the rigidity traps described by Ahuja and Morris Lampert (2001). By internally recognizing the appeal of MOBA games demonstrated by outside enthusiasts, Valve capitalized on the learning taking place in gaming communities. As such, they did not need to create a new style of game (in this case, a MOBA) from scratch to capture significant returns from innovation. They did not even need to be alert to the micro-learning processes regarding how to properly design such a game. They simply needed to appropriate the experimentation *already* occurring in the informal communities that had emerged in the wake of widespread modding appeal. In doing so, they went on to profit from one of the most innovative and commercially successful games to date and incorporated new capacities for learning that likely will benefit them well into the future.

Likewise, the developers of quasi-modding games simply need to wait and see what their fans ultimately create rather than trying to predict based on industry practice what gamers will desire going forward. Furthermore, MUDDING, while no longer commonplace, still ultimately provides the inspiration for many of the new features we see coming out in games today. Importantly, as Bartle (2003) warns, newer developers may need to take the time to understand the rationale behind certain approaches from this genre so as to avoid the mistakes of the past. Nevertheless, looking back to this seminal and highly innovative period may help developers overcome any apparent rigidities their businesses may face. Looking to Propositions 8.4 and 8.5, the entrepreneurs in these firms exercised good judgment by properly selecting the features that exhibited high potential for a new project given existing internal firm knowledge (thus enhancing the effects of the firm's absorptive capacity on innovation), and the knowledge gained through this iterative process increased the firm's future ability to generate new ideas as well (by opening up new possible modes of thinking internally).

Firms in other highly dynamic industries can learn from these examples as well, and this chapter posits three primary implications for organizations outside of the games industry. First, firms struggling to innovate due to internal rigidities may well benefit from finding similar communities connected to their own industries. By absorbing and incorporating the learning that occurs in such groups, they can take advantage of low-hanging fruit for proven radical changes to their businesses. Second, these communities may also provide a wellspring of useful talent for enhancing a firm's absorptive capacity in useful ways. New hires from this pool of presumably unique and entrepreneurial individuals likely will enhance and diversify an organization's human capital such that future innovation performance becomes more explorative and less exploitative. Finally, even if a firm chooses to refrain from over-relying on these networks in the ways described earlier (for example, for reasons of legitimacy in the eyes of shareholders), they still may prove useful as a source of unique solutions to specific problems the firm may face. In short, in an age where essentially every discipline attracts hobbyists and technology easily facilitates their interactions, crowdsourced knowledge provides a uniquely useful tool for enhancing organizational innovation.

Conclusion

In conclusion, highly dynamic or entrepreneurial industries demand that firms within them consistently innovate, particularly in an explorative (as opposed to exploitative) fashion. This, consequently, requires that firms continuously learn from the environment and others operating within a given space. To explain how this learning process occurs then, researchers have frequently turned to the highly influential ACAP construct in the literature, as it provides an extremely intuitive means of understanding organizational capabilities for learning. However, while informative, the concept suffers when subjected to theoretical and empirical criticism related to various organizational rigidities developed internally within the firm.

As such, this chapter contributes to the ongoing rich discussion of ACAP by considering how informal external networks, specifically the consumer-oriented communities that comprise the "wisdom of the crowd," might help organizations in highly dynamic industries overcome the internal rigidities they face in terms of innovation. Furthermore, it sheds light on how certain legal and economic policies, such as those related to intellectual property, affect this underlying process. In particular, it considers three broad types of modding—traditional modding, quasi-modding, and MUDDING. In each, game developers utilize the lessons learned in these more *ad hoc* environments to create polished products with some truly innovative features.

First, I show how a professionally developed game, *Dota 2*, came into existence due to a distinctly user-generated learning process facilitated by communities of coders (traditional modding). As such, the game developer overcame the rigidities associated with learning through ACAP by relying on outsourced information from informally organized groups rather than on practices standard within the industry, in order to capitalize upon a unique form of explorative innovation. Consequently, they generated immense value for the gaming community and reinforced their own ACAP with unique insights unlikely to emerge within already path-dependent formal organizations.

Next, I look to a slightly less recognized brand of modding embodied by titles such as *Minecraft*, *Little Big Planet* and, more recently, *Assassin's Creed Odyssey*. While the platforms in these cases come from the respective game developers themselves, the learning taking place consists of an emergent process of players contributing their own unique ideas to the ultimate evolution and success of the underlying game. Despite possessing inherent creative boundaries, this approach still enables firms within the industry to capitalize upon a more diverse and potentially innovative source of knowledge and, consequently, bolster their absorptive capacity for future entrepreneurial endeavors.

Lastly, I consider a predecessor to modern-day notions of modding (that is, MUDDING) and explain its relevance for the emergence of MMORPGs. The importance of MUDs rests in their reliance on text-based gameplay that facilitates a practically limitless playground of imagination. With this, users engage in elaborate world-building unimpeded by many of the technical limitations involved with bringing visible and audible virtual worlds to life, such as those showcased by most video games today. As such, the capacity for truly innovative activities, in many ways, remains unmatched by this early form of modding. Though its primary successors (that is, MMORPGs such as *EverQuest*) eschewed such a platform for graphical capabilities and more complex player mechanics, they owe their origins to the early creative efforts of MUDDERs. This evolution, thus, highlights yet another way in which firms within the gaming industry turned to its player community to bolster both its innovative potential and overall absorptive capacity.

For the gaming industry broadly, all of this reinforces what should be a pretty intuitive idea for most—player demands provide the ultimate guide for creating value! Modding as an art form allows players to express what they most want games to be and, given this, they also provide a highly useful metric for determining the most profitable development paths to pursue. Not only this, they help illustrate the cultural landscape gamers inhabit. While not all-encompassing, such a vivid portrayal fosters an appreciation of both the gaming community's desires and ultimate vision for the future of this dynamic medium.

Finally, looking at these ideas also provides more insight for further refining entrepreneurial theory, from both the economic and management perspectives. The Austrian economist Friedrich Hayek once stated (speaking on the importance and application of local knowledge to solving economic problems), "To assume all the knowledge to be given to a single mind … is to disregard everything that is important and significant in the real world" (Hayek, 1945, p. 530). Certainly, success in any entrepreneurial endeavor requires learning from outside actors and, in many cases, allowing those same actors to make important strategic decisions (or at least provide relevant information for such decisions). In addition, firms seeking to enhance their innovative capabilities and remain profitable absolutely must pay attention to such external sources of learning. To these ends, I submit that, for industries in highly dynamic or entrepreneurial environments, more attention needs to be given to the relative potential of crowdsourced networks to generate that learning.

References

Ahuja, G., and C. Morris Lampert. 2001. "Entrepreneurship in the Large Corporation: A Longitudinal Study of How Established Firms Create Breakthrough Inventions." *Strategic Management Journal* 22 (6–7): 521–543.

Aken, J. E. V., and M. P. Weggeman. 2000. "Managing Learning in Informal Innovation Networks: Overcoming the Daphne-Dilemma." *R&D Management* 30 (2): 139–150.

Alexandra, H. 2019, June 11. "Assassin's Creed Odyssey's Story Creator Is Simple but Fun." *Kotaku*. Accessed on June 20, 2019. https://kotaku.com/assassins-creed-odysseys-story-creator-is-simple-but-fu-1835424798.

Allen, J., A. D. James, and P. Gamlen. 2007. "Formal versus Informal Knowledge Networks in R&D: A Case Study Using Social Network Analysis." *R&D Management* 37 (3): 179–196.

Anklam, P. 2005. *The Social Network Toolkit: Building Organisational Performance Through Collaborative Communities*. London, UK: Ark Group.

Arakji, R. Y., and K. R. Lang. 2007. "Digital Consumer Networks and Producer-Consumer Collaboration: Innovation and Product Development in the Video Game Industry." *Journal of Management Information Systems* 24 (2): 195–219.

Aribi, A., and O. Dupouët. 2015. "The Role of Organizational and Social Capital in the Firm's Absorptive Capacity." *Journal of Knowledge Management* 19 (5): 987–1006.

Baker, W. E., A. Grinstein, and N. Harmancioglu. 2016. "Whose Innovation Performance Benefits More from External Networks: Entrepreneurial or Conservative Firms?" *Journal of Product Innovation Management* 33 (1): 104–120.

Baldwin, C., C. Hienerth, and E. von Hippel. 2006. "How User Innovations Become Commercial Products: A Theoretical Investigation and Case Study." *Research Policy* 35 (9): 1291–1313.

Bartle, R. A. 2003. *Designing Virtual Worlds*. 1st ed. Indianapolis, Ind: New Riders.

———. n.d. "MUD History, Who Invented MUD's, How MUD's Were Invented." Accessed on January 7, 2020. https://www.livinginternet.com/internet/d/di_major.htm.

Benner, M. J., and M. Tushman. 2002. "Process Management and Technological Innovation: A Longitudinal Study of the Photography and Paint Industries." *Administrative Science Quarterly* 47 (4): 676–707.

Boettke, P. J. 1990. "The Theory of Spontaneous Order and Cultural Evolution in the Social Theory of F.A. Hayek." *Cultural Dynamics* 3 (1): 61–83.

———. 2012. *Living Economics: Yesterday, Today, and Tomorrow*. 1st ed. Oakland, CA: The Independent Institute.

Bogers, M., A. Afuah, and B. Bastian. 2010. "Users as Innovators: A Review, Critique, and Future Research Directions." *Journal of Management* 36 (4): 857–875.

Bogers, M., and J. West. 2012. "Managing Distributed Innovation: Strategic Utilization of Open and User Innovation." *Creativity and Innovation Management* 21 (1): 61–75.

Browder, R. E., H. E. Aldrich, and S. W. Bradley. 2019. "The Emergence of the Maker Movement: Implications for Entrepreneurship Research." *Journal of Business Venturing* 34 (3): 459–476.

Buchanan, J. M. 1965. "An Economic Theory of Clubs." *Economica* 32 (125): 1–14.

Casper, K. 2017. "How to Install PC Game Mods: A Beginner's Guide." *PCWorld*, November 17, 2017. Accessed on June 18, 2019. https://www.pcworld.com/article/3237246/how-to-install-pc-game-mods.html.

Chang, Y. Y., Y. Gong, and M. W. Peng. 2012. "Expatriate Knowledge Transfer, Subsidiary Absorptive Capacity, and Subsidiary Performance." *Academy of Management Journal* 55 (4): 927–948.

Cohen, W. M., and D. A. Levinthal. 1990. "Absorptive Capacity: A New Perspective on Learning and Innovation." *Administrative Science Quarterly* 35 (1): 128–152.

Cross, R., and A. Parker. 2004. *The Hidden Power of Social Networks: Understanding How Work Really Gets Done in Organizations*. Boston, Mass: Harvard Business Review Press.

D'Amico, D. J. 2015. "Spontaneous Order." In *The Oxford Handbook of Austrian Economics,* edited by Peter J. Boettke and Christopher Coyne. New York, NY: Oxford University Press, pp. 115–142.

D'Amico-Wong, L. "The Decline of League of Legends." GINX Esports TV, August 31, 2018. Accessed on June 26, 2019. https://ginx.tv/lol/decline-of-league-of-legends/.

Dean, P. 2014. "The Story of DOTA." *Eurogamer*, April 6, 2014. Accessed on May 4, 2019. https://www.eurogamer.net/articles/2011-08-16-the-story-of-dota-article.

Dey, T., J. L. Massengill, and A. Mockus. 2016. "Analysis of Popularity of Game Mods: A Case Study." In *Proceedings of the 2016 Annual Symposium on Computer-Human Interaction in Play Companion Extended Abstracts*. New York: Association for Computing Machinery, pp. 133–139.

Dyer, A. 2016. "History of PC Game Mods." *NVIDIA*, March 18, 2016. Accessed on June 18, 2019. https://www.nvidia.com/en-us/geforce/news/history-of-pc-game-mods/.

El-Nasr, M. S., and B. K. Smith. 2006. "Learning through Game Modding." *Computers in Entertainment* 4 (1): 1–20.

Ferguson, A. 1782. *An Essay on the History of Civil Society.* 5th ed. London: T. Cadell.

Foss, N. J., and P. G. Klein. 2012. *Organizing Entrepreneurial Judgment: A New Approach to the Firm*. Cambridge, UK: Cambridge University Press.

———. 2015. "Introduction to a Forum on the Judgment-Based Approach to Entrepreneurship: Accomplishments, Challenges, New Directions." *Journal of Institutional Economics* 11 (3): 585–599.

Foss, N. J., P. G. Klein, and C. Bjørnskov. 2019. "The Context of Entrepreneurial Judgment: Organizations, Markets, and Institutions." *Journal of Management Studies* 56 (6): 1197–1213.

Frank, A. 2016, November 28. "Final Fantasy 15 Was Announced 10 Years Ago. Here's How the World's Changed Since." *Polygon*, November 28, 2016. Accessed on June 26, 2019. https://www.polygon.com/2016/11/28/13764684/final-fantasy-15-development-time-timeline.

Franke, N., and E. von Hippel. 2003. "Satisfying Heterogeneous User Needs via Innovation Toolkits: The Case of Apache Security Software." *Research Policy* 32 (7): 1199–1215.

Franke, N., and S. Shah. 2003. "How Communities Support Innovative Activities: An Exploration of Assistance and Sharing among End-Users." *Research Policy* 32 (1): 157–178.

García-Villaverde, P. M., J. Rodrigo-Alarcón, M. J. Ruiz-Ortega, and G. Parra-Requena. 2018. "The Role of Knowledge Absorptive Capacity on the Relationship between Cognitive Social Capital and Entrepreneurial Orientation." *Journal of Knowledge Management* 22 (5): 1015–1036.

Grayson, N. 2015. "The First Big Game That Brought Mods to Consoles." *Kotaku*, June 24, 2015. Accessed on June 18, 2019. https://kotaku.com/the-first-big-game-that-brought-mods-to-consoles-1713716040.

Hardin, G. 1968. "The Tragedy of the Commons." *Science* 162 (3859): 1243–1248.

Hayek, F. A. 1945. "The Use of Knowledge in Society." *The American Economic Review* 35 (4): 519–530.

Heller, M. A., and R. S. Eisenberg. 1998. "Can Patents Deter Innovation? The Anticommons in Biomedical Research." *Science* 280 (5364): 698–701.

Hervas-Oliver, J.-L., J. Albors-Garrigos, B. de-Miguel, and A. Hidalgo. 2012. "The Role of a Firm's Absorptive Capacity and the Technology Transfer Process in Clusters: How Effective Are Technology Centres in Low-Tech Clusters?" *Entrepreneurship & Regional Development* 24 (7–8): 523–559.

Holcombe, R. 2006. *Entrepreneurship and Economic Progress.* 1st ed. New York, London: Routledge.

Hsu, D. H., and R. H. Ziedonis. 2013. "Resources as Dual Sources of Advantage: Implications for Valuing Entrepreneurial-Firm Patents." *Strategic Management Journal* 34 (7): 761–781.

Knight, F. H. 1921. *Risk, Uncertainty and Profit.* Boston, NY: Houghton Mifflin Company.

Kreiner, K., and M. Schultz. 1993. "Informal Collaboration in R & D. The Formation of Networks across Organizations." *Organization Studies* 14 (2): 189–209.

Lakhani, K. R., and E. von Hippel. 2004. "How Open Source Software Works: 'Free' User-to-User Assistance." In *Produktentwicklung mit virtuellen Communities: Kundenwünsche erfahren und Innovationen realisieren,* edited by C. Herstatt and J. G. Sander, pp. 303–339.

Letzter, R. 2015. "Online Communities Are Changing Video Games to Make Them Better, Weirder, and Much More Wonderful." *Business Insider*, July 20, 2015. Accessed on March 30, 2019. https://www.businessinsider.com/video-game-modding-2015-7.

Livingston, C., T. Hatfield, D. Papiz, and J. Macgregor. 2019. "The Best Skyrim Mods." *PC Gamer*, May 11, 2019. Accessed on June 18, 2019. https://www.pcgamer.com/best-skyrim-mods/.

Lüthje, C. 2004. "Characteristics of Innovating Users in a Consumer Goods Field: An Empirical Study of Sport-Related Product Consumers." *Technovation* 24 (9): 683–695.

Marabelli, M., and S. Newell. 2014. "Knowing, Power and Materiality: A Critical Review and Reconceptualization of Absorptive Capacity." *International Journal of Management Reviews* 16 (4): 479–499.

Miller, W. G. 2018. "The Role of Spontaneous Order in Video Games: A Case Study of Destiny." *Cosmos+Taxis* 5 (3+4): 63–72.

Mises, Ludwig von. 1949. *Human Action: The Scholar's Edition*. Auburn: Ludwig von Mises Institute.

Mises, Richard von. 1981. *Probability, Statistics, and Truth.* 2nd ed. New York, NY: Dover.

Olivetti, J. 2011. "The Game Archaeologist Plays with MUDs: The History." *Engadget*, April 5, 2011. Accessed on June 17, 2019. https://www.engadget.com/2011/04/05/the-game-archaeologist-plays-with-muds-the-history/.

Ostrom, E. 2002. "Common-Pool Resources and Institutions: Toward a Revised Theory." In *Agriculture and Its External Linkages: Vol. 2. Handbook of Agricultural Economics*, edited by Bruce L. Gardner and Gordon C. Rausser, pp. 1315–1339.

Packard, M. D., B. B. Clark, and P. G. Klein. 2017. "Uncertainty Types and Transitions in the Entrepreneurial Process." *Organization Science* 28 (5): 840–856.

PC Gamer. 2017. "The Best Total Conversion Mods." *PC Gamer*, August 28, 2017. Accessed on June 18, 2019. https://www.pcgamer.com/the-best-total-conversion-mods-ever/.

Poor, N. 2014. "Computer Game Modders' Motivations and Sense of Community: A Mixed-Methods Approach." *New Media & Society* 16 (8): 1249–1267.

Posen, H. E., and J. S. Chen. 2013. "An Advantage of Newness: Vicarious Learning despite Limited Absorptive Capacity." *Organization Science* 24 (6): 1701–1716.

Postigo, H. 2007. "Of Mods and Modders: Chasing down the Value of Fan-Based Digital Game Modifications." *Games and Culture* 2 (4): 300–313.

———. 2008. "Video Game Appropriation through Modifications: Attitudes Concerning Intellectual Property among Modders and Fans." *Convergence* 14 (1): 59–74.

Prescott, S. 2017. "The Dota 2 International Prize Pool Has Comfortably Broken Its Record." *PC Gamer*, August 8, 2017. Accessed on June 26, 2019. https://www.pcgamer.com/the-dota-2-international-prize-pool-has-comfortably-broken-its-record/.

Schmidt, T. 2010. "Absorptive Capacity—One Size Fits All? A Firm-Level Analysis of Absorptive Capacity for Different Kinds of Knowledge." *Managerial and Decision Economics* 31 (1): 1–18.

Shah, S. K. 2006. "Motivation, Governance, and the Viability of Hybrid Forms in Open Source Software Development." *Management Science* 52 (7): 1000–1014.

Shah, S. K., and M. Tripsas. 2007. "The Accidental Entrepreneur: The Emergent and Collective Process of User Entrepreneurship." *Strategic Entrepreneurship Journal* 1 (1–2): 123–140.

Solomon, D. 2014. "How Two Game Fans Became Developers on LittleBigPlanet 3." *Fast Company*, October 30, 2014. Accessed on June 26, 2019. https://www.fastcompany.com/3037700/how-two-game-fans-became-developers-on-littlebigplanet-3.

Sotamaa, O. 2010. "When the Game Is Not Enough: Motivations and Practices among Computer Game Modding Culture." *Games and Culture* 5 (3): 239–255.

Stasiukaitis, B. 2017. "A Beginner's Guide to MOBAs: Best Games, Terminology & More." *Cultured Vultures*, October 30, 2017. Accessed on June 26, 2019. https://culturedvultures.com/beginners-guide-mobas-best-games-terminology/.

Statista. 2019. "DOTA 2 global MAU 2019." *Statista.* Accessed on May 6, 2019. http://www.statista.com/statistics/607472/dota2-users-number/.

SteamCharts. 2019a. "Dota 2—Steam Charts." Accessed on June 26, 2019. https://steamcharts.com/app/570#1y.

———. 2019b. "League of Legends—Steam Charts." Accessed on June 26, 2019. https://steamcharts.com/app/20590#All.

Stubbs, M. 2017. "Dota 2's $100 Million Milestone, Visualised." *RedBull,* June 23, 2017. Accessed on June 26, 2019. https://www.redbull.com/se-en/dota-2-100-million-milestone-visualised.

Sun, P. Y. T., and M. H. Anderson. 2010. "An Examination of the Relationship between Absorptive Capacity and Organizational Learning, and a Proposed Integration." *International Journal of Management Reviews* 12 (2): 130–150.

Superannuation. 2014. "How Much Does It Cost to Make a Big Video Game?" *Kotaku,* January 15, 2014. Accessed on June 26, 2019. https://kotaku.com/how-much-does-it-cost-to-make-a-big-video-game-1501413649.

Tietz, R., P.D. Morrison, C. Lüthje, and C. Herstatt. 2005. "The Process of User-Innovation: A Case Study in a Consumer Goods Setting." *International Journal of Product Development* 2 (4): 321–338.

Todorova, G., and B. Durisin. 2007. "Absorptive Capacity: Valuing a Reconceptualization." *Academy of Management Review* 32 (3): 774–786.

Tortoriello, M. 2015. "The Social Underpinnings of Absorptive Capacity: The Moderating Effects of Structural Holes on Innovation Generation Based on External Knowledge." *Strategic Management Journal* 36 (4): 586–597.

von Hippel, E. 1976. "The Dominant Role of Users in the Scientific Instrument Innovation Process." *Research Policy* 5 (3): 212–239.

———. 2005. "Democratizing Innovation: The Evolving Phenomenon of User Innovation." *Journal Für Betriebswirtschaft* 55 (1): 63–78.

———. 2006. *Democratizing Innovation.* Cambridge, Mass: The MIT Press.

Walker, A. 2016. "League of Legends Made More Revenue in 2015 than CSGO, Dota 2 and World of Warcraft Combined." *Kotaku,* January 28, 2016. Accessed on May 4, 2019. https://www.kotaku.com.au/2016/01/league-of-legends-made-more-revenue-in-2015-than-csgo-dota-2-and-world-of-warcraft-combined/.

Watts, S. 2019. "E3 2019: Assassin's Creed Odyssey Story Creator Mode Out Now, Discovery Mode Coming This Fall." *GameSpot,* June 13, 2019. Accessed on June 20, 2019. https://www.gamespot.com/articles/e3-2019-assassins-creed-odyssey-story-creator-mode/1100-6467623/.

Welch, D. E., and L. S. Welch. 2018. "Developing Multilingual Capacity: A Challenge for the Multinational Enterprise." *Journal of Management* 44 (3): 854–869.

West, J., and S. Gallagher. 2006. "Challenges of Open Innovation: The Paradox of Firm Investment in Open-Source Software." *R&D Management* 36 (3): 319–331.

Wiens, K., and G. Gordon-Byrne. 2017. "The Fight to Fix It." *IEEE Spectrum* 54 (11): 24–29.

Zahra, S. A., and G. George. 2002. "Absorptive Capacity: A Review, Reconceptualization, and Extension." *Academy of Management Review* 27 (2): 185–203.

9

Levels without Bosses?

Entrepreneurship and Valve's Organizational Design

Ulrich Möller and Matthew McCaffrey

The video game industry has often been surrounded by controversy and, in fact, has been a repeated target of public outcry over the past forty years or so. Until recently, however, it was typically the content of games that invited criticism, most infamously in the debate about the effects of video game violence on children (Egenfeldt-Nielsen, Smith, and Tosca, 2020, pp. 273–297). Yet in the last decade, the controversy has shifted to the business of video games and to questions about the economics and ethics of game production and distribution (for example, McCaffrey, 2019). As a result, academic researchers in the social sciences and humanities are increasingly turning their attention toward the major development and publishing companies and the ways that their organizations evolve in response to far-reaching social, economic, and technological changes (O'Donnell, 2017).

One of the key players in the industry is Valve Corporation, an enigmatic and idiosyncratic company that offers a fascinating example of nontraditional economic organization. Valve is a "flat" company without a management hierarchy or traditional boss roles: instead of top-down organization and management, Valve employees are free to work on whatever projects they choose and to convince other employees to join collaborative groups. Decision-making is thus "democratized" rather than centralized in key management positions. This peculiar structure, or lack thereof, seems to challenge conventional ideas about organization not only in the video game business but also business in general. We say "seems to" because, as we will explain, the company's story is more complicated than either its supporters or critics tend to acknowledge.

Despite Valve's distinctive and even extreme approach to organizing, research on the company is limited to only a few papers (for example, Felin and Powell, 2016; Puranam and Håkonsson, 2015) that paint a somewhat scattered and incomplete picture of its operations. In this chapter, we will integrate and expand on this work to explore Valve's economic organization and discuss the challenges it faces. We thereby provide a clearer and more comprehensive story of this organization, while also providing a foundation for future research on the gaming industry as well as on economic organization more generally. Companies such as Valve challenge our "pet theories" in strategy and management (Birkinshaw, 2015), and, by doing so, they provide valuable opportunities to discuss their limitations and oversights. In particular, we use our survey of Valve's unique organization to draw implications for theories of entrepreneurship, projects, strategy formation, and organizational capabilities. To do this, we draw on a range of publicly available data and first-hand accounts of the company, as well as available secondary literature. We start by providing a short account of Valve's history, business, and organization. We then discuss its organizational design in light of current theory, arguing that it is not an organizational anarchy but rather employs a set of powerful rules, before highlighting potential problems of its design. Building on this discussion, we derive implications for strategy, capabilities, and projects showing that while Valve's organization enables continuous experimentation and innovation, it also limits the kind of projects and products it can pursue. Finally, we use the case of *Half-Life 3*, a highly-demanded-yet-never-made video game, as an example of challenges organizations such as Valve face.

Valve's Economic Organization: Theory and History

Valve was founded in 1996 by Gabe Newell and Mike Harrington, former Microsoft employees who wanted to launch a video game studio. The company's first game, *Half-Life*, was released in 1998 to widespread commercial and critical acclaim and has enjoyed a lasting impact on the artistry and mechanics of game design. It was followed by a variety of successful titles including *Team Fortress* (1999), *Counter-Strike* (2000), *Half-Life 2* (2004), *Portal* (2007), and *Left 4 Dead* (2008), each of which eventually became a franchise in its own right. Alongside these projects, the company also experimented with a wide range of software, middleware, and hardware, with varying degrees of success. One of the first of these experiments was the popular Source engine, a middleware product Valve used for its own games and licensed to other developers. By far its most commercially successful venture, however, has been Steam, an online sales platform and community hub. Steam was launched in 2003 and was initially intended to deliver updates and patches to existing software. Over time, however, it evolved into a platform store featuring thousands of games from third-party and independent developers as well as Valve itself. As a result of its success, in the past decade Valve has moved away from in-house game development and has focused instead on Steam and on pursuing growth in new areas such as virtual reality (VR). Gabe Newell's personal wealth is estimated at around $3.5 billion (Forbes, 2019), and despite employing around 400 people, the company's market value is rumored to be far larger. The Steam library now boasts more than 33,000 games and, as of 2017, sales revenue through the platform was estimated at around $4.3 billion (Gough, 2020). There is little doubt then that the company is one of the great success stories of the gaming industry, which has always been highly uncertain and prone to sudden reversals of fortune, even among its leading firms.

The company's economic organization plays an important role in its past success. From its earliest days, Valve has worked along very different lines and with a radically different vision than most other companies in the gaming industry (Birdwell, 1999; Abrash, 2012)[1]. Valve "was designed as a company that would attract the sort of people capable of doing the initial creative step, leave them free to do creative work and make them want to stay" (Abrash, 2012). "Leave them free" means every employee can allocate his or her time to freely chosen projects rather than being directed by managers (Valve, 2012). The driving force behind this organizational design is the idea that software products in general and games in particular depend on creative and innovative ideas, not on routine work (Abrash, 2012) and that hierarchy stifles unorthodox thinking. In 2012, Valve published its employee handbook, which outlines its general approach, explains employee responsibilities, and provides an overview of the work process. The handbook gives researchers the clearest idea of how the business works—in theory at least. A wide range of interviews, first-hand accounts, and news articles on the company have also appeared over the years that offer further insight into the company and how its organization affects its market performance. Together, these resources provide a fascinating case study of the costs and benefits of the "boss-less" firm and especially what it means for entrepreneurship, innovation, and economic performance.

---

[1] Some of Valve's company blogs are no longer available in their original form, but may be accessed through the Internet Archive at the links provided.

The primary feature of Valve's organizational design is the freedom for employees to work on whatever they want. Each employee is allowed and encouraged to allocate their time and ideas where they think best. Employees can choose the projects they want to work on and which tasks and responsibilities they want to take on. They can furthermore initiate projects, gather resources, and even release subsequent products without managerial oversight. However, there are some measures in place that guide this form of self-organization. Most notably there is the "rule of three," which states that a project can only be initiated if at least three employees agree to work on it. Similarly, for a product to be released, at least three employees have to agree. As we will see, this simple rule provides a powerful way to shape, select, and reevaluate project ideas. Another notable feature of Valve's organization is its policy of employee remuneration based on peer review. The salary of each employee is set based on evaluation of his or her contributions and skills by other employees. It is important to note that management, although taking part in these processes, does not have superior decision power. Whether this model "works" will be discussed later; for now, we turn to some theoretical foundations of Valve's design.

Entrepreneurship, Management, and Decision-Making at Valve

Academic research about Valve's organization tends to revolve around a central theme: decision-making. Who decides what the company should produce, when, for whom, and to what standard? In traditional firms, these questions are answered (*a*) by the management hierarchy, which conveys the internal wishes of the company's owners and (*b*) indirectly by the system of market prices, which conveys the external wishes of consumers. These two forces are united by ***entrepreneurship***. Entrepreneurs are the ultimate decision-makers in a firm, the ones who govern the management structure (Mises, 2007 [1949]; Foss and Klein, 2012; Foss, Klein, and McCaffrey, 2019). As we will see, many of the mysteries associated with companies such as Valve can be solved by considering the role of entrepreneurs.

What do entrepreneurs do, exactly? Typically, the traits most associated with entrepreneurship are innovative thinking, the creation of new business ideas, and taking action to carry out those ideas. Valve's model invokes all of these in one way or another, but in this chapter we will focus mainly on the last one: taking action. Anyone can have a good idea, but it takes much more than an idea to be a successful entrepreneur. The stated goal of Valve's organizational design is the generation of innovative ideas, yet the implementation of that design strongly implies idea execution as well, as it grants employees the right to allocate company resources to their projects—it even allows for shipping new games and features without consulting management (Valve, 2012).

One theme of the rich literature on entrepreneurship is the deployment of resources (Mataja, 1966 [1884]; Mises, 2007 [1949]; Foss and Klein, 2012; Bylund, 2016; Möller and McCaffrey, unpublished). In this view, entrepreneurs use their knowledge and subjective impressions to imagine a future state of the world, especially one in which a problem has been solved or a need has been met. They then decide how to combine and allocate scarce resources to make this future into reality. Crucially, because entrepreneurial action happens over time, there is no way to know in advance if decisions will be successful. For this reason, we say that entrepreneurs "bear uncertainty." They make decisions without strict rules or guidance, relying instead on their own predictions about the future. We call this decision process *entrepreneurial judgment* (Knight, 1964; Foss and Klein, 2012; Foss, Klein, and McCaffrey, 2019). Ultimately, good judgment—that is, correct predictions about how to satisfy consumers in the future—determines which entrepreneurs succeed and which ones fail and, likewise, which earn profits and which go bankrupt. One important implication of this view is that being an entrepreneur goes hand in hand with owning resources, because ownership grants decision-making authority and gives entrepreneurs something to risk in the first place. In Valve's case, over 50 per cent of its shares are owned by founder and CEO Gabe Newell, with the rest owned by minor shareholders (Chiang, 2011). As such, the problem of decision-making for the company falls to them. This might seem strange, given that the company is supposed to be organized without a central decision-maker or group of them. Crucially though, entrepreneurs need not make all day-to-day choices to govern a business: they can delegate authority as well. We could say that entrepreneurs exercise "original judgment" while delegating to managers and other employees "derived judgment" (Foss, Foss, and Klein, 2007). In this sense, we can look at large, complex firms as elaborate networks of decision-making power, all of which can be traced back to the owner-entrepreneurs. Valve is an extreme example of delegation, as almost all aspects of the entrepreneurial function are given to its employees. Even core decisions such as selecting projects and allocating firm resources are delegated. This implies that even strategy formation—an area that is almost entirely regarded as a responsibility of upper management—lies in the hands of the employees.

There are two decisions that cannot be separated from entrepreneurs, however. The first is the decision to delegate itself: even if every subsequent hiring or firing is delegated, the initial decision power remains with the entrepreneur, even if it is seldom utilized (Rothbard, 1962). This "judgment about judgment" stays with the owner-entrepreneur (Knight, 1964). In Valve's case, Newell holds the ultimate authority, as he reserves the right to hire and fire (Puranam and Håkonsson, 2015; Keighley, 2020, Chapter 2). The initiation and execution of these processes, however, are fully delegated to the employees (Roberts, 2013). In practice, Newell takes a hands-off approach to day-to-day decisions, to the point that there are projects he wants to pursue that are never begun because employees are not interested. Yet although top-down decisions are rare, they do happen (Keighley, 2020, Chapter 3).

The second choice relates to profit and loss. Because profit and loss are incurred by entrepreneurs (Mataja, 1966 [1884]; Knight, 1964; Mises, 2007 [1949]), not managers or other employees, it is the entrepreneurs who ultimately decide what to do with profits. Even if a company allocates all profit to its employees, the final decision to implement or revoke such a system remains with the entrepreneur. In practice, Valve uses a remuneration system that determines salaries and bonuses via a peer-review process. Yet this process only indirectly and partially links profits to employee performance because it is grounded in the subjective evaluations of employees, which may or may not represent actual contributions to company success. This highlights the more practical problem of matching individual contributions to firm outcomes. Furthermore, it is unclear how much profit is allocated among the employees and how the allocation is determined. Anonymous Glassdoor reviews suggest that Newell and the board keep a significant portion themselves, making them the entrepreneurs both in theory and in practice.

Self-Organization and Decision-Making

Valve's particular way of organizing appears to be novel and even extreme, and it is certainly uncommon. Yet the basic ideas behind it are not new and have been applied in the past by companies such as Morningstar, W. L. Gore, and Oticon. They also align with more recent concepts such as the "Holacracy" system used by Zappos (Bernstein et al., 2016). In the literature on multinational corporations, the concept of "heterarchy" has been used for companies that grant their subsidiaries substantial discretion (Birkinshaw, 2000). In fact, the vanishing of formal hierarchies has been predicted repeatedly over the past few decades (Foss and Dobrajaska, 2015). However, several widely praised examples of organizations without hierarchies—such as Oticon (Foss, 2003), W. L. Gore (Hamel, 2007), Medium.com (Doyle, 2016), and GitHub (Burton et al., 2017)—ultimately abandoned their original designs and introduced centralized decision-making. In any case, because these ideas have been around for some time, organization theory has something useful to say about them that helps put Valve's particular design into perspective.

Organizations are multi-agent systems with identifiable boundaries and system-level goals toward which the agents of the system work (Puranam, Alexy, and Reitzig, 2014). Boundaries and goals jointly define the identity of the organization. Organizing is a problem-solving process that relies on agents with a limited capacity to access and process information (bounded rationality) and who are self-interested. Compressing several decades of organization research, Puranam, Alexy, and Reitzig (2014) derive four universal problems of organizing that agents face:

- task division—mapping goals to tasks and sub-tasks
- task allocation—mapping agents to tasks
- reward provision—mapping rewards to agents
- information provision—mapping information to agents

While the first two involve the general problem of the division of labor and specialization, the last two imply questions about cooperation, coordination, and integration.

How does Valve's way of organizing solve these universal problems? In Valve, task division is non-centralized and relies on employees proposing and pursuing their own projects. Interestingly, even goals and strategies themselves are set by employees, who choose where and how to contribute (we return to this problem in the section "The Implications of Valve's Organization for Strategy"). The task dimension therefore loosely resembles a market for the employees' time and skills (Varoufakis, 2012). Rewards at Valve are handled by a peer-review remuneration system in which each employee ranks every other employee from the projects in which they are involved. The review covers several dimensions, including overall skill, productivity, contribution to product, and contribution to the group (Valve, 2012). The project team rankings are then pooled company-wide and employees' salaries are adjusted according to their rank. Information provision is achieved by cross-team meetings, the employment of knowledge-sharing tools (Birdwell, 1999; Valve, 2012), peer reviews, and the social process of project initiation (Felin, 2015). Coordination and monitoring are therefore not top-down procedures implemented by management but bottom-up processes of social interaction among employees. This shows that Valve is not merely a "flat organization" but rather distributes power among its employees and grants them full autonomy, creating a "polyarchy" (Felin and Powell, 2016). This in turn involves employees bearing responsibility, making employee selection one of the most important requirements of ultimate decision-making. This is clearly acknowledged by Valve itself (Birdwell, 1999; Valve, 2012).

Does this combination of self-organization and peer review make Valve a structureless, organizational anarchy? No. There are powerful rules and norms in place to prevent people from doing what they want with impunity. In fact, some of these are quite formal. Felin and Powell (2016), for example, highlight self-selection and the "rule of three," which states that for a project to be started or a product to be shipped, at least three employees have to agree to participate. Both rules serve as "social proofs" that filter, transform, and shape ideas and products. The process of negotiations and assessments enables knowledge sharing through discourse and thereby provides an important mechanism for integration and coordination (Felin and Powell, 2016). Other methods are more informal, such as the culture of high performance that is imposed through rigorous employee selection and wages that are significantly above industry average (Foss and Dobrajaska, 2015). These boundaries together provide a set of rules of different strength that coordinate individual actions, making Valve a rule-based organization (Burton et al., 2017). In addition, there is a substantial emergent informal structure with strong influencers that have more authority over project selection and execution than others (Reiner, 2017; Keighley, 2020).

The idea that boss-less firms are completely without structure or hierarchy is often a misconception that can be illuminated by organization theory (Bernstein et al., 2016). Puranam and Clement (2017), for example, show that some structure performs better than no structure because a minimal structure works as a guide for emerging processes. The existence of a rule-based structure and to some degree even a formal hierarchy within Valve is illustrated eloquently by its handbook, which states that although no one in the company is a boss, "Gabe [Newell] is the most not your boss" (Valve, 2012). As discussed earlier, Newell retains original judgment within the firm.

Problems

Despite the company's financial success, Valve's organization has been the subject of much debate, and since its handbook was published in 2012, researchers have become increasingly interested in the costs and unintended consequences of adopting a boss-less structure. In general, critics argue that Valve's greatest strengths can also be its greatest weaknesses. For instance, as explained earlier, self-selection and the rule of three can be powerful coordinating mechanisms that force project ideas to gather social proof of plausibility and feasibility as well as undergo a process of negotiation, transformation, and shaping (Felin, 2015). This process utilizes local knowledge, fosters information sharing, and reduces individual biases. However, in doing so it may simply be exchanging individual for collective biases, for example, by encouraging group-think and shared cognitive frames. These result from homophily, the tendency to bond with others based on similarity (Felin and Powell, 2016).

Furthermore, project-selection decisions may depend on the popularity of projects, the likability and reputation of the people initiating them, and interpersonal conflicts rather than more objective metrics such as expected profitability (Foss and Dobrajaska, 2015; Puranam and Håkonsson, 2015). In this sense, self-organization and the rule of three overemphasize personal characteristics such as extroversion and salesmanship, and personal relations such as loyalties that may overshadow a project's true market potential. This may be the case with Linux gaming, for instance, which is still an active project at Valve despite an extremely low adoption rate of around 0.84 per cent (Valve, 2019c), hinting that profitability concerns do not drive all internal ventures. Moreover, since remuneration and employment depend on peer assessment, employees are incentivized to reduce risk-taking and innovativeness and instead favor "safe" projects because they are less uncertain and more likely to succeed and will gather commitments more easily (Puranam and Håkonsson, 2015). One of Valve's more recent game projects, *Dota Underlords*, is an instructive example: it simply makes an already highly successful modification of *Dota 2* into a stand-alone game.[2] Also, because peer assessment inevitably makes personal characteristics and relations quite important, it can incentivize employees to "invest" in people who are more focused on showmanship and maintaining a superficial reputation than creating value for consumers (Foss and Dobrajaska, 2015).

[2] See Chapter 8 for further discussion of the relationship between modders and the gaming industry.

Taken together, these factors represent an informal hierarchy in which the ideas and attitudes of influential groups of employees replace formal structure and management (Puranam and Håkonsson, 2015; Foss and Dobrajaska, 2015; Keighley, 2020, Chapter 3). Several personal accounts from former Valve employees argue that this is indeed the case, with some even likening the company's culture to a schoolyard complete with cliques and bullying (Warr, 2013). This claim is repeated by several anonymous Glassdoor reviews, positive and negative. Unsurprisingly, some reports suggest that Newell is one of the most influential figures in the company (Reiner, 2017), a fact Valve itself playfully acknowledges with its remark that he "is the most not your boss" (Valve, 2012). An anonymous employee explains that there is "a body of influencers and decision makers [within the company]. When I say decision makers, Gabe is probably the king of that group. When he proclaims where the wind blows, it just blows that way. If you fight it for too long, you are going to find yourself either out or executed or just exiled" (quoted in Reiner, 2017). This highlights a critical weak spot in some flatter organizational designs: while decentralization, autonomy, and self-organization can be empowering and motivating, they are also highly dependent on power relations (Felin and Powell, 2016).

Valve's particular kind of organization and culture requires and attracts a specific kind of individual, and employees are likely to be similar with regard to education, social background, and personal interests. While this can reduce conflict because there are fewer divergent views (Foss and Dobrajaska, 2015), it can also for the same reason amplify homophily and the problem of collective biases in project selection, as there is a limited diversity of opinion from which to choose (Felin and Powell, 2016). This could mean that, as in the case of GitHub (Burton et al., 2017), because Valve's vision and values[3] attract high-performing and highly autonomous people, its success should not only be fully attributed to its unique design and processes but also to self-selection by employees. Yet the promise of fitting in a well-designed organization is itself a reason to select into it: it is not an independent variable but part of the motivation to find employment and, therefore, also an influence on a firm's success.

Puranam and Håkonsson (2015) as well as Krogh and Geilinger (2015) argue that the consensus-driven process of the rule of three can reduce the speed of decision-making. In fact, there have been cases of Valve taking a long time to respond to complaints about ethically problematic games being published on

[3] With apologies for the alliteration.

Steam (McWhertor, 2014; Valve, 2019b). A lack of overall coordination can also lead to duplicated efforts without effective knowledge sharing (Puranam and Håkonsson, 2015; Felin and Powell, 2016). Felin and Powell (2016) argue that Valve's project rules can provide such knowledge integration. However, Burton et al. (2017) argue that the rule of two implemented at GitHub may have led to inefficiencies and wasted resources because self-selection does not ensure maximum value creation for the firm.

Lastly, there is a problem of scalability (Birkinshaw, 2015; Puranam and Håkonsson, 2015; Felin, 2015). Generally, the need for coordination rises as a company expands, leading start-ups to establish more formal structures. Birkinshaw (2015) argues that the problems listed earlier will become more prevalent during a growth period, leading management to become fully occupied with firefighting, dispute-solving, and ensuring coherence between products. However, as Krogh and Geilinger (2015) and Puranam, Alexy, and Reitzig (2014) point out, minimal formal organization works better for large open-source projects. Moreover, Varoufakis (2012) argues that if Valve's organizational design is viewed as a market for time, it should be able to scale indefinitely. Valve itself is aware of the scale issue and was surprised to find itself employing about 400 employees in 2012 (Varoufakis, 2012). However, the number of employees does not seem to have changed much since then: in 2014 there were still around 400 (Puranam and Håkonsson, 2015) and in 2016 about 360 (Chalk, 2016), with some firings in between (Cifaldi, 2013; Chapple, 2013). This may suggest that there was in fact an employment threshold past which coordination problems became more prevalent, reducing the efficiency of the organizational design, or at least, employees believed that more people would lead to more problems and were therefore reluctant to hire more. Similar firms have experienced thresholds of this type. GitHub, for instance, changed its organizational design around the time it exceeded 300 employees (Burton et al., 2017), Morningstar has employed around 400 (Hamel, 2011), and W. L. Gore has tried to keep each operation site at about 200 (Hamel, 2007). On the other hand, Zappos appears to perform well with over 1,500 employees (Feloni, 2016). Another more mundane explanation for the employee bottleneck may simply be that Valve cannot find and retain enough employees that fit well with its particular organizational design and culture.

The Implications of Valve's Organization for Strategy

Valve made several crucial strategic decisions over the years that shaped and changed its business. Most notable was the development of Steam and the subsequent change in the company's business model to add game distribution to its key activities. Other notable choices include the decision to focus on competitive multiplayer games with social features, on hardware development (Steam Machines, controllers, VR), and on Linux support. While some of these decisions were more successful than others, it is interesting how they made progress to completion given Valve's particular way of organizing. When employees can propose and pursue any kind of projects they like without serious constraints, the resulting products shape the firm's strategy. This implies that it is really Valve's employees who make its strategic decisions.

This kind of bottom-up strategic decision-making is quite rare and is not studied much in the literature (Foss, Klein, and McCaffrey, 2019, pp. 45–47). Yet strategy is one of the most important areas of decision-making in a firm because it determines key facets of the business model and its positioning, that is, the sources of the firm's profit. This is why it is usually ascribed to top management (Foss and Dobrajaska, 2015). However, the contribution of employees is sometimes acknowledged. Several decades ago, Mintzberg (1978) was already arguing that realized strategies do not come only from deliberate initiatives by top management but through emergent strategy originating in micro activities and strategizing-in-practice. Another view was provided by Burgelman (1983), who argued that a project can either be aligned or not with the overall strategy of the firm, with the former representing *induced* and the latter *autonomous* strategic activities. In a more recent study, Mirabeau and Maguire (2014) bring both views together by proposing autonomous strategic activities as the microfoundation of emergent strategy. They highlight three key activities required to turn an autonomous project into an emergent strategy: mobilizing support and acquiring resources, legitimizing the project by manipulating the prevailing strategic context, and changing the structural context by creating new teams and establishing new routines and procedures. Similar activities have been described by Birkinshaw (2000) for subsidiary managers of multinational corporations hoping to successfully complete projects that are not initially sanctioned by the company headquarters.

In both cases, strategic behavior lies outside the formal allocation of decision rights and, in Birkinshaw's (2000) subsidiary initiative concept especially, it comes down to a fight between a headquarters and a subsidiary. For Valve, however, the key activities are built into their organizational design as employees are not only allowed but asked to initiate projects, create teams, and gather support and resources to bringing them to fruition. This suggests that Valve mostly, if not exclusively, uses emergent strategies based on autonomous activities. However, the extant literature treats autonomous activities as strategically nonaligned (Burgelman, 1983). Since Valve's organizational design demands autonomous activities, it does not seem plausible to regard all projects at Valve as nonaligned with a prevailing concept of strategy. This would contradict basically every project that contributes to Steam, for example. Valve thus provides an example of strategic activities that are deliberate and aligned with the prevailing strategy of the firm yet are emergent in the sense that they arise out of micro activities of employees, not top-management initiatives. The prevailing strategy of the firm is itself an emergent strategy.

The strongest example of this emergent strategy is Steam. Initially developed to make it easier to deliver updates to the multiplayer game *Counter-Strike*, Valve's employees realized that it could also be used to digitally distribute games and they imagined that there might be a market for such a platform (Felin and Powell, 2016). This happened without management direction or classical market research and analysis (Valve does not even have a marketing department). The most important and successful shift in Valve's strategy and business model was thus imagined and executed by its employees. Other examples include Valve's initiative to enter the living room—traditionally, the domain of video game consoles and companies such as Sony, Microsoft, and Nintendo—by streaming PC games to televisions (TVs), and the related Steam Machine, a Linux-based PC with controllers designed for TVs. This support for Linux is aimed at becoming more independent from Microsoft's Windows (BBC, 2012) and may not only be driven solely by commercial reasoning but also by the passions of Valve developers, making it almost a form of social entrepreneurship. Another interesting example is Valve's internal struggle between virtual and augmented-reality devices. There have been projects developed for both, yet the augmented-reality project was eventually shut down, with the people involved leaving to found a new venture (Hollister, 2013).

Mirabeau and Maguire (2014) highlight another condition for autonomous activities to become emergent strategy: discourse. Discourse is actually the necessary precursor to the key activities listed earlier. Mirabeau and Maguire (2014) found that to become part of emergent strategy, projects need to be actively and passively related and sold to other employees and to management. Examples might include defining problems or processes that get adopted or presenting projects at town hall–style meetings. The active relation is obvious given Valve's organizational design and the rule of three (Felin, 2015). Initiating a project requires two other employees to be convinced of its value and willing to commit their time to it. The same holds for shipping a finished product. Further, Felin and Powell (2016) add an important aspect of the rule of three and role of dialogue. During the process of convincing others to start a project, that project is likely to be adjusted and transformed due to ideas coming in from other participants and along with any conditions they set in exchange for committing their time. Strategy arising from this process is therefore emergent on another dimension, as has been suggested before. It is collective but not necessarily majority strategic decision-making.

The Implications of Valve's Organization for Capabilities

Entrepreneurship and delegating decision power are linked to the concepts of dynamic and ordinary capabilities (Möller and McCaffrey, unpublished; Teece, 2012). Dynamic capabilities in particular overlap with entrepreneurial judgment (Foss and Klein, 2012) as they enable firms to adapt resources to changes in the environment (Teece, Pisano, and Shuen, 1997). Felin and Powell (2016), who were able to look into Valve's internal workings in more detail, argue that the comprehensive form of delegating entrepreneurship that the company employs is particularly well-suited for developing dynamic capabilities. Both self-selection and social proof contribute. Self-selection drives active search for new attributes and their value-creating prospects, utilizes local knowledge, and increases engagement with the project (Sloof and Siemens, 2019). At the same time, social proof improves knowledge sharing, learning, coordination, and search by varying, discussing, and challenging project ideas. Yet ordinary capabilities are also related to the degree of freedom employees have because this freedom is a key factor in the creation and enactment of capabilities (Salvato, 2009; Felin et al., 2012).

Ordinary capabilities describe the ability of a firm to produce an output (Amit and Schoemaker, 1993) and are associated with repeatable patterns of action, that is, routines (Winter, 2003). The possession of capabilities contributes to competitive advantage (Zollo and Winter, 2002), which is represented by profit (Foss and Knudsen, 2003). Contrary to this thinking, Valve is highly successful and generates large profits while also being deliberately designed to avoid repetition (Abrash, 2012). Indeed, several accounts suggest that Valve struggles with routine tasks. For instance, it has frequently had problems providing high-quality customer support and, rather than build this capability internally, it has outsourced it to call centers all over the world (Valve, 2019a) and to the Steam community itself. Another example relates to quality control: any developer can publish a game using Steam, which requires Valve to check in a routinized manner whether game content is legal and is morally and ethically acceptable. However, instead of building a team to perform these checks, Valve has introduced a broad policy regarding what content is allowed on Steam—essentially, anything that is not illegal (Valve, 2018). This rule was tested in early 2019 when a controversy and protest surrounded Valve over a "rape simulation game" that was available on Steam. The company reacted late and made an exception to its previous rule by banning the game, but only after a wave of bad publicity (Valve, 2019b). A similar incident that was also resolved late in a nonroutine way occurred in 2014 when Valve employees first decided to ban a game but were overruled by Newell (McWhertor, 2014).

Routines are generative systems that may emerge without being explicitly designed (Pentland and Feldmann, 2008). Therefore, despite these examples and Valve's deliberate avoidance of routinization, there may nevertheless be routines. There are two possible levels within Valve's organizational structure where they could exist. First, when ideating and selecting projects and, second, during project execution. At the level of project ideation and selection, routines may be found in the stages of challenging, variating, and enhancing proposed ideas. Yet given the heterogeneity of employees and the principle of self-selection, the social proof process is, although rule-based, more likely to be spontaneous.

During project execution, repeated, patterned actions can emerge when groups of employees regularly work together (Cohendet and Llerena, 2008) and apply best practices as well as common project management and software development approaches (Becker, 2004). However, these routines are likely to be unstable because team members can join and leave whenever they want, each new project requires adjustments to an existing routine, and transferring routines from one project to another is far from trivial. Switching team members changes the way a routine is performed even if its structure remains the same, as routines are not independent from the individuals that perform them (Felin et al., 2012). Miller, Choi, and Pentland (2014) show that changing just one individual has an impact on routine performance and losing an individual with key knowledge may even mean losing the routine. Furthermore, a new team member may have different skills that make it possible to change the composition of tasks thereby changing its structure. This is even more the case when team members are added or lost. Projects, moreover, also differ with regard to size, scope, complexity, and goals. Finally, routines are local as they arise out of a specific context with specific requirements (Becker, 2004). This makes them inherently difficult to transfer between projects (Narduzzo and Warglien, 2008). Reasons for this include incomplete understanding of the routine (Szulanski and Winter, 2002), tacit knowledge (Nonaka and Takeuchi, 1995), or a misfit between routine and new context (Madhok, 1997). Therefore, while routines may emerge at Valve, they are likely to be temporary and exist only within a specific project.

The fact that Valve is nonroutine but does nevertheless have a sustained competitive advantage poses a challenge to capability theory. One major problem is that ordinary capabilities as sources of competitive advantage are conceptualized solely as repeated patterned actions and thereby fail to explain organizations that deliberately avoid routines and emphasize spontaneous creative action. Similar arguments have been made by Salvato and Rerup (2011) and Obstfeld (2012). Another problem is that dynamic capabilities are conceptualized as only indirectly creating competitive advantage through the reconfiguration of existing ordinary capabilities and resources (Helfat and Peteraf, 2003; Teece, 2007). This misses the more direct role entrepreneurial imagination and action play in the generation of profits (Möller and McCaffrey, unpublished; Foss and Klein, 2012). Both lead to the inability of capability theory to explain Valve's sustained competitive advantage. Regarding its organizational design as successfully organizing derived entrepreneurial judgment may lead to a more satisfying explanation.

Valve's success is indicated by its profits and market share, both of which are considerable. Along with Felin and Powell (2016), we argue that Valve's performance is due to its ability to create ideas and transform them into successful projects, "successful" meaning they satisfy customer demand. This is achieved by employees balancing explorative and exploitative entrepreneurial functions of innovation, coordination, and arbitrage (Freiling, 2008; Freiling and Schellhowe, 2014). Valve's competitive advantage then is the result of correctly imagining customer wants and deploying resources accordingly; in other words, exercising judgment (Möller and McCaffrey, unpublished). This is not the result of routines but of correctly combining resources in expectation of changing customer preferences. However, routines and capabilities play an important role as they are the means to enhance an already existing competitive advantage by increasing the efficiency of resource combinations (Möller and McCaffrey, unpublished; Mataja, 1966 [1884]). Valve's approach of encouraging the search for ideas and giving full decision rights to its employees while coordinating efforts via social interaction seems to do well in the tasks of imagining customer preferences and deploying resource combinations accordingly. This does not imply that all projects that are begun are successfully shipped; in fact, many are not (Reiner, 2017). The rule of three, while providing an initial hurdle, is easy enough to overcome to foster comprehensive experimentation (Felin, 2015; Krogh and Geilinger, 2015), while at the same time preventing projects with bad prospects of completion. External control by other employees (Puranam and Håkonsson, 2015) and self-selection further give Valve the ability to stop unpromising projects quickly. Costly mistakes can thereby be decreased, yet not fully prevented, as shown by failed projects such as the Steam Machines or the game *Artifacts*. While Felin and Powell (2016) see this organizational design as particularly suited for the creation of dynamic capabilities, we argue that it is better seen as a way to organize diverse derived judgment. Valve's organizational design motivates and channels individual judgments in a way that lets it continuously anticipate customer demands, generate considerable profits, and thereby create sustained competitive advantage.

Implications for projects: *Half-Life 3* confirmed?

"Is there ever going to be a *Half-Life 3*?" is a persistent question from devoted gamers who long for a sequel to the highly successful series that made Valve and Gabe Newell icons in the gaming industry. Although a new *Half-Life* would almost certainly be successful financially, Valve has been reluctant to develop it. There are certainly good reasons not to; after all, multiplayer-focused games such as *Dota 2* and larger projects such as the Steam platform generate more income than individual titles such as *Half-Life* ever could. There are also natural incentives at play, as potential developers may fear that they cannot meet the high expectations of the community. Accounts from within Valve do indicate that the most important influencers have been uninterested (Reiner, 2017). However, we would like to propose another hypothesis, namely, that Valve's particular way of organizing has made it difficult to develop *Half-Life 3*.

Video games are complex software products consisting of many different and interdependent parts. These include game mechanics, graphics, visual design, and story, among others. Story is of particular importance because it requires planning and organizing a specific sequence of events and must be complete when the game is sold (Keighley, 2020, Chapters 11 and 14).[4] This is not the case with all services produced by Valve, however. Steam, the distribution and community platform, is a highly complex product that can easily be divided into

[4] See the discussion in Chapter 2.

individual projects with low or even no interdependence and that do not require a specific order or time frame to be delivered. Steam's community functions are largely unrelated to its shop functions, for instance. Similarly, most of the games Valve has developed, especially in recent years, are modular multiplayer titles such as *Dota 2*, *Counter-Strike*, and *Left 4 Dead* that can easily be developed as independent projects. *Portal*, a single-player title with only a rudimentary story, was shorter and less complex than the *Half-Life* games.

The development of *Half-Life 3* is extremely complex though. First, full-length, AAA games require many different parts to design; second, there are high expectations from both consumers and developers that these parts be of very high quality and also contain innovative features; third, as a story-driven game, these parts have to be in a specific order; and fourth, the game must be complete when shipped. This requires a minimum number of team members along with considerable development time and coordination. Most of these requirements relate to procuring and retaining resources, especially team members and their time. A game such as *Half-Life 3* must include many different features and innovations, and many specializations are needed to develop these. While Valve does not make use of job descriptions or predefined roles (Valve, 2012), employees nevertheless have a limited number of areas in which they are confident they can contribute value to the project and to the company generally. It is a truism that human capital, just like ordinary capital, is heterogeneous: not all knowledge or skill is equally suited to all tasks. A higher minimum number of team members is required for a full *Half-Life* game than for many other projects, and since there is an internal market for team members' time, it is more difficult to initialize, coordinate, and complete such a game. Furthermore, because of the finite nature and the general size and complexity of a *Half-Life* game, a significantly large time frame is required for completion. This is a more difficult sell for employees than shorter commitments because there are always other projects available and team members can always choose to leave. Besides general demands from team members in long-term projects, such as endurance or a sufficient degree of social fit, Valve's remuneration system incentivizes more immediate results. Although they are not completely determined by the market success of projects after release, individual contributions are far easier to evaluate using objective external data such as sales figures. Since the review process happens once a year, every project with a longer time horizon will be more difficult to sell because remuneration becomes more uncertain. Typically, large AAA games require up to three years of development even with a sufficiently sized team contributing 100 per cent of its time (and, toward the end of the development cycle, frequently working overtime). This suggests that, from a remuneration perspective alone, *Half-Life 3* will be enormously difficult to complete without a centralized effort within Valve.

This raises an important question though: if the barriers to creating AAA games are so high within Valve, how did the company ever produce the original *Half-Life*, let alone other major titles? The most plausible answer is that Valve's organizational design has developed and adapted over the years, and its development has gone hand-in-hand with the company's move away from traditional game design. In fact, besides having a general vision of full delegation, the organizational problems described earlier were not in place when *Half-Life* was developed, when the company's organizational form was better adapted to fit the requirements of the project at hand. Birdwell (1999), for example, describes the development of the "cabal" system at Valve in reaction to the deeply unsatisfactory first version of *Half-Life*. This system was initially used for one AAA game and then later applied to others. Yet several features of Valve's current system were missing at this early point—there were still job descriptions and roles, there was no practice of proposing and creating major projects, the peer feedback system was not in place, and so on. These crucial aspects of Valve's current model were added between 1999 and 2012, when Valve's handbook for new employees brought them to light (Valve, 2012). *Half-Life 2* came to market in 2004 and Valve's organization at that point was probably still better suited for undertaking complex projects. Moreover, *Half-Life 2* had an important marketing function, as it was intended to draw users to Steam. That the organization changed more significantly over the following years can be inferred from experience with *Half-Life 2* Episodes 1 and 2. These mini-sequels to *Half-Life 2* were released in 2006 and 2007. Although they used the same technological foundation, they were far shorter and considerably less complex than their predecessor. A third episode was planned but never finished (Keighley, 2020), and the much hoped-for *Half-Life 3* was experimented with in at least five different projects before being abandoned (Keighley, 2020). Newell even stated in an interview that the two finished episodes should be regarded as *Half-Life 3* (Bramwell, 2007). This suggests that in this period, Valve's organizational design was already changing such that highly complex AAA projects were becoming quite difficult. In 2011, when Valve must have already reached the state described by its handbook, Newell commented that the episodic distribution model would be replaced by continuous updates over Steam, suggesting that modular multiplayer titles were more in favor at the company (Crossley, 2011). Finally, in 2015, Newell added that going back to complex finite single-player games, and dismissing lessons learned from continuous multiplayer games and titles such as *Portal 2*, would only happen when many people came together and had a very good reason why (Keighley, 2015).

There seem to be limits to what Valve's organizational design can achieve in terms of products and projects. *Half-Life 3* lay beyond this threshold, at least for many years, until organizational inertia was overcome. None of the concepts made it very far, and as one employee has explained, every failure reduced the commitment to subsequent new *Half-Life 3* games (Reiner, 2017). This suggests that although Valve's particular way of organizing allows for initiating large and complex projects, it can also prevent them from taking off, with each failed attempt making it harder to gather the team members needed to move forward.

Valve has shifted from an organizational design that mirrored the interdependent structure of its projects to one in which projects are constrained by its organizational design. There is some irony in this as the creation of Valve's current model was sparked by an unsatisfactory version of the original *Half-Life*, a game that became a huge success. However, each further adaptation and advancement of the model made it more difficult for Valve to work the same kind of magic again.

Half-Life: Alyx

Nevertheless, in November 2019 Valve surprised the gaming community by announcing the return of the *Half-Life* franchise after a twelve-year hiatus. The game it announced was not the hoped-for *Half-Life 3*, however, but a prequel to *Half-Life 2* called *Half-Life: Alyx*. The game is a VR exclusive distributed for free with the purchase of Valve's own VR headset. Pundits had long predicted that the company would never return to its flagship intellectual property, so the announcement was met with equal parts excitement and confusion about the future of the franchise. More importantly, the production of *Half-Life: Alyx* (*HL:A*) sheds some fascinating light on the issues discussed in this paper.

During the final months of the game's production, Valve granted full access to its premises to journalist Geoff Keighley, who documented the development process and extensively interviewed employees about Valve's history and inner workings from around 2006 to 2020. What he discovered dramatically illustrates our narrative about Valve's development as a company. As he bluntly explains,

"The company's self-professed, no-hierarchy organizational structure has led to inefficiencies and periods of creative drought" (Keighley, 2020, Introduction).

In the late 2000s, Valve was enjoying a series of financial and critical successes in game development and publishing. Yet its Source engine, which had powered its most popular games, was outdated and in dire need of replacement. Work began on Source 2, and the development of some projects, especially *Half-Life 2: Episode 3*, was put on hold until they could be transferred. However, Source 2's development took far longer than expected, and even while it was still unfinished, numerous Valve teams tried to use it for a wide range of projects. A lack of centralized direction in the company meant that too many demands were put on the emerging technology: "The invisible, self-directed hand of Valve had suddenly led the company in a dizzying array of directions" (Keighley, 2020, Chapter 3). The result was a multitude of different visons for the new engine, none of which could be realized. A series of projects, including some concepts for *Half-Life* games, were scrapped, and employees recount how, once there were few ongoing projects left, it became more difficult to propose new ones (Keighley, 2020, Chapter 3). By 2013, Valve had entered a period of extreme lack of focus that its employees called "The Wilderness" (Keighley, 2020, Chapter 3).

During this period, Gabe Newell's vision for the company was also changing as he became more interested in hardware-based projects, including VR (Keighley, 2020, Chapter 2). His ultimate authority as entrepreneur was reflected in Valve's lack of successful new game development. Yet his vision came as a surprise to many new employees who joined the company at this time specifically to create new games. The general feeling among the staff was that Valve needed to regroup:

> Most of the time, your job at Valve is to make great games. But sometimes, since there is no real management layer, employees have to take on the "people stuff" to steer the invisible hand of Valve in a particular direction. By early 2016, it was becoming clear to [employees] that an intervention of sorts was needed to help re-spark Valve's creative output. (Keighley, 2020, Chapter 5)

Several employees expressed similar sentiments about what was wrong at the company and what was required to fix it:

> "There were just too many things going on at the company to feel like we were healthy as an organization";

> "We sort of had to collectively admit we were wrong on the premise that you will be happiest if you work on something you personally want to work on the most... Instead, we decided as a group that we would all be happier if we worked on a big thing, even if it's not exactly what we wanted to work on"; "It was an inversion of the usual thinking... But we needed to put the health of the company first." (quoted in Keighley, 2020, Chapter 5)

"Cultural conversations" took place to discuss how to refocus. And the eventual development of *HL:A* was, in a way, an attempt to remedy the disappointment of those newer employees who wanted to get back into game development. As one staff member explained, the creation of *HL:A* was in some ways "the story of how we fixed Valve" (quoted in Keighley, 2020, Chapter 1).

Interviews with project leaders reveal that *HL:A* began development around 2016. It was not therefore one of the many *Half-Life* projects in development after the release of *Half-Life 2*; in fact, employees were for some time intimidated and even terrified at the prospect of suggesting a new *Half-Life* project. Instead, the team that eventually developed *HL:A* began with the desire to respond to customer demand for a flagship VR game to complement Valve's foray into that market. *HL:A* was not originally intended to be a *Half-Life* title; instead, it was first and foremost an open-ended experiment with VR that subsequently evolved.

Felin (2015) notes that tipping points play an important role in an organizational design based on self-organization. He sees such a point in the rule of three and the social proof required to start a project (Felin and Powell, 2016). The development of *HL:A* and the previously failed *Half-Life 3* experiments indicate, however, that there is a second tipping point reached when a running project becomes stable and promising enough that gathering additional required resources becomes easy.

Customer demand for a flagship VR title was accompanied by Valve's realization that their hardware would be far less valuable without a supporting AAA game. This must have been a major concern given that several of Valve's other highly visible hardware projects, such as Steam Machines, had failed. VR experimentation provided a strong motivation not only to start the *HL:A* project, and hence reach the first tipping point, but also surpass it. The initial liftoff was eased by the fact that the team did not have a *Half-Life* title in mind but rather wanted to experiment with VR. Furthermore, since Valve had invested heavily in VR over the years, there was an initial group already available with relevant skills and interest and was, therefore, easy to recruit.

The initial team was able to create a ten-minute playable prototype that was well received by testers, who even played it in ways that were not intended. This early success was crucial for the further development of the project because it made it possible to move from the initial experimental stage into full development and, hence, to overcome the second threshold. There were three reasons for this. First, the prototype could be played by potential new team members, providing a proof of concept. Second, the reaction of the testers showed what could be done and what possibilities lay within the scope of the project. Third, it signaled leadership and a working team organization able to get the project done (thereby again highlighting the importance of informal hierarchies). As one interviewee argued, this fit with the desire of many newer Valve employees to work on a *Half-Life* project. At this point, recruiting new team members became, to the surprise of team leaders, quite easy. This is because the existing state of the project significantly reduced the perceived costs of commitment for the employees. With over fifty people working on *HL:A*, about one-eighth of Valve's employees, it was the largest team the company had ever seen.

Altogether, *HL:A* was initially less the result of purposeful creation and more of the lucky coincidence of a need for a specific product, a strong motivation to create it, an open-ended and experimental development approach, and the availability of skilled employees. Together these were able to produce the prototype that in turn transformed an experiment into a major *Half-Life* game. While this is a cause for joy among fans, it also highlights the difficulties and hurdles that must be overcome in an organization such as Valve in order to make such projects happen.

Conclusion

Although Valve is not the organizational utopia sometimes depicted in the popular business press, its particular model does provide many learning opportunities for scholars working in economics, organization, entrepreneurship, and strategy. As Birkinshaw (2015) noted, Valve provides a stress test for our "pet theories" in these disciplines.

Organizations with little or no hierarchy are not intrinsically more or less efficient or capable of developing sustained competitive advantages; instead, their effectiveness is heavily context-dependent. Each firm must find the appropriate balance between the demands of customers, the requirements of producing specific services, and the costs of organizing employee knowledge and skills. Valve has so far done a good job of striking this balance, although, as we show, there are some ways in which the flat approach to organization can limit a company's potential. We argue that the unique organization design that grants full autonomy to every employee and rests on self-organization in combination with a peer-review-based remuneration system struggles with large, complex, long-term projects because they are too costly for the individual employee. Moreover, while companies such as Valve abolish hierarchy on paper, the result tends to be the replacement of formal with informal hierarchies, and the development of influential teams and cliques.

What can our discussion tell us about Valve's future in the games industry? Steam has dominated the PC distribution market for years, but its dominance may be coming to an end. Competitors that operate using traditional business models, such as the Epic Games Store, may put Valve at a disadvantage by exploiting its slow reaction times, a direct result of its consensus-driven decision-making process (Krogh and Geilinger, 2015; Puranam and Håkonsson, 2015). Furthermore, with Epic attacking Steam by emphasizing the significantly lower costs for game developers of using its own platform, as well as by collecting exclusive distributions rights for AAA games (especially sequels to highly successful titles), Valve may need to react more quickly and consistently in order not to lose significant market share. Foss and Dobrajaska (2015) explain that when decisions are highly time-dependent, coordination of interdependencies becomes more important and, therefore, key knowledge should be centralized using top management. Burton et al. (2017) additionally argue that without environmental selection pressures, such as competition, any organizational design can work. The success until now of Valve and its organizational design may, therefore, be facilitated by a lack of competition to force fast reactions and innovation. The coming years will reveal if Valve has been successful because of or despite its unique way of organizing.

References

Abrash, M. 2012. "Valve: How I Got Here, What It's Like, and What I'm Doing." *Valvesoftware*. Accessed on March 1, 2020. http://blogs.valvesoftware.com/abrash/valve-how-i-got-here-what-its-like-and-what-im-doing-2/.

Amit, Raphael, and Paul J. H. Schoemaker. 1993. "Strategic Assets and Organizational Rent." *Strategic Management Journal* 14 (1): 33–46.

Baldwin, C. Y. 2015. "In the Shadow of the Crowd: A Comment on 'Valve's Way'." *Journal of Organization Design* 4 (2): 5–7.

BBC. 2012. "Valve Boss Gabe Newell Calls Windows 8 a 'Catastrophe'." *BBC*, July 26, 2012. https://www.bbc.com/news/technology-18996377.

Becker, M. C. 2004. "Organizational Routines: A Review of Literature." *Industrial and Corporate Change* 13 (4): 643–677.

Bernstein, E., J. Bunch, N. Canner, and M. Lee. 2016. "Beyond the Holacracy Hype." *Harvard Business Review* 94 (7–8): 38–49.

Birdwell, K. 1999. "The Cabal: Valve's Design Process for Creating Half-Life." *Gamasutra*, December 10, 1999. Accessed on January 5, 2021. http://www.gamasutra.com/view/feature/131815/the_cabal_valves_design_process_.php.

Birkinshaw, J. 2000. *Entrepreneurship in the Global Firm*. London: SAGE Publications.

———. 2015. "What Lessons Should We Learn from Valve's Innovative Management Model?" *Journal of Organization Design* 4 (2): 8–9.

Bramwell, T. 2007. "Opening Valve." *Eurogamer*, September 8, 2007. Accessed on January 5, 2021. https://www.eurogamer.net/articles/i_valve_060606.

Burgelman R. A. 1983. "A Model of the Interaction of Strategic Behavior, Corporate Context, and the Concept of Strategy." *Academy of Management Review* 8 (1): 61–70.

Burton, R. M., D. D. Håkonsson, J. Nickerson, P. Puranam, M. Workiewicz, and T. Zenger. 2017. "GitHub: Exploring the Space between Bossless and Hierarchical Forms of Organizing." *Journal of Organizational Design* 6 (10): 1–19.

Bylund, P. L. 2016. *The Problem of Production*. New York: Routledge.

Cifaldi, F. 2013. "Several Out of Work as Valve Makes 'Large Decisions' about Its Future." *Gamasutra*, February 13, 2013. Accessed on January 5, 2021. http://www.gamasutra.com/view/news/186592/Several_out_of_work_as_Valve_makes_large_decisions_about_its_future.php#.URvysqVjt8H.

Chalk, A. 2016. "Valve Denies Wrongdoing in Skin Gambling Legal Rumblings: 'No Factual or Legal Support for These Accusations'." *PCGamer*, October 18, 2016. Accessed on January 5, 2021. https://www.pcgamer.com/valve-misses-deadline-to-respond-to-washington-state-gambling-regulator-but-says-its-coming-soon/.

Chapple, C. 2013. "[Update] Holtman Latest to Leave in Valve Twist, Says Source." *Develop*, February 13, 2013. https://web.archive.org/web/20170525135008/http://www.develop-online.net/news/update-holtman-latest-to-leave-in-valve-twist-says-source/0114043.

Chiang, O. 2011. "The Master of Online Mayhem." *Forbes*, February 9, 2011. Accessed on January 5, 2021. https://www.forbes.com/forbes/2011/0228/technology-gabe-newell-videogames-valve-online-mayhem.html#7c326ca93ac0.

Clement, J., and P. Puranam. 2017. "Searching for Structure: Formal Organization Design as a Guide to Network Evolution." *Management Science* 64 (8): 3879–3895.

Cohendet, P., and P. Llerena. 2008. "The Role of Teams and Communities in the Emergence of Organizational Routines." In *Handbook of Organizational Routines*, edited by M. C. Becker. Cheltenham, UK: Edward Elgar, pp. 256–277.

Crossley, B. 2011. "The Valve Manifesto." *Develop*, May 9, 2011. Accessed on March 1, 2020. https://web.archive.org/web/20110513224713/http://www.develop-online.net/features/1184/The-Valve-manifesto.

Doyle, A. 2016. "Management and Organization at Medium." *Medium*, March 4, 2016. Accessed on January 5, 2021. https://blog.medium.com/management-and-organization-at-medium-2228cc9d93e9.

Egenfeldt-Nielsen, Simon, Jonas Heide Smith, and Susana Pajares Tosca. 2020. *Understanding Video Games: The Essential Introduction*. 4th ed. New York: Routledge.

Felin, T. 2015. "Valve Corporation: Strategy Tipping Points and Thresholds." *Journal of Organization Design* 4 (2): 10–11.

Felin, T., N. J. Foss, K. H. Heimeriks, and T. L. Madsen. 2012. "Microfoundations of Routines and Capabilities: Individuals, Processes, and Structure." *Journal of Management Studies* 48 (8): 1351–1374.

Felin, T., and T. C. Powell. 2016. "Designing Organizations for Dynamic Capabilities." *California Management Review* 58 (4): 78–96.

Feloni, R. 2016. "Zappos CEO Tony Hsieh Explains Why 18% of Employees Quit during the Company's Radical Management Experiment." *Business Insider*, January 15, 2016. https://www.businessinsider.de/zappos-ceo-tony-hsieh-on-holacracy-transition-2016-1.

Forbes. 2019. "Gabe Newell." https://www.forbes.com/profile/gabe-newell/#4b0f41347da0.

Foss, N. J. 2003. "Selective Intervention and Internal Hybrids: Interpreting and Learning from the Rise and Decline of the Oticon Spaghetti Organization." *Organization Science* 14 (3): 331–349.

Foss, N. J., and M. Dobrajaska. 2015. "Valve's Way: Vayward, Visionary, or Vouguish?" *Journal of Organization Design* 4 (2): 12–15.

Foss, N. J., K. Foss, and P. G. Klein. 2007. "Original and Derived Judgment: An Entrepreneurial Theory of Economic Organization." *Organization Studies* 28 (12): 1893–1912.

Foss, N. J., and P. G. Klein. 2012. *Organizing Entrepreneurial Judgment: A New Approach to the Firm*. Cambridge: Cambridge University Press.

Foss, N. J., P. G. Klein, and M. McCaffrey. 2019. *Austrian Perspectives on Entrepreneurship, Strategy, and Organization*. Cambridge: Cambridge University Press.

Foss, N. J., and T. Knudsen. 2003. "The Resource-Based Tangle: Towards a Sustainable Explanation of Competitive Advantage." *Managerial and Decision Economics* 24 (4): 291–307.

Freiling, J. 2008. "SME Management: (What) Can We Learn from Entrepreneurship Theory?" *International Journal of Entrepreneurship Education* 6 (1): 1–19.

Freiling, J., and C. L. Schellhowe. 2014. "The Impact of Entrepreneurial Orientation on the Performance of Internationalization." *Journal of Entrepreneurship, Management and Innovation* 10 (4): 169–199.

Gough, Christina. 2020. "Steam Gaming Platform: Statistics and Facts." *Statista*, October 16, 2020. https://www.statista.com/topics/4282/steam/.

Hamel, G. 2007. *The Future of Management*. Brighton, MA: Harvard Business School Press.

———. 2011. "First, Let's Fire All the Managers." *Harvard Business Review* 89 (12): 48–60.

Helfat, C. E., and M. A. Peteraf. 2003. "The Dynamic Resource-Based View: Capability Lifecycles." *Strategic Management Journal* 24 (10): 997–1010.

Hollister, S. 2013. "How Two Valve Engineers Walked Away with the Company's Augmented Reality Glasses." *The Verge*, May 18, 2013. https://www.theverge.com/2013/5/18/4343382/technical-illusions-valve-augmented-reality-glasses-jeri-ellsworth-rick-johnson.

Ireland, R. D., M. A. Hitt, and D. G. Sirmon. 2003. "A Model of Strategic Entrepreneurship: The Construct and Its Dimensions." *Journal of Management* 29 (6): 963–989.

Kano, L., and A. Verbeke. 2015. "The Three Faces of Bounded Reliability: Alfred Chandler and the Microfoundation of Management Theory." *California Management Review* 58 (1): 97–122.

Keighley, G. 2015. "Valve: A Conversation with Gabe Newell and Erik Johnson." *Gamslice*, audio interview. https://soundcloud.com/gameslice/valve.

———. 2019. "The Final Hours of *Half-Life: Alyx* – Behind Closed Doors at Valve Interview." *The Game Awards*, November 21, 2019. YouTube video, 22:00. https://www.youtube.com/watch?v=-9K0eJEmMEw.

———. 2020. "The Final Hours of *Half-Life: Alyx*." *Steam*, ebook. https://store.steampowered.com/app/1361700/HalfLife_Alyx__Final_Hours/.

Knight, F. H. 1964. *Risk, Uncertainty and Profit*. New York: August M. Kelley.

Krogh, G. V., and N. Geilinger. 2015. "Valve's Organization: Opportunities and Open Questions." *Journal of Organization Design* 4 (2): 18–19.

O'Donnell, Casey. 2017. "'Show Me the Money!': Shifting Fields of Capital in the Global Game Industry." In *The Evolution and Social Impact of Video Game Economics*, edited by Casey B. Hart. Lanham, MD: Lexington, pp. 1–13.

Madhok, A. 1997. "Cost Value and Foreign Market Entry Mode: The Transaction and the Firm." *Strategic Management Journal* 18 (1): 39–61.

Mataja, V. 1966 [1884]. *Der Unternehmergewinn: Ein Beitrag zur Lehre von Gütervertheilung der Volkswirtschaft*. Osnabrück: Otto Zeller.

McCaffrey, M. 2019. "The Macro Problem of Microtransactions: The Self-Regulatory Challenges of Video Game Loot Boxes." *Business Horizons* 62 (4): 483–495.

Miller, K. D., S. Choi, and B. T. Pentland. 2014. "The Role of Transactive Memory in the Formation of Organizational Routines." *Strategic Organization* 12 (2): 109–133.

Mintzberg, H. 1978. "Patterns of Strategy Formation." *Management Science* 24 (9): 934–948.

Mises, Ludwig von. 2007 [1949]. *Human Action: A Treatise in Economics*. 4th ed. Indianapolis: Liberty Fund.

Mirabeau, L., and S. Maguire. 2014. "From Autonomous Strategic Behavior to Emergent Strategy." *Strategic Management Journal* 35 (8): 1202–1229.

Möller, U., and M. McCaffrey. "Entrepreneurship and Firm Strategy: Integrating Resources, Capabilities, and Judgment through an Austrian Framework." *Entrepreneurship Research Journal*, forthcoming.

Narduzzo, A., and M. Warglien. 2008. "Conducting Experimental Research on Organizational Routines." In *Handbook of Organizational Routines*, edited by M. C. Becker. Cheltenham, UK: Edward Elgar, pp. 301–324.

Nonaka, I., and H. Takeuchi. 1995. *The Knowledge-Creating Company*. Oxford: Oxford University Press.

Obstfeld, D. 2012. "Creative Projects: A Less Routine Approach toward Getting New Things Done." *Organization Science* 23 (6): 1571–1592.

Pentland, B. T., and M. S. Feldman. 2008. "Designing Routines: On the Folly of Designing Artifacts, while Hoping for Patterns of Action." *Information and Organization* 18 (4): 235–250.

Puranam, P., O. Alexy, and M. Reitzig. 2014. "What's 'New' About New Forms of Organizing?" *Academy of Management Review* 39 (2): 162–180.

Puranam, P., and D. D. Håkonsson. 2015. "Valve's Way." *Journal of Organization Design* 4 (2): 2–4.

Reiner, A. 2017. "Searching for Half-Life 3." *Gameinformer*, January 11, 2017. Accessed on January 5, 2021. https://www.gameinformer.com/b/features/archive/2017/01/11/searching-for-half-life-3.aspx.

Roberts, R. 2013. "Varoufakis on Valve, Spontaneous Order, and the European Crisis." *EconTalk*, February 25, 2013. Accessed on January 5, 2021. http://www.econtalk.org/varoufakis-on-valve-spontaneous-order-and-the-european-crisis/.

Rothbard, M. N. 1962. *Man, Economy, and State: A Treatise on Economic Principles*. Princeton, NJ: Van Nostrand.

Salvato, C. 2009. "Capabilities Unveiled: The Role of Ordinary Activities in the Evolution of Product Development Processes." *Organization Science* 20 (2): 384–409.

Salvato, C., and C. Rerup. 2011. "Beyond Collective Entities: Multilevel Research on Organizational Capabilities." *Journal of Management* 37 (2): 486–490.

Schumpeter, J. A. 1983. *The Theory of Economic Development: An Inquiry into Profits, Capital, Credit, Interest, and the Business Cycle*. New Brunswick/London: Transaction Publishers.

Shane, S., and S. Venkatamaran. 2000. "The Promise of Entrepreneurship as a Field of Research." *Academy of Management Review* 25 (1): 217–226.

Sloof, R., and F. A. von Siemens. 2019. "Effective Leadership and the Allocation and Exercise of Power in Organizations." *The Leadership Quarterly*. https://www.sciencedirect.com/science/article/pii/S1048984318303199.

Szulanski, G., and S. Winter. 2002. "Getting It Right the Second Time." *Havard Business Review* 80 (1): 62–69.

Teece, D. J. 2007. "Explicating Dynamic Capabilities: The Nature and Microfoundations of (Sustainable) Enterprise Performance." *Strategic Management Journal* 28 (13): 1319–1350.

———. 2012. "Dynamic Capabilities: Routines versus Entrepreneurial Action." *Journal of Management Studies* 49 (8): 1395–1401.

Teece, D. J., G. Pisano, and A. Shuen. 1997. "Dynamic Capabilities and Strategic Management." *Strategic Management Journal* 18 (7): 509–533.

Valve. 2012. "Handbook for New Employees." Valve Corporation, Bellevue, WA.

———. 2018. "Who Get's To Be on the Steam Store." *Valve*, June 6, 2018. Accessed on January 5, 2021. https://steamcommunity.com/games/593110/announcements/detail/1666776116200553082.

———. 2019a. "GDC 2019: Steam Business Update." *Valve*, March 29, 2019. YouTube video, 46:31. Accessed on January 5, 2021. https://www.youtube.com/watch?v=wrvr02SiHY4.

———. 2019b. "Rape Day Will Not Ship on Steam." *Valve*, March 7, 2019. Accessed on January 5, 2021. https://steamcommunity.com/games/593110/announcements/detail/1808664240304050758.

———. 2019c. "Steam Hardware- and Software Survey May 2019." *Valve*. Accessed on March 1, 2020. https://store.steampowered.com/hwsurvey.

Varoufakis, V. 2012. "Why Valve? Or, What Do We Need Corporations for and How Does Valve's Management Structure Fit into Today's Corporate World?" *Valve Economics*. Accessed on March 1, 2020. http://blogs.valvesoftware.com/economics/why-valve-or-what-do-we-need-corporations-for-and-how-does-valves-management-structure-fit-into-todays-corporate-world/.

Warr, P. 2013. "Former Valve Employee: 'It Felt a Lot Like Highschool'." *Wired*, September 7, 2013. Accessed on January 5, 2021. https://www.wired.com/2013/07/wireduk-valve-jeri-ellsworth/.

Winter, Sidney G. 2003. "Understanding Dynamic Capabilities." *Strategic Management Journal* 24 (10): 991–995.

McWhertor, M. 2014. "Hatred Is Back on Steam Greenlight (Update)." *Polygon*, December 16, 2014. Accessed on January 5, 2021. https://www.polygon.com/2014/12/16/7406713/hatred-returns-to-steam-greenlight-valve.

Zenger, T. R. 2015. "Valve Corporation: Composing Internal Markets." *Journal of Organization Design* 4 (2): 20–21.

Zollo, Maurizio, and Sidney G. Winter. 2002. "Deliberate Learning and the Evolution of Dynamic Capabilities." *Organization Science* 13 (3): 339–351.

About the Contributors

Robert S. Cavender grew up in St. Louis, Missouri, but now lives in Gettysburg, Pennsylvania, where he teaches courses in economic development, political economy, history of economic thought, and microeconomics as a visiting assistant professor of economics at Gettysburg College. Robert was a Mercatus Fellow at George Mason University, where he received his Doctorate as well as his MA in economics in 2015 and 2012, respectively. He received his BSc in economics from Missouri State University in 2010. Robert is currently working on research pertaining to the political economy of development, as well as the economics of nongovernment institutions of cooperation. Most recently, his work took him to the Syrian refugee camps on the northern border of Jordan, where he conducted research on the institutions that have evolved to facilitate cooperation in the camps. Aside from writing, teaching, and arguing about economics, philosophy, and politics, Robert also enjoys online gaming, reading fantasy fiction, hiking, riding his bicycle around the Gettysburg battlefields, and playing the piano and classical guitar.

Stephen Davies is Head of Education at the Institute of Economic Affairs and senior fellow at the American Institute for Economic Research. He taught for thirty years at the Department of History and Economic History, Manchester Metropolitan University. His published works include *The Wealth Explosion: The Nature and Origins of Modernity*, *The Dictionary of Conservative and Libertarian Thought*, and *Empiricism and History*. His research interests include the history and trajectory of complex orders, the western esoteric tradition and the history of the idea of the Devil, the politics and sociology of the contemporary radical right, and the intellectual and political history of liberalism. He is currently finishing a book on the Malthusian understanding of the history of civilisations and the premodern world.

Peter C. Earle is a PhD candidate in economics at the University of Angers and a research fellow at the American Institute for Economic Research. His research focuses on financial markets, monetary policy, virtual and cryptocurrencies, and economic measurement. Before becoming an economist, he spent two decades as a trader in global financial markets and is the founder of Intangible Economics, LLC, a game economy and cryptocurrency consultancy.

Zachary Gochenour is a lecturer in economics at James Madison University. He holds a PhD in economics from George Mason University. His research focuses on using economics to study politics, law, and history, and he has also published on the economics of immigration.

Matthew McCaffrey is associate professor of entrepreneurship in the Alliance Manchester Business School at the University of Manchester. He holds a BA in literature, and an MSc and PhD in economics. His research focuses on entrepreneurship and the institutions under which it thrives, as well as innovation and the economics of games and the gaming industry. He is the author or editor of five books, most recently *Austrian Perspectives on Entrepreneurship, Organization, and Strategy*, co-authored with Nicolai J. Foss and Peter G. Klein (Cambridge University Press, 2019). He has been playing games for twenty-five years and writing about them for nearly a decade.

William Gordon Miller is a doctoral student in entrepreneurship at Baylor University. Originally from Atmore, Alabama, Gordon earned his BSc in music education at Troy University in 2014. Upon completion of this degree, he pursued other interests in libertarian and classical liberal philosophy through various work opportunities in the Washington DC metropolitan area, most notably with the Charles Koch Institute. Shortly thereafter, he returned to Troy University to continue his formal education, earning his master's degree in economics in 2017. His current research focuses on how entrepreneurs make use of online communities to facilitate new methods of learning as well as how this process impacts the greater economic and entrepreneurial landscape.

Ulrich Möller is a PhD candidate in the Department of Small Business and Entrepreneurship (LEMEX) at the University of Bremen. His research lies at the intersection of entrepreneurship, organization, and strategy. His PhD thesis looks into entrepreneurship in established companies, its organizational preconditions, and its implications for management and strategy. He particularly focuses on the microfoundations of management thought, delegation, and the performance implications of organizational design choices. He is also a business development manager at a large German tech company.

Robert Conan Ryan holds a PhD in business administration from the University of Pittsburgh. His work centers around competitive strategy (competitive dynamics, radical innovation strategy, gray economy strategy), neo-Schumpeterian economics (paradigmatic change; emerging technological trajectories), and business ethics (the social construction of credibility, belief networks, and stakeholder management). His work has received honors from such institutions as the Academy of Management, the Product Development and Management Association, and the American Institute for Economic Research.

Solomon Stein is a senior fellow for the F. A. Hayek Program for Advanced Study in philosophy, politics, and economics. He received his PhD in economics from George Mason University in 2015, and is an alumnus of the Mercatus PhD Fellowship program. His work focuses on the history of economic thought, particularly the development of the contemporary market process tradition. Along with this work, he is also involved in assisting the George Mason University Library's Special Collections and Archives in collecting the papers of James M. Buchanan.

Index